The Greengrocer's Kitchen:
Vegetables and Herbs

PETE LUCKETT

The Greengrocer's Kitchen

Vegetables and Herbs

Best Wishes

Pete Luckett

Woodleedoo!!

GOOSE LANE

Published by Goose Lane Editions with the assistance of the Department of Canadian Heritage and the New Brunswick Department of Economic Development, Tourism and Culture, 1999.

Edited by Laurel Boone.
Photography by Julian Beveridge.
Food preparation by Don Mailman.
Styling by Julian Beveridge and Julie Scriver.
Pete Luckett photo © John Sherlock Photographer. Reproduced with permission.
Illustrations by Judi Pennanen.
Cover and book design by Julie Scriver.
Printed in Canada by Friesens.
10   9   8   7   6   5   4   3   2   1

Canadian Cataloguing in Publication Data

Luckett, Pete, 1953-

The greengrocer's kitchen

Includes index.
ISBN 0-86492-231-0

1. Cookery (Vegetables)   2. Cookery (Herbs)   I. Title.

TX801.L82 1999   641.6'5   C99-950044-9

Goose Lane Editions
469 King Street
Fredericton, New Brunswick
CANADA E3B 1E5

Contents

Introduction

When I left school at the age of sixteen to seek my fortune in the world of produce, the High Street greengrocer, the market trader, and the barrow boy still ruled the roost. Business was brisk in my hometown of Nottingham, England, and I landed a job with one of the best. Pat Britton came from a long line of greengrocers, and he knew that the only way to learn was from the bottom up. For a princely four pounds a week (half of which went to my mum), I was up at dawn hauling fifty-pound sacks of spuds or sorting through mountains of near-frozen Brussels sprouts.

Such is the life of the apprentice. Just when I was pondering a career change, Pat decided to give me a go at doing the shop window. All the fruit had to be polished to a shine, then nestled in tissue paper, stacked carefully into pyramids, and tweaked until it "had the look." I was hooked. No matter that it took several hours to get it just right or that it had to be done over every three days. The satisfaction I felt every time I passed by that display window kindled a spark. I still take pride in our produce displays at the Frootique, and the hand-lettered signs — "pick o' the crop," "ripe 'n' ready," "sweet and juicy" — remind me how I got my start.

Well, those were the simple days. I soon realized that the successful greengrocer must be part artist, part accountant, part botanist, and part PR man. Ten years later, I started my own business in Saint John, New Brunswick. The soil was good, and soon my twelve-foot stall grew into a bumper crop of four shops and a wholesale warehouse. In 1992, I sold up to my brother, Dave, my sister, Kate, and her husband, Geoff, and moved to Nova Scotia. I opened my flagship market in Bedford in 1992, which has grown to over 13,000 square feet and houses a British-style butcher, a European delicatessen, and Pete's Power Juice Bar, along with dairy and grocery sections and, of course, the largest selection of fresh fruits and vegetables in Atlantic Canada. I also operate Tooodleeedooo!! The Best of Britain, an eclectic British store featuring specialty foods and giftware.

The success of my businesses has enabled me to launch into yet another arena as a keynote speaker, consultant, and media personality. My story of "budding" success was picked up early in my career and eventually blossomed into regional and national TV appearances and syndicated newspaper columns. Today I enjoy travelling throughout Canada and the US, delivering presentations to a wide variety of organizations. I take real pleasure in sharing my experiences with other businesses on everything from cutting-edge produce trends to my grass-roots approach to customer service.

There are always dozens of people behind any successful project. As this book is really the culmination of my years in the produce business, my specific thanks go to those people who have been there, in one way or another, from the beginning. My dad, Bill Luckett, encouraged (in the strongest sense of the word) a heavy-duty work ethic in all his children, which has been the driving force behind my success. Pat Britton, my mentor, opened a door that has led to places neither of us dreamed of. My good pal Bobby Demerchant supported my first venture in the Saint John City Market, for which I am truly grateful. I have been extremely fortunate to find staff members who share the same vision for success; to all, past and present, I extend my gratitude. And without the love and support of my wife, Sue, who has put up with more early mornings and late nights than anyone should have to, I would be lost.

For help specifically with *The Greengrocer's Kitchen*, I am very thankful to Ross and Willa Mavis, owner-chefs of Inn on the Cove, Saint John, New Brunswick, for their generous contribution of microwave instructions. And I owe a particular debt of gratitude to Jennifer Lambert for her invaluable help in putting this book together.

Pete Luckett
1999

Vegetables

The world of produce has seen a dramatic shift since I came to Canada almost twenty years ago. The variety of fruits and vegetables now available is due in part to the ever increasing number of ethnic groups who are making their homes here, creating a demand for vegetables that soon find their way from the "exotic" to the ordinary. After all, it wasn't that long ago that the majority of my customers viewed an avocado with some suspicion! Innovations in cooling and refrigeration techniques, as well as sophisticated transportation systems, have also changed what we buy and eat. Seasonal produce is, for the most part, a thing of the past. Just as our home-grown asparagus is coming to an end, the growing season begins in the southern hemisphere in countries such as Chile and Peru, and then shifts slowly northwards into Mexico, California and Washington, ensuring that we enjoy this "luxury" vegetable year round. When I talk of peak local growing seasons, I'm generally referring to those periods when produce is at its height here in the Maritimes. The growing season across Canada can vary by up to a month, especially in our national "banana belt," southwestern Ontario. However, if you keep an eye on your local greengrocer or supermarket's produce section, you'll soon figure out when and what home-grown produce is available in your neck of the woods. Local produce usually means fresher, and can — but does not always — mean better value for money.

Although we may be more adventurous in our eating habits than even ten years ago, there are still many vegetables that people pass by, sometimes unsure how to cook them, other times not entirely certain what they are! While this is not a guide to the "exotica" of the produce world, I've tried to include most of the vegetables and herbs one is likely to find at an upscale supermarket. For those readers with a botanical bent, I should acknowledge that many of the entries are, properly speaking, fruits or berries rather than vegetables. Members of the squash family, including cucumbers and pumpkins, are actually fruits, as are beans, peas, avocados, and those "culinary vegetables" belonging to the nightshade family: eggplants, peppers, and tomatoes. If I were to leave out all those vegetables that are in fact botanical fruit, there would be some pretty large holes in this book, not to mention in my produce section!

The following pages are an attempt to guide you through the produce department, from choosing and storing vegetables to cooking and eating them. Much of it is common sense, some of it can be taught, and some must be experienced. Actually cooking and eating an artichoke is entirely different than reading about it, although one's first experience can be made easier with a few tips! The recipes that accompany each section are designed with a view to showcasing particular vegetables. Use them to inspire your own creations. Don't be afraid to experiment, whether it be with a new vegetable or a different approach to cooking an old favourite.

Artichokes

Artichoke aficionados consider this vegetable food for the gods. Its botanical name, *Cynara scolymus*, is in honour of Cynara, a beautiful woman who, according to Greek mythology, was transformed into an artichoke plant by a jealous god. A bit hard to swallow, perhaps, but artichokes are nothing if not legendary. First written about over 2000 years ago, they were considered a luxury item at the height of the Roman Empire, and then fell into obscurity until they were reintroduced in Italy during the Renaissance. Our modern globe artichoke is derived from this plant, which was introduced to California by Spanish explorers in the late 1900s. Today, Castroville, California, claims to be the artichoke capital of the world and certainly produces the lion's share of all artichokes eaten in North America.

Technically a thistle, the artichoke plant grows as high as six feet, resembling a giant fern. The artichokes are the immature flower buds, which, if left to grow, transform into huge purple flowers. The name artichoke comes in a circuitous way from the Arabic *al kharshuf,* meaning "the thistle," which was borrowed by the Spanish (*alcahofa*), corrupted by the Italians (*articiocco*), and nicked by the French (*artichaut*), until the English finally adopted it as artichoke. It worked out nicely, since the artichoke has both a heart and a choke. Not surprisingly, the heart is found at the centre of the artichoke, the tender, pale, nutty-flavoured inner leaves. To get to the heart you have to scrape off the "choke," a light layer of fuzz, which I don't suggest you eat.

Artichokes are available sporadically all year long, with their peak season being in the spring, from March through May. Look for firm, compact heads, heavy for their size, with thick, clear skins. The tough outer leaves may be bright green or purplish-red. In the late fall, artichokes sometimes have bronze markings on their leaves, which means they've been kissed by the first frost and may promise a sweeter flavour, since their maturation process has been slowed. Artichokes are picked when mature, and size has nothing to do with taste. Large artichokes are easier to stuff, medium-sized ones are good for dipping and steaming, and the smallest are easiest to prepare as the choke is not developed (they're delicious sautéed or marinated and tossed with pasta). Fresh, unwashed artichokes can be kept in a plastic bag in the refrigerator for up to a week. The leaf tips are spiny, so handle with care.

Preparing — or eating — artichokes can be a little daunting the first time, but it's not as difficult as it looks, and artichokes make a great ice-breaker at a dinner party. I first ate fresh artichokes at my pals' place in Saint John. In hindsight, I was amazed at their capacity to consume just about 100% of the artichoke — thistle ends, choke, and all! At the time, however, I was pretty unsophisticated and too shy to ask questions, so I came away with ravaged and bloody lips! If you've never had them before, here's what to do: Pluck the leaves off one at a time, dip the thick end in a sauce, and then scrape the flesh off using your *teeth*. Once you get to the choke, scrape it away to reveal the prize, which is easiest to eat with a knife and fork.

Artichokes are a great source of potassium and a good source of fibre and vitamin C. At only 47 calories a pop, you can't get enough of these fun-filled vegetables.

STEAMED ARTICHOKES
Rinse the artichokes, slice an inch or so from the tops, and trim the stems to the base. Remove and discard the toughest outer leaves.

Steam the artichokes in a saucepan large enough to allow them to sit side by side on the bottom. Add water to come halfway up the artichokes, plus 1 tablespoon of lemon juice for each artichoke. Bring to a gentle boil, cover, and cook for 20-50 minutes, depending on size; they're done when the leaves pluck off easily and a fork or knife tip can be easily inserted into the base. Drain and serve at once.

Three Dipping Sauces for Artichokes

I like artichokes best when steamed and served with a tasty dipping sauce. Each one of these recipes makes enough sauce for four large artichokes. You could also try a hollandaise sauce (page 71).

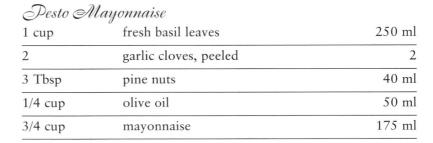

Pesto Mayonnaise

1 cup	fresh basil leaves	250 ml
2	garlic cloves, peeled	2
3 Tbsp	pine nuts	40 ml
1/4 cup	olive oil	50 ml
3/4 cup	mayonnaise	175 ml

Combine everything except the mayonnaise in a food processor, and pulse until it forms a paste. Add the mayonnaise, and blend until smooth. Refrigerate until needed.

Avgolemono (Greek Lemon and Egg Sauce)

1 1/4 cups	chicken broth	300 ml
1/3 cup	dry white wine	80 ml
3	egg yolks	3
3 Tbsp	freshly squeezed lemon juice	40 ml
1 Tbsp	snipped fresh chives	15 ml
	salt and freshly ground black pepper	

Combine the chicken broth and wine in a small saucepan, and bring to a boil over a high heat. Simmer rapidly until the liquid has reduced by about half.

Beat together the egg yolks and lemon juice in a bowl, and then gradually whisk in about 1/4 cup of the hot liquid. Reduce the heat, and pour the egg mixture into the saucepan, whisking constantly until the sauce thickens. If it's a bit lumpy, strain it through a sieve. Season to taste with salt and pepper, and stir in the chives. Serve warm.

Anchovy Browned Butter

1/2 cup	unsalted butter	125 g
1 Tbsp	freshly squeezed lemon juice	15 ml
2 tsp	anchovy paste	10 ml
	salt and paprika	

Heat the butter until lightly browned, making sure it doesn't burn, and then stir in the remaining ingredients. Serve warm.

Artichokes with White Wine and Pancetta

SERVES 4

Cook artichokes in a light wine stock and then use it as a dipping sauce.

1/4 cup	olive oil	50 ml
2	shallots, chopped finely	2
2 oz	pancetta, chopped	50 g
1 cup	dry white wine	250 ml
2 Tbsp	freshly squeezed lemon juice	25 ml
1 Tbsp	chopped fresh oregano	15 ml
	salt and freshly ground black pepper	
4	large artichokes, washed and trimmed	4

Heat the olive oil in small skillet or frying pan. Sauté the shallots and pancetta for 2-3 minutes, and then pour in the wine, lemon juice, and oregano. Season to taste with salt and pepper, and bring to a simmer.

Spread apart the artichoke leaves, and remove the small inner leaves and choke. Position the artichokes upright in a saucepan. Pour the wine sauce into the open tops of the artichokes, and bring to a boil. Cover and simmer for about 45 minutes, until tender. Remove the artichokes from the saucepan, and serve at once with any of lovely sauce left in the pan.

IN THE MICROWAVE
Make the sauce, place the prepared artichokes in a microwave-safe dish, and pour the sauce over them. Cover with a loose lid or vented plastic wrap. Microwave on high 15-18 minutes, basting once or twice, until tender. Let stand 3-5 minutes, and enjoy.

Artichokes Stuffed with Bacon and Parmesan

SERVES 4

4	large artichokes, washed and trimmed	4
4 Tbsp	olive oil	60 ml
6	strips bacon, chopped	6
2	shallots, peeled and chopped finely	2
1	garlic clove, peeled and chopped finely	1
3/4 cup	bread crumbs	175 ml
1/2 cup	freshly grated parmesan cheese	125 ml
1/2 cup	chopped fresh parsley	125 ml
	salt and freshly ground black pepper	

2 Tbsp	melted butter	25 ml
1/2 cup	chicken broth	125 ml
1/2 cup	white wine	125 ml

MICROWAVED ARTICHOKES
Brush rinsed and trimmed artichokes with lemon juice to prevent discolouring. Wrap individually in plastic wrap pierced with a fork. Microwave on high for 4-5 minutes per artichoke. You know they're done when the leaves come off easily and the base is tender. Let stand 3-5 minutes before eating.

Steam the artichokes for 20-50 minutes, until the leaves can be pulled apart. Drain and cool.

Meanwhile, heat the olive oil in a pan, and sauté the bacon, shallots, and garlic for 5 minutes. Remove from the heat, and stir in the bread crumbs, parmesan, and parsley. Season with salt and pepper to taste. Set aside.

Preheat the oven to 375°F (190°C). Remove the choke from each artichoke, and spread the leaves apart, pushing the stuffing into the cavities and between the leaves. Set the artichokes upright in a shallow baking dish. Brush them with melted butter, and pour the broth and wine into the dish. Bake for 30-45 minutes, basting frequently, until tender. Serve at once.

Arugula

Arugula is an excellent source of vitamins A and C and iron. You can also eat it to give a calcium boost to your diet.

Arugula is one of the stellar greens that have made North Americans dive into their salad bowls with new gusto. Europeans have been eating and cooking this pungent leaf for centuries (Italian *rucola*, French *roquette*, English *rocket*), but it wasn't until fairly recently that we could find arugula at our local supermarkets. Arugula has a complex flavour that reminds me of roast beef, pine nuts, and pepper. Its tender green leaves are not just for the salad bowl. They add a welcome bite and dynamic flavour to soups and sauces, as well as dishes that feature starches, such as potatoes, rice, or pasta.

Arugula can be bought year-round, and will generally be found with either the lettuces or the fresh herbs. It comes in bunches, often with its roots still attached. Its emerald-green leaves, which look similar to dandelion leaves, will not be crisp, but neither should they appear limp or wilted. Despite its robust flavour, arugula is delicate and very perishable. If you wrap the roots in paper towel (first removing any elastic bands or twist-ties) before popping the arugula in a plastic bag, it will keep in the refrigerator for two or three days at the most. You'll need to rinse the leaves thoroughly before using as they can hold traces of grit. Slicing the roots off beforehand will get rid of a lot of it, but rinse the leaves in a sink full of cold water, and then spin or pat them dry. If the leaves are large, you may want to tear them in half; otherwise leave them whole.

I never serve the leaves by themselves, but add them to almost any kind of salad, cold or warm, to give it some zing. I also like to add a handful to potato dishes (casseroles, salads, and plain old mashed), and stir whole leaves into creamy pasta sauces.

Fettucini with Arugula Pesto

Arugula has a slightly hot, mustard-like flavour with a hint of pine, which works very well as a substitute for the basil traditionally used as the base for pesto sauce. If you're using dried pasta, reduce the quantity by half and cook according to package instructions.

2 pounds	fresh fettucini	1 kg
3-4 Tbsp	shaved or grated parmesan cheese, for garnish	40-60 ml

For the pesto:

1 cup	lightly packed arugula leaves	250 ml
1/2 cup	parsley	125 ml
1	garlic clove, peeled	1
2 Tbsp	toasted pine nuts	25 ml
1/3-1/2 cup	virgin olive oil	80-125 ml
1/4 cup	grated parmesan cheese	50 ml
	salt	

To make the pesto: Combine the arugula, parsley, garlic, and pine nuts in a food processor or blender, and pulse to form a coarse paste. Continue pulsing while gradually adding enough olive oil to make a loose purée. Mix in the parmesan cheese, and season with salt to taste.

Bring a large pot of salted water to the boil and cook the fettucini for 3-4 minutes, until just tender. Drain and toss with the pesto. Garnish with extra parmesan cheese, and serve at once.

Arugula Salad with Grilled Sweet Onion Rings

3	large sweet onions, peeled and cut in thick slices	3
1/4 cup	olive oil	50 ml
1 tsp	brown sugar	5 ml
3	bunches arugula, rinsed, dried and torn in bite-sized pieces	3

Grilled sweet onions provide a lovely contrast to the peppery taste of arugula.

1/4 cup	shaved fresh parmesan cheese	50 ml
2 Tbsp	freshly squeezed lemon juice	25 ml
2 Tbsp	toasted pine nuts (optional)	25 ml
	salt and freshly ground black pepper	

Preheat the broiler and move an oven rack to the highest position.

Arrange the sliced onion on an oiled baking pan, and drizzle generously with more olive oil. Season with the brown sugar, salt, and pepper, and grill for 5-8 minutes, until the onion slices are just beginning to char. Turn them over, and grill the other sides, brushing them with a little more olive oil and seasoning. Remove from the oven, allow to cool, and then separate into rings. Mix the remaining olive oil with the lemon juice, and toss with the onions, arugula, and pine nuts (if using) in a serving bowl. Serve at once.

Warm Arugula and New Potato Salad

SERVES 2

Choose the smallest potatoes you can find for this recipe. Once cooked, they are grilled with cheese on top of a bed of arugula, causing the leaves to wilt and resulting in a wonderful warm salad.

1 pound	small new potatoes, wiped clean	500 g
2	bunches arugula, rinsed, dried, and torn in bite-sized pieces	2
1 Tbsp	olive oil	15 ml
1 tsp	freshly squeezed lemon juice	5 ml
6 oz	Brie cheese, sliced thinly	175 g
	salt and freshly ground black pepper	

Bring a large pot of lightly salted water to a boil, and add the potatoes. Bring back to a boil, and cook for 10-15 minutes, until tender. Drain and set aside.

Preheat the broiler. Toss the arugula leaves with the olive oil and lemon juice in a shallow baking dish. Slice the cooked potatoes in half if they are larger than bite-sized, and lay them on top of the arugula. Place the cheese on top, season with a little salt and pepper, and slide the dish under the broiler. Grill for a minute or two, until the cheese melts. Serve at once.

IN THE MICROWAVE
You can easily cook the potatoes in the microwave. Put them in a microwave-safe dish with 1/2 cup of water and 1/2 teaspoon salt, and cook on high power for 7-8 minutes, or until tender. Let stand for 3 minutes, and drain.

Asparagus

It wasn't that long ago that the arrival of asparagus was the harbinger of spring. Those first slim and tender green shoots announced the end of winter and were celebrated with reverence, in light of both their limited availability and their high cost. Now, thanks to modern transportation and innovations in post-harvest cooling methods, asparagus can grace our tables most of the year. Beginning in the southern hemisphere in October, in countries such as Chile and Peru, the asparagus season shifts gradually northwards to Mexico, then to California and Washington, before our own home-grown asparagus is harvested in May. Late-season or secondary Canadian asparagus is available into August and even September.

Even so, despite our global economy, asparagus is considered the Rolls-Royce of vegetables, and though it's better value than ever before, we still approach those delicate spears with some veneration. And rightly so, for local seasonal produce is almost always superior to imports, and like other vegetables, asparagus begins to lose its sweetness almost from the moment it is cut. So the arrival of domestic asparagus does indeed call for celebration.

Early asparagus tends to be pencil thin and crunchy, while later crops produce thicker, juicier spears. Choose asparagus with smooth, straight stems of a uniform colour and compact or tightly furled and pointed tips. Most of our asparagus ranges in colour from pale to emerald green. Occasionally you'll find white asparagus. Popular in France, these pale spears are grown underground, "blanched" by the earth to prevent photosynthesis from occurring and producing colour. Asparagus that is allowed to grow just above the surface of the earth usually has mauve or purple tips. In any case, avoid asparagus with ruffled tips or wrinkled, flaccid spears with desiccated stem ends. When harvested too late, asparagus will be tough and fibrous and taste bitter or grassy.

To prepare asparagus for cooking, simply rinse it very quickly under cold running water, and pat dry. Debating whether to trim or snap off the ends and whether to peel or not to peel can consume an entire dinner conversation among asparagus aficionados. The simple answer is that you should remove as little of the stems as possible, either slicing them off a scant inch from the ends or bending them until they snap naturally. Thin young spears shouldn't need peeling, but you can save the length of thicker spears by paring them thinly about half way to the tips. Either way, save the trimmings for stock, as they lend a rich and earthy flavour to soups and sauces. Asparagus is best used as soon as you get it home from the market, but if you must wait, treat the stems like cut flowers, placing them upright in a jar of tepid water. For longer storage, wrap the stem ends in wet paper towel and store in a plastic bag in the crisper section of your refrigerator for up to four days.

As the tender tips cook more quickly than the stem ends, the best way to cook asparagus is standing up — the asparagus, that is; you can kick back with something restorative while you wait. An asparagus steamer is a worthwhile investment for a true lover of the robust vegetable, but you can also tie the spears in small bunches (six or eight) and stand them upright in a tall stock-pot or, as I do, in an old coffee pot, using a piece of foil to create a domed lid. See the instruction on page 18.

ASPARAGUS IN
THE MICROWAVE
Arrange 1 pound (500 g) of asparagus in even layers in a 12 x 18 inch glass baking dish, with the tips towards the centre. Add 1/4 cup (50 ml) water, cover, and cook on high for 3-4 minutes. Rearrange the spears, moving those on the outside to the middle and vice versa. Cook for another 3-4 minutes, until tips are barely tender.

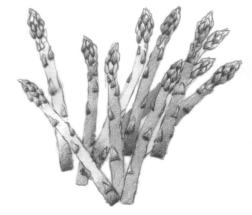

**AVOCADO, MANGO, AND
SHRIMP SALAD WITH MESCLUN**
page 22

CASSAVA FRITTERS
page 43

ROSEMARY AND BLACK
OLIVE FOCACCIA
page 176

EGGPLANT AND RED PEPPER PASTA
page 62

I like to stick half-a-dozen asparagus spears between two slices of crusty white bread and treat myself to a heavenly sandwich. Alternatively, soft-boil an egg and enjoy a sophisticated version of toast soldiers, dipping the cooked spears into the gooey yolk and adding a sprinkle of salt on the way up to your mouth.

Roasted Asparagus with Parmesan

SERVES 4-6

When you're weary of steamed asparagus dripping in butter, try eating it as the Italians do, roasted with olive oil and parmesan cheese. You can also cook it this way on the barbecue and serve it alongside grilled chicken or fish.

2 pounds	asparagus spears, rinsed and trimmed	1 kg
1/4 cup	virgin olive oil	50 ml
1/2 cup	grated fresh parmesan cheese	125 ml
	salt and freshly ground black pepper	

Preheat the oven to 350°F (180°C).

Blanch the asparagus in boiling water for 1-2 minutes, then immediately plunge into ice-cold water, rinse, and pat dry.

Arrange the asparagus on a large sheet of foil, drizzle with olive oil, and season to taste. Fold the foil over the sides and top, pinching to seal. Bake for 15 minutes, then open the foil and sprinkle the asparagus with the parmesan. Leave unsealed and cook for 5 minutes more. Serve piping hot.

Asparagus and Pasta Salad

SERVES 4

Serve this creamy salad on top of a bed of slightly bitter salad leaves, such as mesclun. As with most pasta salads, the flavour deepens if it is left in the refrigerator for at least an hour and preferably overnight.

1 lb	asparagus spears, trimmed and chopped in 1-inch (2.5 cm) lengths	500 g
2 cups	cooked and drained rotini	500 ml
1/2 cup	finely chopped celery	125 ml
1/2	green pepper, seeded and chopped finely	1/2
1/2	small English cucumber, chopped finely	1/2
1	scallion, chopped finely	1

For the dressing:

1 cup	mayonnaise	250 ml
1/2 cup	plain yogurt	125 ml
2 Tbsp	freshly squeezed lemon juice	25 ml
1 Tbsp	chopped fresh dill	15 ml
1 tsp	garlic salt	5 ml
	freshly ground black pepper	

Steam the asparagus spears for about 5 minutes, until just tender. Drain, plunge in cold water, drain again, and pat dry with paper towel.

Blend together the dressing ingredients in a large bowl, and then gently fold in the cooked pasta, chopped celery, green pepper, cucumber, scallion, and asparagus. Cover and refrigerate for at least 1 hour before serving.

Pan-Fried Asparagus with Mustard-Garlic Hollandaise Sauce and Crisp Pancetta

SERVES 4-6

The robust flavour of asparagus takes well to pan-frying and is complemented beautifully by this flavourful version of the classic hollandaise sauce. I like the delicate smokiness of pancetta, but you can substitute thin strips of bacon. Garlic takes on a wonderfully mellow flavour when roasted (see page 74), so don't be alarmed at the quantity in the sauce.

2 lb	asparagus spears, washed and trimmed	1 kg
2 Tbsp	virgin olive oil	25 ml
12	thin slices pancetta	12
	chopped fresh parsley, to garnish (optional)	

For the sauce:

1	whole bulb of garlic	1
3	egg yolks	3
1 Tbsp	freshly squeezed lemon juice	15 ml
1/4 cup	prepared Dijon mustard	50 ml
1/2 cup	virgin olive oil	125 ml
	salt and freshly ground black pepper	

To make the sauce: Remove the loose outer skin of the garlic bulb, then wrap it in foil. Roast it in a preheated 350°F (180°C) oven for about 25 minutes, or until it feels soft when pressed. Allow to cool, and then separate

HOW TO STEAM ASPARAGUS
In an asparagus steamer, stock pot, or unused coffee pot, bring enough water to come an inch or so up the asparagus stems to a rapid boil. Add the asparagus and cover immediately. Cook for 4-10 minutes, depending on the thickness of the stems.

No matter what domestic tragedy occurs in the meantime, *don't* overcook it. The asparagus is ready when the tips are tender, so don't sacrifice the most flavourful bit for the rest.

Pat the asparagus dry with a tea towel or paper towel. Serve on warm plates with a drizzle of melted butter and a squirt of lemon juice.

the cloves and squeeze them into the bowl of a food processor or electric mixer, discarding the skins. Add the egg yolks, lemon juice, and mustard to the garlic. Pulse or beat slowly to mix, then gradually add the olive oil, a few drops at a time, until well combined. Season to taste with salt and pepper, and transfer the sauce to the top of a double boiler set over simmering water. Stir constantly until the sauce thickens, remove from the heat, and set aside. Give it another stir before serving.

Heat the 2 tablespoons of olive oil in a large frying pan or skillet over a medium heat, then sauté the asparagus in batches, turning it frequently for about five minutes, until just tender. If the spears brown slightly, all the better. Remove with a slotted spoon, and pat dry with paper towel, keeping the cooked spears warm in the oven while you finish sautéing the remaining asparagus. You can add a little extra oil to the pan between batches if necessary.

Now raise the temperature, and quickly sauté the pancetta until crisp. Divide the asparagus among four serving plates, placing a generous dollop of sauce alongside each serving. Top each plate with two or three slices of pancetta, and garnish with a sprinkling of parsley, if desired.

Asparagus Risotto

SERVES 4 AS A MAIN COURSE
OR 6-8 AS A SIDE DISH

1/2 lb	asparagus spears, trimmed and cut in 1/2-inch (2.5-cm) lengths	250 g
2 Tbsp	butter	40 ml
1 Tbsp	virgin olive oil	15 ml
2 large	shallots, chopped finely	2
1/4 cup	dry white wine	50 ml
1 cup	risotto rice (arborio, carnaroli, or roma)	250 ml
2 1/2 - 3 cups	chicken stock, or half-and-half chicken broth and water	625-750 ml
1/2 cup	grated fresh parmesan	125 ml
	salt and freshly ground black pepper	
	finely chopped fresh parsley, to garnish	

Risotto has become a very trendy restaurant dish, but a lot of people are shy to cook their own. Don't be — although you can't leave the stove while it's cooking, there is very little preparation involved, and nothing beats a freshly cooked risotto, especially one with asparagus and parmesan. The key to a great risotto is to use the right rice, sometimes labelled "risotto" rice, but usually called arborio, carnaroli, or roma. Use a heavy-based saucepan, add the stock slowly, and stir constantly. Risotto should be creamy in texture, but still be al dente — a little firm in the centre.

Set aside the asparagus tips and melt the butter and oil in a heavy-based saucepan over a medium heat. Sauté the chopped shallots for 5 minutes, until golden brown. Stir in the chopped asparagus stems and cook for 1-2 minutes. Stir in the wine, raise the heat, and cook quickly, stirring frequently until the liquid has almost evaporated.

Stir the rice into the saucepan, coating the grains thoroughly. Add 1/2 cup of chicken stock, reduce the heat to medium-low, and cook for about 5 minutes, stirring constantly, until the liquid is absorbed. Add another 1/2 cup of stock, and continue to cook, stirring constantly. Continue this way until all but 1 cup of stock is absorbed, and season to taste with salt and pepper. Then add the asparagus tips with 1/2 cup of the remaining stock. Cook for 5 minutes, until the stock is absorbed and the rice is tender but not mushy, adding the remaining 1/2 cup of stock if necessary. Stir in the cheese, season again if necessary, and serve at once, garnished with chopped fresh parsley.

Avocados

Technically fruit, avocados grow on trees that bear some botanical kinship to the glossy-leafed laurel. Also known as avocado pears, due to their shape, or alligator pears, because of the lizard-like skin of certain varieties, their name actually comes from the Aztec word *ahuacatl*. A New World fruit native to Central America (famous for guacamole), avocados are now produced also in California, Florida, the West Indies, South Africa, Australia, and Israel. The Israelis were the first to develop a mobile, chariot-like lift that enables pickers to move rapidly up, down, and around the trees, choosing only those avocados prime for harvesting. Avocados are a bit of an anomaly in the world of produce, as they can ripen only after they're picked, and instead of sweetening as they mature, they develop a high fat content, which gives them their buttery, velvet texture and rich, nutty taste.

There are many varieties of avocados, but the Hass, imported from Mexico and California, is by far the most popular and most commonly available. Small and pear-shaped, it has a dark, purplish skin, knobbly in texture, and beautiful creamy flesh — like eating butter out of a shell. The Fuertes avocado, which comes mainly from Florida, has a smooth bright green skin and a drier flesh, with only about half the fat of the Hass variety.

It's a rare thing to find a perfectly ripe avocado in the supermarket, so buy them a few days before you need them. Avoid very soft fruit and those with blemished or dented skins. Although a slightly over-ripe avocado can be used in sauces or dips, after a certain point the flesh will have turned black and taste slightly rancid. Leave unripened avocados on a windowsill or countertop until they "give" when pressed gently, and refrigerate for one or two days if you're not eating them right away. I recommend allowing avocados to come back to room temperature before eating, as their flavour is less pronounced when they are cold. And never refrigerate an under-ripe avocado, as it will become brown and streaky.

To prepare an avocado for eating, slice it in half lengthways around the centre stone, then give it a slight twist to pull the halves apart. Holding the half with the stone in the palm of one hand, press a sharp knife blade into the stone and twist gently to remove it. You can scoop out the flesh using a spoon, or peel off the skin and slice or chop the flesh. Use cut avocados as soon as possible, as the flesh begins to darken almost immediately. Rubbing cut surfaces with lemon juice will prevent the fruit from discolouring for 1-2 hours.

I used to claim that eating cooked avocados would be like drinking ice-cold Guinness — neither abomination would ever pass my lips. However, having travelled a fair bit in Central America, I've learned that avocados are

Avocados are a good source of vitamins E, B6, and folate, and contain moderate quantities of vitamin C and potassium. However, their high fat content — while of the healthy, monounsaturated variety — does leave them further behind in the weight loss game than most fruits and vegetables. Half a medium-sized avocado contains about 200 calories.

an excellent last-minute addition to soups and stews. Still, the perfect way to eat a ripe avocado is simply drizzled with balsamic vinegar, with perhaps a large black olive set in the centre of each half. The creamy texture and high fat content of avocados makes them good salad partners with acidic fruits such as pineapple, tomato, pink grapefruit, mango, and papaya, and sliced avocado with chopped cilantro makes a great garnish for grilled mackerel.

Avocado, Tomato, and Bocconcini Salad

SERVES 4

This Mediterranean salad — insalata tricolore in Italian — echoes the colours of the Italian flag. The flavours of sweet, ripe tomatoes, rich, nutty avocado, and peppery fresh basil combine to complement perfectly the creamy mellowness of "baby" mozzarella, or bocconcini. Bocconcini comes in small balls, usually kept fresh in a light brine. Serve this salad with crusty ciabatta bread to mop up the juices and vinaigrette.

4-6	ripe tomatoes, sliced thinly	4-6
2	ripe avocados, peeled, stoned, and sliced thinly	2
10 oz	bocconcini, drained and halved	300 g
1/2 cup	fresh basil leaves, left whole	125 ml

For the vinaigrette:

1	garlic clove	1
1/2 tsp	salt	2 ml
1 1/2 tsp	Dijon mustard	7 ml
2 Tbsp	balsamic vinegar	25 ml
1/3 cup	extra virgin olive oil	80 ml
2 Tbsp	chopped fresh basil leaves	25 ml
1 Tbsp	chopped fresh tarragon	15 ml
1/2 tsp	freshly ground black pepper	2 ml

To prepare the vinaigrette: Crush the garlic and salt to a paste in a mortar and pestle or with the flat side of a knife blade. Combine the garlic with the remaining vinaigrette ingredients in a small jar with a tightly fitting lid, and shake thoroughly.

Arrange the tomato and avocado slices in concentric, overlapping circles on a large platter, inserting the whole basil leaves throughout. Scatter the bocconcini halves on top, drizzle the dressing over everything, and serve at once.

Avocado, Mango, and Shrimp Salad with Mesclun

SERVES 4

2	avocados, peeled, stoned, and sliced thickly	2
1	large mango, peeled and sliced thickly	1
1 lb	cooked salad shrimp, rinsed and drained	500 g
12 oz	mesclun	375 g

For the dressing:

1	garlic clove, chopped finely	1
1	shallot, chopped finely	1
1/4 cup	freshly squeezed orange juice	50 ml
2 Tbsp	freshly squeezed lime juice	25 ml
2/3 cup	vegetable oil	150 ml
1 Tbsp	chopped fresh parsley	15 ml

Combine the dressing ingredients in a bowl, and whisk to blend. Gently fold the avocado, mango and shrimp into the dressing. Arrange the salad leaves on a serving platter or individual plates, and slide the dressed salad over top. Serve at once.

Avocado Salsa

SERVES 4 AS A SIDE DISH

1	ripe but firm large avocado, peeled, stoned, and chopped finely	1
2	ripe but firm large tomatoes, chopped finely	2
1/2	small red onion, chopped finely	1/2
1	finger hot pepper, chopped very finely	1
2 Tbsp	finely chopped fresh cilantro	25 ml
2 Tbsp	freshly squeezed lime juice	25 ml
	a dash of Tabasco sauce	
	salt and freshly ground black pepper	

This salad-cum-dip is the perfect accompaniment to grilled salmon. It's also great as a garnish for piping hot bowls of chili — with a dollop of sour cream, of course. Chop the vegetables finely, but not so finely that they turn into mush when stirred together.

Combine all the ingredients in a bowl, and season to taste. Cover and set aside for at least 1 hour to allow the flavours to develop.

Beans

POD AND SHELL BEANS

Despite the mountains of beans available in the Frootique each summer, every year I plant about forty scarlet runner beans in my own garden. Rarely sold commercially, these prolific climbers (they'd grow up your leg if you stood still long enough) produce an enormous yield of delicious, crunchy beans, as well as gorgeous red flowers. But even if you don't grow your own, there are plenty of other varieties available at the supermarket.

Once upon a time, all fresh beans were referred to as string beans, whether yellow or green, because of the tough thread running down the length of the pod. Children were set the endless task of pulling the fibrous strings from the beans before dinner. In time, botanists developed a new, threadless strain of bean, and children were free to play throughout the long days of summer. Fairy tales do come true. Now we divide beans into two groups, pod beans and shell beans.

Shell beans include fava (broad) beans and cannellini. Most shell beans grown commercially are dried, and we commonly purchase them cooked and canned or rehydrate them and use them in dishes such as Boston baked beans. However, if you're able to find them fresh, young shell beans can be cooked and eaten pod and all, and have a tender, starchy quality that's enhanced by a bit of butter and black pepper. If they are longer than three inches, you'll probably need to shell them. I find shelling them after boiling works best, since it mellows the bitterness of older beans.

Pod beans include endless varieties but only three types: snap beans, wax beans, and pole beans. Snap or green beans are available year-round, coming from Florida, California, Georgia, and sometimes Mexico, but you'll find the freshest and tastiest beans during your local growing season. Snap beans are pale to dark green in colour, have smooth skins and a pleasant curve, and are more or less round in cross-section. They range from the tiny, tender, three-inch variety, which the French call *haricots verts*, to a good eight inches in length.

Wax or yellow beans are not grown as widely, and aside from local summer bounties, they're available sporadically throughout the rest of the year. Similar in shape to snap beans, they can be any colour from a pale, almost translucent yellow, to a deep golden hue. The freshest wax beans will have slightly green tips. Wax beans have a mild, buttery flavour.

Pole beans resemble flattened green snap beans with slightly coarser skin. They're not commonly available at supermarkets; you are more likely to find them in season at farmers' markets, roadside stands, or, if you're lucky, in a neighbour's garden. (Don't come knocking at my door.)

When buying pod beans, choose small, firm ones with good colour, a silky texture, and no blemishes. If they look wilted or bend easily, give them a miss. As a grocer, I don't encourage wholesale slaughter of my beans, but you might want to give one or two a test; if they break easily with a simple snap, they're fresh and tender. Snap and wax beans will keep in the refrigerator for up to four days.

HOW TO PREPARE POD BEANS
Rinse well in cold water and then snap off or trim the stem ends. Cook small beans whole, and slice larger ones in pieces. Steam or boil them in lightly salted boiling water for 3-8 minutes, depending on their size, until just tender. You want them to retain their snap, so don't overcook them. Serve at once, drizzled with butter or a vinaigrette and sprinkled with salt and freshly ground black pepper.

If you're using your beans cold or in a recipe, blanch them in boiling water for 1 minute, then plunge them into cold water to stop the cooking process and preserve their fresh colour.

YARD-LONG BEANS
(CHINESE BEANS, DAU GOK)

I'm going to cheat a bit here and sneak in a personal favourite that isn't really a bean at all. The yard-long bean may look like an overgrown green bean, but in fact it's a pea, not a bean, and the flavour is distinctly different. Yard-long beans are neither crisp nor sweet nor juicy; instead, they're rather chewy and nutty, and their flavour intensifies when they're fried, braised, or stewed. They're great when stir-fried in sesame oil with garlic, ginger, and a splash of soy sauce.

Grown mostly in Asia and available year-round, yard-long beans are actually harvested when they reach about 1 1/2 feet (45 cm), with the peas still immature. Slender and flexible, they can be pale or deep green — the lighter coloured variety is generally more tender. Choose small, skinny beans, with no rusty patches. They won't be snappy, like green beans, but neither should they be too limp or dry. Yard-long beans are more perishable than green beans and should be used within two days of purchase. In the meantime, store them in a plastic bag in the refrigerator.

HOW TO PREPARE
YARD-LONG BEANS
Rinse well in cold water, trim the ends, and slice on the diagonal in short lengths. Don't bother boiling or steaming these beans; they won't thank you for it. Yard-long beans benefit from slow braising, which in fact will cause them to become crunchier, developing a nut-like flavour.

Spanish Mixed Bean Stew with Picada

SERVES 4-6

Picada, a mixture of garlic, bread crumbs, herbs, and toasted nuts, is used in Spain to thicken and flavour soups and stews.

3 cups	water	750 ml
1/4 cup	white wine	50 ml
1	bay leaf	1
2 tsp	cumin seeds, toasted and crushed	10 ml
1 tsp	salt	5 ml
1	large carrot, peeled and cubed	1
1	large apple, cored and cubed	1
1 cup	green or yellow beans, trimmed and halved	250 ml
1/2 cup	canned chickpeas, drained	125 ml
1/2 cup	canned cannellini, flageolet, or white beans, drained	125 ml
1/2 cup	snow peas, trimmed	125 ml
1/2 cup	fresh or frozen peas	125 ml
	freshly ground black pepper	
	chopped fresh parsley, to garnish	

TOASTED SEEDS
The flavour of cumin seeds is much more pronounced once they are toasted. Simply heat them in a small covered pan until they begin to dance around.

For the picada:

4 Tbsp	toasted hazelnuts	60 ml
2 Tbsp	toasted pine nuts	25 ml
2 Tbsp	dried bread crumbs	25 ml
1	garlic clove, crushed	1
1/2 cup	fresh parsley	125 ml

Bring the water, wine, bay leaf, cumin seeds, and salt to a boil in a large saucepan. Add the carrot and apple, and reduce the heat. Simmer for 5 minutes. Stir in the beans, chickpeas, canned beans, snow peas and peas, and cook for 5 minutes longer.

Meanwhile, place the ingredients for the picada in a food processor or blender, and pulse until the mixture forms a paste. Add a tablespoon of liquid from the stew to the paste to thin it out, and then stir the picada into the stew. Simmer for 5 minutes more, adding extra water if necessary. Season to taste with salt and pepper, garnish with fresh parsley, and serve.

Beans with Walnut Vinaigrette

SERVES 4

A mixture of yellow and green beans adds a bit of colour to the table. If you don't have walnut oil, increase the amount of olive oil and add an extra tablespoon of crushed nuts.

1 lb	beans, trimmed and cut in 2-inch (5-cm) lengths	500 g
1 Tbsp	walnut pieces, to garnish	15 ml

For the vinaigrette:

1	shallot, chopped	1
2 Tbsp	finely chopped walnuts	25 ml
1/2 tsp	coarse sea salt	2 ml
1/4 tsp	freshly ground black pepper	1 ml
2 tsp	Dijon mustard	10 ml
3 Tbsp	balsamic vinegar	40 ml
1/3 cup	olive oil	60 ml
1/4 cup	walnut oil	50 ml

To prepare the vinaigrette: Combine the ingredients in small jar with a tightly fitting lid, and shake thoroughly.

Bring a large pot of salted water to a rapid boil, and drop in the beans.

Bring back to a boil, and cook, uncovered, for 3-8 minutes, until the beans are just tender. Drain and plunge into cold water, drain again, and toss with the walnut vinaigrette. Garnish with walnut pieces and serve at once, or refrigerate and serve chilled.

Stir-Fried Yard-Long Beans

SERVES 4

Yard-long beans take longer to cook than snap beans, but they will retain their crunchy texture even after a combination of stir-frying and braising. Adding almonds just before serving accentuates the nutty flavour of the beans.

2 Tbsp	peanut oil	25 ml
1 lb	yard-long beans, trimmed and cut diagonally in 2-inch (5-cm) lengths	500 g
1-inch	piece of fresh ginger, peeled and chopped finely	2.5-cm
1	garlic clove, peeled and chopped finely	1
1 Tbsp	soy sauce	15 ml
3 Tbsp	water	40 ml
1/3 cup	toasted slivered almonds	60 ml

Heat the oil in a wok or large stir-fry pan. Add the beans, ginger, and garlic, and stir-fry for about 5 minutes, until the beans turn bright green. Reduce the heat, and add the soy sauce and water. Cover and simmer for 5-7 minutes, until the beans feel tender when pierced with a fork. Stir in the almonds, and serve at once.

MICROWAVED BEANS
Put a pound (500 g) of prepared green or wax beans in a 2-litre casserole dish with 1/2 cup of water. (Do not salt!) Cover and cook on high until tender, 6-8 minutes, stirring once, and let stand, covered, for 2 minutes.

Beets

Many people believe that beets grow in jars on their grandmother's pantry shelves. Not true. These globe-shaped beauties are the sweetest of the root vegetables as well as the most colourful. However, I have to admit that, with the exception of pickled beets, this is one of the few vegetables I've never grown to like. But beet lovers will tell you that there's nothing like the fresh article — steamed lightly, roasted or baked, or even sautéed with garlic and a smidgen of caramelized onions.

There are four main beet varieties: the sugar beet, from which most of our white sugar is processed; the mangold, harvested for livestock feed; the leaf beet, or Swiss chard, which is grown for its greens (see page 141-143); and the common or garden beet, which is the vegetable in question here. The garden beet is available almost year-round, but its growing season is during the summer and early fall. New beets arrive with their leafy greens still attached, which can be eaten raw in salads, stir-fried, or braised slowly to bring out their mild flavour.

Beets can be round or elongated, and they can vary in colour from white, gold, or pale pink to the more common rich purple-red. When choosing beets, look for smooth, unblemished skins, firm texture, and a vibrant tone. The more regular the shape the better, as misshapen roots can indicate toughness or a bitter flavour. The condition of the tops is important only if you plan on using them, in which case you want young, thin-ribbed greens with fresh, clean leaves. Beet greens should be removed and used as soon as possible. The beets themselves can be kept for up to a month in a perforated plastic bag in the refrigerator. You can peel and shred really small, young raw beets for salads or stir-fries. Smaller beets will be more tender, suitable for eating steamed or stir-fried, while the larger, older beets benefit from boiling, roasting or braising, all of which take about the same amount of time.

To prepare beets, trim the stems and tails about a finger's width from the beet — any closer and you risk nicking the skin and causing the beet to bleed during cooking.

Rinse the beets under cold running water, rubbing them with your hands to remove any grime. Cook them whole and unpeeled so the colour and nutrients don't leach into the water. Depending on their size, beets will take 20-60 minutes to cook, whether boiled, steamed, or roasted. They are ready when they feel tender when pierced with a fork or knife tip.

Blanch boiled beets in cold water to speed up the cooling process and to make sure the skins will slip off easily.

Serve small beets whole and larger beets sliced; toss in butter or olive oil with a squeeze of lemon juice, a sprinkling of salt and paprika, and some freshly chopped dill or parsley.

Stir-Fried Beets

SERVES 4

2 Tbsp	butter	25 ml
1 lb	fresh beets, peeled and shredded	500 g
	zest and juice of 1 lemon	
1 Tbsp	chopped fresh cilantro	15 ml
	salt and freshly grated black pepper	
	sour cream, to garnish	

Heat the butter in a large frying pan, and sauté the shredded beets for about 2 minutes to heat through. Stir in the lemon juice and zest, and season with salt and pepper to taste. Garnish with chopped cilantro, and serve at once.

For a slightly different flavour and texture, place the butter and shredded beets in a glass dish, and microwave for 1-2 minutes, until heated through. Then stir in the lemon juice and zest, season, garnish, and serve.

Braised Beets with Apples and Nutmeg

SERVES 4

5	fresh beets, cooked, peeled and cut in 1/2-inch (1-cm) cubes	5
3	tart apples, cored and cut in 1/2-inch (1-cm) cubes	3
1	small onion, sliced thinly	1
2 Tbsp	butter	25 ml
	zest and juice of 1/2 lemon	
2 tsp	sugar	10 ml
1 tsp	salt	5 ml
1/2 tsp	freshly grated nutmeg	2 ml

Preheat the oven to 350°F (180°C). Lightly grease a shallow casserole or baking pan.

Toss together the beets, apples, and onion. Dot with butter, and sprinkle with the lemon juice and zest, sugar, salt, and nutmeg. Cover and bake for 30 minutes. Remove the cover, give the mixture a stir, and cook for 10-15 minutes more. Serve hot.

MICROWAVE BRAISING
The microwave does a nice job on this recipe. Prepare the ingredients as directed in a microwave-safe casserole, adding 1 tablespoon of water. Cover and microwave on high for 8-10 minutes, until apples and onion are soft. Let stand 2-3 minutes, and serve.

Bountiful Summer Borscht

SERVES 4-6

2 Tbsp	butter	25 ml
1	onion, chopped	1
1	garlic clove, chopped finely	1
1	carrot, peeled and cubed	1
1	potato, peeled and cubed	1
1 lb	beets, peeled and grated	500 g
2	tomatoes, skinned, seeded and chopped	2
2 Tbsp	balsamic vinegar	25 ml
1/2 tsp	sugar	2 ml
5 cups	chicken stock	1.25 L
1 lb	cabbage, cored and shredded	500 g
1	large cooked beet	1
1 Tbsp	freshly squeezed lemon juice	15 ml

This is a lighter version of the traditional heavy Russian soup. Because the vibrant purple colour of the beets turns brownish when cooked, grate an extra cooked beet into the soup just before serving to liven it up.

salt and freshly ground black pepper	
sour cream	
fresh snipped chives	

Melt the butter in a large saucepan, and sauté the onion and garlic for 5 minutes, until softened but not browned. Stir in the cubed carrot and potato and the shredded beets, and cook for 5 minutes more. Add the tomatoes, vinegar, sugar, and 1 cup of stock. Bring to a simmer, and cook for 15 minutes. Now stir in the cabbage and the remaining stock. Bring back to a simmer, and cook for 20 minutes, stirring occasionally.

Peel the cooked beet, and shred it directly into the soup. Season to taste with lemon juice, salt, and pepper, and leave over a low heat for 5 minutes more. Top each serving with a swirl of sour cream and a sprinkling of chives.

Bok Choy

Bok choy, also known as pak choi, is another entry in the growing list of vegetables with sometimes-confusing names. Although bok choy is at once Asian and a cabbage, it is not the same as either Chinese cabbage or napa (see page 36). In appearance it looks like a pale version of Swiss chard, with thick, silvery-white central stalks and slightly furled bluish-green leaves. Its flavour is mildly hot and cabbage-like, making it a perfect foil for the sweet and spicy flavours of Asian cooking. Unlike Chinese cabbage, which is ideal for eating raw in salads, bok choy is better when cooked briefly; its leaves become brilliant green and their flavour more intense, while its stalks remain succulent and crunchy.

Once found only in Asian specialty markets, bok choy is now readily available year-round in most supermarkets. There are a number of different varieties, but usually bok choy will be fairly squat, with large, wide leaves, or else have longer stems with narrow leaves. The chubby variety is great in soups, and the more elegant-looking kind is ideal for stir-fries, as the abundant stems provide a second vegetable. Either way, look for firm, white stalks and crisp, vivid leaves. Avoid any that appear tired or wilted, as bok choy is extremely perishable and there is no way of reviving it. You should also look out for "baby" bok choy, or "hearts," which are ideal for braising or steaming and serving whole.

Because bok choy does not keep well, use it as soon as possible after purchase and within two days at the most. Until then, keep it in a plastic bag in the refrigerator. Bok choy is wonderful stir-fried (on its own or in combination with other vegetables) in a little peanut or sesame oil, seasoned with garlic, ginger, and a splash of soy sauce. Or take advantage of the numerous Chinese, Thai, and other bottled Oriental sauces available to make a quick, easy, and flavourful stir-fry. Shredded leaves can be tossed into a soup or stew at the end of cooking, or you can braise the stems in chicken stock until barely tender, and then stir in the leaves a few minutes before serving. The key to cooking bok choy is to keep it quick and simple.

HOW TO PREPARE BOK CHOY
Trim and discard the base. Strip the leaves from the stalks, and rinse and spin or pat them dry. Chop or tear the leaves, and slice the stalks on the diagonal, keeping all the pieces bite-sized. As the leaves need very little cooking, add them to the wok or steamer just a few seconds before serving.

Bok Choy with Shiitake Mushrooms

SERVES 4

Serve this stir-fry with aromatic jasmine or basmati rice and a pot of green tea for a quick and easy Asian meal.

8-12	shiitake mushrooms, cleaned and trimmed	8-12
1	large bok choy, rinsed and trimmed	1
1/4 cup	chicken stock	50 ml
1/4 cup	rice wine or dry sherry	50 ml
1 Tbsp	oyster sauce	15 ml
2 tsp	sesame oil	10 ml
1 tsp	sugar	5 ml
2 tsp	cornstarch	10 ml
	freshly ground black pepper	
2 Tbsp	peanut or vegetable oil	25 ml
2	garlic cloves, chopped finely	2
1	large shallot, chopped finely	1

Bok choy is rich in vitamins A and C and is a good source of potassium. Feel free to eat as much as you like — at only 30 calories a cup, this green is a dieter's delight.

If the shiitakes are very large, slice them thickly; halve or quarter smaller mushrooms. Separate the leaves from the stems of the bok choy. Slice the stems diagonally in 2-inch (5-cm) lengths, and shred the leaves.

Combine the stock, rice wine or sherry, oyster sauce, sesame oil, sugar, and cornstarch in a small bowl, and blend thoroughly.

Heat the oil in a wok or large stir-fry pan over a high heat. Add the garlic and shallot, and sauté for 30 seconds. Stir in the mushrooms and bok choy stems, and stir-fry for about 3 minutes. Add the leaves and cook for 1 minute more, and then stir in the blended stock mixture. Cook for 1-2 minutes, stirring frequently to glaze the vegetables. Serve at once.

Hot and Sour Steamed Bok Choy

SERVES 4

1	large bok choy, rinsed and trimmed	1
3 Tbsp	rice vinegar	40 ml
1 tsp	Asian chili sauce	5 ml
2 tsp	sesame oil	10 ml
2 tsp	toasted sesame seeds	10 ml

Because the leaves cook more quickly than the stems, they should be added a few minutes later so they don't turn soggy.

1 tsp	sugar	5 ml
1 tsp	salt	5 ml

IN THE MICROWAVE

After washing and shredding the bok choy, place it in a covered casserole. Microwave on high for 6-8 minutes, stirring once. Let stand for 2-3 minutes before tossing with the remaining ingredients.

Strip the leaves from the stems, and shred finely. Slice the stems on the diagonal in 1/2-inch (1-cm) strips. Place the stems in a steamer basket over an inch (2 cm) of boiling water. Cover and steam for 4 minutes, and then add the leaves and cook for 2 minutes longer. Combine the remaining ingredients in a serving bowl, and then add the cooked bok choy. Toss to coat and serve at once.

Broccoli

Broccoli is an excellent source of vitamin A, calcium, potassium, and folate, and a single serving contains more vitamin C than a glass of orange juice. However, to retain its nutrients, broccoli should be cooked in as little water as possible or, even better, munched raw.

COOKING TIP

Cook broccoli and its more pungent relatives uncovered for the first few minutes to let the sulphuric gases escape. This will eliminate the strong smell these vegetables sometimes produce, and it will also help to retain the vibrant green colour.

If you forget to buy your loved one roses on Valentine's Day, consider presenting him or her with a head of broccoli. It's a beauty of a vegetable, a vibrant bouquet of florets and budding sprouts that tastes as great as it looks. And once you're done admiring it, you've got any number of options. Eat it raw, with a creamy dip; steam it just until tender, and then drizzle with melted butter; braise it with garlic, anchovies, and wine; or stir-fry it in a black bean sauce. Now *that's* a recipe for passion.

Broccoli is a member of the cabbage family, a sort of cousin to cauliflower, Brussels sprouts, collard greens, and kale. We can thank Italy for this magnificent vegetable (broccoli is Italian for "small shoots"), and in particular the Calabrians, from whom broccoli gets its other name, calabrese. North America produces very good broccoli, and I have to say that the stuff grown here in the Maritimes is the best I've ever eaten. Available year-round, broccoli peaks when the weather is cool, from late summer to early spring. Broccoli is sometimes offered pre-wrapped in cellophane, but it's preferable to buy it loose, both because you can see what you're getting and because wrapped vegetables tend to deteriorate more quickly. Look for heads with small, tightly closed bud clusters and firm but tender green stalks. The buds should be dark green, with a purple or bluish haze. Avoid heads that are sprouting or yellow in colour and stalks that look either woody or rubbery. As with most vegetables, the best thing you can do with broccoli once it's in your kitchen is to eat it. Broccoli is very perishable, but it will keep in good condition for about three days when stored in a plastic bag in the refrigerator.

To prepare broccoli, rinse it under cold running water and shake dry. Cut the stalk at its base and peel off any tough or fibrous skin. You can remove the florets, cutting them off at the base of their stems, and slice the peeled stalk and florets into equal-sized pieces for even cooking. The stems will take a few minutes longer to cook, so add them to the pan first. Broccoli can be boiled in a small amount of lightly salted water for 3-5 minutes or steamed for 8-12 minutes. Either way, leave the lid off the pot for the first few minutes. You can also boil or steam whole heads of broccoli. Peel the stalks and slit them up to the base just below the florets, then boil for 6-8 minutes, or until tender but still crisp. To steam whole heads, stand them upright in an inch or two of boiling water, then cover and cook for 10-15 minutes. If you're parboiling broccoli for use in a recipe, rinse it under cold running water to halt the cooking process, and drain well. And if you're inviting me round for supper, just remember that while I love broccoli cooked *al dente*, I may not be able to refrain from making a horrible face if presented with a plate of soft, overcooked florets.

Broccoli with Garlic and Anchovies

SERVES 4-6

Garlic and anchovies sautéed in olive oil and butter make a wonderfully piquant dressing for crisp, steamed broccoli or for raw or blanched florets. Either way, have a loaf of crusty bread on hand to soak up the extra juices.

2 Tbsp	butter	25 ml
6	garlic cloves, chopped finely	6
10	canned anchovies, drained and chopped	10
3/4 cup	virgin olive oil	175 ml
1 lb	broccoli, trimmed and cut in spears	500 g

Melt the butter in a saucepan over a medium heat, and sauté the garlic until softened but not browned. Stir in the anchovies, and cook for 1 minute. Gradually add the olive oil, stirring constantly, and simmer for 10 minutes.

Blanch the broccoli in lightly salted boiling water for 3-5 minutes, until barely tender. Drain and transfer to a serving bowl. Pour the anchovy sauce over top, and serve at once.

Stir-Fried Broccoli with Black Bean Sauce

SERVES 4

1 Tbsp	peanut or vegetable oil	15 ml
1	onion, sliced thinly	1
1 lb	broccoli, trimmed and cut in spears	500 g
3 Tbsp	water	40 ml
1 Tbsp	black bean sauce	15 ml
1 tsp	sugar	5 ml
2 tsp	sesame seeds (optional)	10 ml

Heat the oil in a wok or large stir-fry pan, and sauté the onions for 2 minutes. Add the broccoli, and stir-fry for 2 minutes more. Add the water, black bean sauce, and sugar, and stir well. Cover and cook for 3 minutes,

BROCCOLI IN THE MICROWAVE

Broccoli cooked in the microwave has a lovely, pure flavour, but getting both stems and florets cooked to perfection is as tricky in the microwave as in the steamer.

Place uniform spears in a round glass baking dish with the tender florets towards the centre and the denser stems pointing outward. Add 1/4 cup of water and a pinch of salt, cover, and cook on high for 5-8 minutes, depending on how much you're cooking and how large the pieces are, until the stems are almost tender. Let stand for 2 minutes before serving.

remove the lid, and cook for 1-2 minutes longer, until the liquid has evaporated and the broccoli is tender but still crisp. Sprinkle with sesame seeds (if using), and serve at once.

Pasta with Creamy Broccoli and Walnut Sauce

SERVES 4

I love the combination of walnuts and broccoli. Chopped walnuts add extra crunch to the sauce, and if you don't have walnut oil on hand, you can substitute olive oil.

1 lb	dried farfalle or fusilli	500 g
1 Tbsp	vegetable oil	15 ml
1 Tbsp	walnut oil	15 ml
1	small onion, chopped	1
1 lb	broccoli florets	500 g
5 oz	cream cheese, cubed	150 g
1 cup	milk	250 ml
1/3 cup	walnut pieces	80 ml
1/2 cup	fresh basil, chopped coarsely	125 ml
	salt and freshly ground black pepper	
2 Tbsp	freshly grated parmesan cheese	25 ml

Cook the pasta according to package directions while you prepare the sauce.

Heat the vegetable and walnut oils in a large saucepan, and sauté the onion for 5 minutes, until softened. Add the broccoli florets, and cook for 5 minutes more. Add the cheese and milk, and cook, stirring frequently, until the cheese melts and the sauce thickens.

Stir in the walnuts and basil, and season to taste with salt and pepper. Toss with the cooked pasta, sprinkle with freshly grated parmesan cheese, and serve at once.

Brussels Sprouts

As with other members of the brassica *species, Brussels sprouts are a cancer fighter, packed with antioxidants.*

"Eat your greens!" My mum's words echo in my ears as if it were yesterday, and I still feel like a bit of a fraud when I hear myself telling my kids the same thing. Greens, when I was growing up, didn't mean Caesar salad or steamed asparagus. Greens meant Brussels sprouts (and my mother meant business). These days I actually like my sprouts, and ironically enough, like many other vegetables of humble origins, they are becoming somewhat fashionable. After all, any vegetable that shares its name with an elegant European city is bound to have a certain mystique. And if you're used to buying Brussels sprouts loose, seeing them on the stalk only enhances their enigmatic personality.

If you're not already enamoured of these doll-sized cabbages, buy a pound and try them again. They have a sweet, nutty flavour, tasting nothing like their giant cousins. However, like other cabbages, Brussels sprouts benefit from either quick cooking or slow braising. Anything between can ruin them, giving them the characteristic sulphuric smell and flavour that lends all cabbages a bad name.

Although available year-round, Brussels sprouts are a cold-weather vegetable, at their best from September through March. They're usually sold loose, but if you have the chance, buy them on the stalk, where they grow in knobbly rows of tiny, hard rosettes. Either way, look for tightly wrapped, bright sprouts; they should be no more than 1 1/2 inches (3 cm) in diameter and feel heavy for their size. Avoid any that seem puffy, with loose or yellowed outer leaves. Store them, unwashed, in a plastic bag in the refrigerator for up to five days. The sooner you use them the better, as their flavour grows more "cabbagey" with age.

To prepare, rinse the sprouts under cold, running water, trim the stems, and remove any loose outer leaves. Trimming the ends too closely will allow the leaves to come apart. Cutting a small cross in the bottom of the stems helps them to cook evenly (and wards off evil spirits for good measure). Small sprouts can be left whole, but larger ones should be halved or even quartered to make sure they cook through before growing soggy on the outside.

If you're stir-frying sprouts, slice them thinly, or you can even separate the leaves, which will cook very quickly in butter or olive oil and are terrific when seasoned with a little ginger and lemon juice.

To cook sprouts, drop them into just enough lightly salted boiling water to cover. Boil for 4-10 minutes, depending on their size, until the stem ends feel tender. Leave the lid off the pan, so that the water evaporates gradually while the steam produced cooks the top layer of sprouts. Drain, drizzle with butter, and then season with salt and lots of black pepper.

To braise sprouts, sauté them in olive oil for a few minutes, add a little white wine or stock, season, and cover. Simmer for 10-15 minutes, until tender.

Brussels sprouts are good roasted around a bird or roast. Parboil the prepared sprouts for 3-5 minutes, drain well, baste with the roasting juices, and nestle them around the roast, giving them 20 minutes to cook.

Sautéed Brussels Sprouts with Bacon

SERVES 4

8	strips bacon, chopped	8
1	onion, sliced thinly (optional)	1
1 lb	Brussels sprouts, trimmed and shredded	500 g

I'm partial to eating these alongside a couple of golden fried eggs with a pint of bitter in front of the telly.

Fry the bacon and onion (if using) in a wok or large frying pan, until the bacon is crisp and the onions are soft and browned. Stir in the shredded sprouts, and cook for 3-4 minutes, until the edges begin to brown. Serve at once.

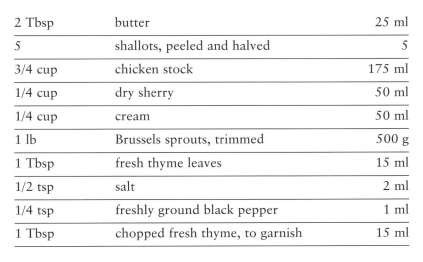

Brussels Sprouts Braised in Sherry and Cream

SERVES 4

2 Tbsp	butter	25 ml
5	shallots, peeled and halved	5
3/4 cup	chicken stock	175 ml
1/4 cup	dry sherry	50 ml
1/4 cup	cream	50 ml
1 lb	Brussels sprouts, trimmed	500 g
1 Tbsp	fresh thyme leaves	15 ml
1/2 tsp	salt	2 ml
1/4 tsp	freshly ground black pepper	1 ml
1 Tbsp	chopped fresh thyme, to garnish	15 ml

Melt the butter in a large, shallow pan or stovetop-safe casserole. Sauté the shallots for about 8 minutes, until golden brown. Add the stock, sherry, and cream, and bring to a boil. Reduce the heat, and stir in the sprouts, thyme, and seasoning. Cover and simmer for 15 minutes, until the sprouts are tender. Sprinkle with the chopped thyme, and serve hot.

Cabbage

All cabbages are extremely rich in vitamin C and are valued for their anti-cancer and antioxidant compounds. To get the most nutritional value from cabbage, munch it raw or lightly cooked. My mother used to make me drink the cooking water from cabbage to prevent me from breaking out in spots. Torture? Yes! But she insisted that's why I missed out on that particular teenage agony!

The cabbage has long been a staple vegetable, but despite its association with oysters and kings, only recently has this humble green become stylish. With the rising popularity of napa and Chinese cabbage, the Savoy, as well as the common red and green cabbages, are also climbing their way up the vegetable totem pole.

The common cabbage, whether red, white, or green, is available year-round, although there is a distinct difference between new and stored. New, or early, cabbages may be conical in shape, and they have tender, juicy leaves with a sweet, mild flavour that stands on its own when steamed or sautéed. Stored, or winter, cabbages are larger and round. Their thicker leaves have a more pronounced flavour and are best eaten raw in salads or slaws, pickled in sauerkraut, or slow-cooked in soups or stews. Red cabbage is particularly tasty when braised slowly with apples, wine, and spices. In any case, when buying these cabbages, choose smooth, firm heads that feel heavy for their size.

In my book, the Savoy is the king of cabbages, and the ones grown in Canada are fit for royalty. Their crinkly leaves peel away easily to reveal tender, pale green hearts, and whether steamed or sautéed, this cabbage needs nothing more than a drizzle of butter and a generous sprinkling of black pepper to bring out its sweet, distinctive flavour. The leaves are very easy to manipulate, making them a good choice for use in cabbage rolls. I also like to stuff raw leaves into sandwiches, and of course Savoy makes a superb coleslaw. Savoy cabbages are slightly softer than the common green or red variety, but they should still have crisp leaves, firmly connected with the stem. Avoid any with pale or blemished leaves.

Chinese cabbage and napa are actually two distinct vegetables, although in taste they are fairly indistinguishable. Chinese cabbage has white ribs that look a bit like celery and smooth, pale green leaves that cling to the stalk. Napa tends to be fatter, with curlier leaves that spring outwards. They both have a hotter flavour than other cabbage varieties, and they cook more quickly. Choose heavy, tightly furled heads with fresh, bright green leaves.

All cabbages stay relatively fresh for about a week when kept in the refrigerator in a plastic bag, although if you're planning on serving cabbage raw, you'd do best to use it within two days of purchase. To prepare, remove any loose or wilting outer leaves and rinse the head under cold running water. Cut common or Savoy cabbages in half and remove and discard the stem core. Slice the cabbage in wedges for steaming or shred for use in braised dishes, slaws, or stir-fries. When cooking cabbage, always leave the lid off for the first few minutes to disperse the sulphuric gases produced by cooking. This will get rid of the "cabbagey" smell that gives the vegetable its bad rap. To retain the vibrant colour of red cabbage, add a splash of vinegar to the cooking water. Steam prepared cabbage for 5-10 minutes, until tender but still crisp. Drain well and serve with a drizzle of melted butter and a squeeze of lemon juice, with plenty of freshly ground black pepper.

HOW TO PREPARE CHINESE CABBAGE AND NAPA
Chinese cabbage and napa need to be treated a little differently from other cabbages, as you're really dealing with two vegetables in one. Cut the leaves away from the ribs, and slice thinly. Chop or slice the ribs as you would celery. If you're stir-frying, add the ribs first because they take a little longer to cook. You can also use both ribs and leaves in salads or add them to soups.

Slow-Braised Red Cabbage with Apples and Cranberries

SERVES 6

3 Tbsp	brown sugar	40 ml
	a generous pinch each of cinnamon, cloves, and freshly grated nutmeg	
	salt and freshly ground black pepper	
1 lb	red cabbage, cored and shredded	500 g
1	large onion, chopped finely	1
1	garlic clove, peeled and chopped finely	1
2	large cooking apples, peeled, cored and chopped	2
1/2 cup	fresh cranberries	125 ml
3 Tbsp	balsamic vinegar	40 ml
1 Tbsp	butter	15 ml

This is a wonderful dish to serve at Christmas. The warm spices and colour are festive, and the dish is even better when made ahead and reheated.

Preheat the oven to 300°F (150°C). Lightly grease a large casserole dish. Mix the sugar, spices, salt, and pepper. Layer the shredded cabbage with the onion, garlic, apples, and cranberries, seasoning each layer with a pinch of the seasoning. Sprinkle the vinegar over top, and dot with butter. Cover and cook for about 2 hours, giving the mixture a stir halfway through cooking. Taste and adjust the seasoning if necessary before serving.

Spicy Savoy Slaw

SERVES 6

The sweet flavour of Savoy cabbage contrasts beautifully with the spicy peppers and zesty cilantro dressing. The flavours will improve if you refrigerate the slaw overnight and then allow it to warm to room temperature before serving.

1	head Savoy cabbage, cored and shredded	1
1	tart apple, cored and sliced	1
1	red onion, peeled and sliced finely	1

For the dressing:

	zest and juice of 1 lime	
1/2 Tbsp	white wine vinegar	7 ml
1/2 cup	olive oil	125 ml
1-2 finger	hot peppers, seeded and chopped very finely	1-2
2 Tbsp	chopped fresh cilantro	25 ml
1 tsp	sugar	5 ml
1/2 tsp	salt	2 ml
	freshly ground black pepper	

To make the dressing: Combine the ingredients in a jar with a tightly fitting lid, and shake well.

Place the shredded cabbage, sliced apple, and red onion in a large bowl. Pour the dressing over top, and toss well. Refrigerate for several hours (preferably overnight), and serve at room temperature.

Hot and Sweet Napa Cabbage

SERVES 4

3 oz	dried rice noodles	75 g
1 Tbsp	peanut or vegetable oil	15 ml
1	onion, sliced finely	1
1	garlic clove, chopped finely	1
1 tsp	grated fresh ginger	5 ml

1	finger hot pepper, seeded and chopped finely	1
1	sweet red pepper, seeded and thinly sliced	1
1	head napa cabbage, trimmed, rinsed, and shredded	1
2 Tbsp	cider vinegar	25 ml
2 Tbsp	brown sugar	25 ml
1/2 tsp	salt	2 ml

Pre-soak the rice noodles according to package directions. Rinse with cold water, drain and set aside.

Heat the oil in a wok or large stir-fry pan, and sauté the onion for 3 minutes. Stir in the garlic, ginger, and hot pepper, and cook for 1 minute more. Add the red pepper and shredded cabbage, and stir to coat. Stir in the cider vinegar and brown sugar, and cook for about 10 minutes, until the cabbage is tender and the liquid has been absorbed. Stir in the drained noodles, and heat through before serving.

Carrots

The carrot was once thought of as a luxury item, extravagant and thrilling. Wild carrots were consumed in ancient Greece as an aphrodisiac, while feathery green carrot tops were worn as plumage in the 17th century, decorating the hats and hair of fashionable young women. It wasn't until the 19th century that carrots became ordinary and took their place beside onions and potatoes as European dietary staples. Although we continue to buy carrots as a matter of course, somehow they've lost the magic they once had.

Carrots can be bought across the country at any time of year. Just as local crops begin to age and grow a little woody, fresh ones arrive from Florida and California, and by the time they are finished, tender, new-crop locals arrive back on the scene. Carrots can usually be purchased loose, bagged, or bunched with their bright green tops. Packages of miniature or baby carrots are also available year-round, already cleaned and ready for use, though some of these are actually ordinary carrots machine-shaped to uniform baby size.

Up until the 19th century, carrots could be pale yellow, bright red, or even purple. The modern carrot, a hybrid, should be a vivid golden-orange colour. Choose the brightest, firmest, best-shaped carrots you can find. Avoid any that are rubbery, tinged with green, or cracked and split. Small carrots will be more tender than large ones, which are older and can be dry or woody. Bunched carrots should have fresh, bright green leaves, which can be removed before storing. (Don't chuck them, as they are a wonderful addition to soups and stocks.) You can refrigerate carrots, unwashed, for up to two weeks.

As most of the valuable nutrients lie just beneath the skin, young carrots should simply be scrubbed, although older ones will need scraping or peeling.

HOORAY FOR CARROTS
Get excited again about the carrot, one of nature's finest surprises. Sweet, crunchy, inexpensive, available year-round, terrific raw or cooked, what more do you want? If you're not seeing the light yet, eat a few more carrots. Chock-full of vitamin A, they've long been touted as an invaluable aid to healthy eyesight, and the same vitamin keeps your bones in good shape as well. And that's not all: carrots also contain vitamin C and potassium.

Young carrots can be left whole, while larger carrots can be chopped, sliced, julienned, or diced. Steam or boil carrots in a minimum of liquid until they are barely tender. Add matchsticks or thinly sliced rounds to a stir-fry. Carrots become sweeter as they cook, and they develop a lovely flavour and velvety texture when braised in butter and a splash of cider. This same natural sweetness makes carrots a popular vegetable for use in baking and desserts.

Microwaving is an excellent method for cooking carrots. It requires so little water that the natural, sweet flavour and the nutrients all remain intact.

Cook whole small baby carrots or sliced, diced, or julienned mature carrots in a microwave-safe casserole with just 2 tablespoons of lightly salted water. Cover with a loose lid or vented plastic wrap, and cook on high for 5-8 minutes, depending on amount and size. Stir once during cooking, and let stand for 3 minutes.

If you've forgotten how extraordinary this vegetable is, put some excitement back into your life. Buy a carrot — heck, buy a bunch — and eat them raw. You'll be glad you did.

Carrot and Orange Soup

SERVES 6

The slightly peppery aniseed flavour of tarragon complements the sweetness of carrots and oranges.

2 Tbsp	butter	25 ml
1	onion, chopped	1
1 lb	carrots, peeled and chopped finely	500 g
2 Tbsp	chopped fresh tarragon	25 ml
4 cups	water or vegetable stock	1 L
	freshly squeezed juice of 1 orange	
	salt and freshly ground black pepper	
1/2 cup	heavy cream or plain yogurt	125 ml

IN THE MICROWAVE
In a large, microwave-safe bowl, cook the butter and onion together on high for 90 seconds, stirring once. Add the carrots, 1 tablespoon of the tarragon, and all the other ingredients except the cream or yogurt. Cover and cook at medium-high for 25-30 minutes, until the carrots are soft.

Purée in a food processor or blender until smooth, and then reheat for 3-4 minutes, until the soup is the temperature you like. Taste, adjust the seasoning, and add the cream or yogurt and the remaining tarragon.

Melt the butter in a large saucepan, and sauté the onion until softened but not browned. Stir in the chopped carrots and 1 tablespoon of tarragon. Cover the pan, reduce the heat to low, and cook for 10 minutes. Add the stock and orange juice, season with salt and pepper, and bring to a boil. Reduce the heat, and simmer for about 25 minutes, until the carrots are very soft. Purée the soup in a food processor or blender until smooth, and then return to the pan and gently reheat. Taste and season again if necessary, and stir in the cream or yogurt and the remaining tablespoon of tarragon.

Sweet and Sour Glazed Carrots

SERVES 4

2 Tbsp	butter	25 ml
1 Tbsp	brown sugar	15 ml
1 lb	carrots, peeled and julienned	500 g
1/4 cup	apple cider	50 ml
2 Tbsp	cider vinegar	25 ml
1 tsp	Dijon mustard	5 ml
1 Tbsp	chopped fresh tarragon or parsley	15 ml

Melt the butter in a wok or large skillet, and sauté the carrots for 5 minutes. Sprinkle with the sugar, raise the heat, and stir-fry until the sugar has dissolved. Add the cider, vinegar, and mustard, and bring to a boil. Reduce the heat, cover partially, and cook for 5-10 minutes, until the carrots are tender and the liquid has evaporated. Sprinkle with the fresh chopped herbs, and serve at once.

Microwave cooking gives a slightly different version of this delicious recipe. Cook the carrots on high with 2 tablespoons of water until tender, about 5 minutes. Drain. In a small bowl, melt the butter, and then stir in the brown sugar, cider, vinegar, and mustard, and microwave on high for 2 minutes, stirring once. Pour this glaze over the carrots, stir to coat, and heat uncovered on high for 15-20 seconds. Garnish with tarragon or parsley, and serve.

Carrot Salad with Apples and Pine Nuts

SERVES 4

Tender young carrots are much juicier than older ones, so you need less dressing. If you're using older carrots, add a little extra yogurt or mayonnaise, and chill for an hour or two before serving.

2	apples	2
1 Tbsp	freshly squeezed lime juice	15 ml
1 lb	carrots, peeled and grated	500 g
1/4 cup	pine nuts	50 ml

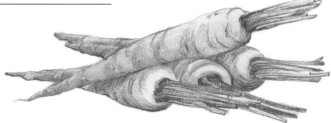

3 Tbsp	olive oil	40 ml
3 Tbsp	vegetable oil	40 ml
3 Tbsp	freshly squeezed lime juice	40 ml
1	garlic clove, crushed	1
2 tsp	honey	10 ml
4 Tbsp	plain yogurt	60 ml
1 Tbsp	chopped fresh cilantro	15 ml
	salt and freshly ground black pepper	

Peel, core, and slice the apples thinly, sprinkling them with the tablespoon of lime juice to prevent them from discolouring. Toss them in a large bowl with the grated carrot and pine nuts.

To make the dressing: Combine the dressing ingredients in a jar with a tightly fitting lid, and shake thoroughly. Pour over the salad and toss well. Serve at once, or chill for a while.

Cassava

Cassava is a hard vegetable to sell to the new taker. Its oddball appearance and general description don't do it any favours. Also called root manioc, it's perhaps best known as the source of the main ingredient in tapioca pudding, which some people find a little yucky (not to be confused with another of cassava's names, yucca). But cassava is a terrific vegetable to cook and eat and makes a pleasant change from the ubiquitous potato. It has a rich, buttery taste, and its dense, starchy character makes it a beautiful addition to soups and stews, thickening and absorbing juices and flavours. Like other tubers, it is great for baking and roasting, and it's a good choice for dumplings, breads, and fritters because of its high gluten content.

Relatively new to North American palates, cassava is revered in southern climes. Native to Brazil, cassava is now cultivated throughout Africa, Asia, the South Pacific, Central and South America, the Caribbean, and Florida. Main supplies for Canadian markets come from the Dominican Republic and Costa Rica, and cassava is available all year round.

The cassava shrub is related to the poinsettia, and it is the swollen roots of the plant that are harvested. Shaped like long, slender sweet potatoes and covered in a tough, brown bark, the tubers can be as heavy as three pounds (1.5 kg). Beneath this rough skin, which is usually waxed before it gets to the supermarket shelves, the flesh is dense and white, turning yellow and almost translucent when cooked. It's important to know what you're getting when buying cassava, as little can be salvaged from a bad one. Look for roots fully covered with dry bark with no cracks, which can be a sign of dryness. Use your nose to check for freshness, and reject any that smell sour or acrid. Most grocers will happily cut cassava open for you to inspect. The flesh should be clean and white; any darkening indicates a vegetable that is past its prime.

HOW TO PREPARE CASSAVA

To boil cassava for eating or use in a recipe, place it whole or halved in lots of cold water, seasoned with lemon juice and garlic. Bring the water to a boil, add salt, and then reduce the heat, keeping the water at a low simmer.

Cook for about 15 minutes before checking for tenderness every few minutes. The cassava is done when a knife tip slips easily through the flesh. Don't overcook it, as cassava can quickly turn into a mass of sticky threads.

Drain well, and serve at once with a knob of butter and some fresh chopped parsley or cilantro or with a spicy salsa.

Unlike other root vegetables, cassava is fairly perishable. Store it in a cool, dark place (not the fridge) for no more than two days. You can cut off just what you need because the exposed surface will heal over, sealing the cut. Simply slice off and discard the scarred end next time you use some. Before peeling cassava, scrub it with hot water to soften the wax. Once peeled, slice the root in half lengthways, remove and discard the fibrous core, and then soak the root in cold water. You can wrap peeled cassava and freeze it for up to one month. If you're cooking cassava whole, remove the core afterwards.

Cassava Kebabs

SERVES 4-6

1 lb	cassava, peeled and cut in 1 1/2-inch (4-cm) cubes	500 g
1	large sweet onion, cut in 12 wedges	1
1	medium-sized zucchini, cut in 1-inch (2.5-cm) slices	1
2	red peppers, cut in 1 1/2-inch (4-cm) squares	2
12	cherry tomatoes	12

These kebabs can be broiled in the oven or grilled on a barbecue. They're good served with aromatic basmati rice.

For the marinade:

1	finger hot pepper, seeded and chopped finely	1
2	green onions, chopped finely	2
2	garlic cloves, chopped finely	2
2 Tbsp	freshly squeezed lime juice	2
1/4 cup	olive oil	50 ml
3 Tbsp	soy sauce	40 ml
1 Tbsp	tomato paste	15 ml
1 tsp	ground allspice	5 ml

Place the cassava in a saucepan, and cover with water. Bring to a boil, and add a pinch of salt. Boil for 10-15 minutes, until barely tender. Drain well.

Meanwhile, combine the marinade ingredients in a large bowl. Toss the prepared vegetables, including the cassava, in the marinade. Cover and refrigerate for at least 1 hour, so the flavours will be well absorbed by the vegetables.

Preheat the broiler or barbecue.

Drain the vegetables, reserving the marinade. Thread them on 12 skewers, and broil or grill for about 15 minutes, turning frequently and basting with the reserved marinade. Serve at once.

Cassava in Coconut and Tomato Sauce

SERVES 6

2 lb	cassava, peeled and cut in 2-inch (5-cm) pieces	1 kg
2 Tbsp	peanut oil	25 ml
1	onion, chopped finely	1
2	garlic cloves, chopped finely	2
1	finger hot pepper, seeded and chopped finely	1
1 tsp	sugar	5 ml
6	plum tomatoes, skinned and chopped coarsely	6
2/3 cup	unsweetened coconut milk	150 ml
2 Tbsp	freshly squeezed lime juice	25 ml
1/4 cup	fresh chopped cilantro	50 ml
	salt and freshly ground black pepper	

Cassava is a good source of iron and potassium. Half a cup of cooked cassava contains about 90 calories.

Place the prepared cassava in a saucepan, and cover with cold water. Bring to a boil, and add a large pinch of salt. Reduce the heat and simmer for about 15-20 minutes, until just tender. Drain and set aside.

Meanwhile, heat the peanut oil in a large skillet, and sauté the onion and garlic for 5 minutes, until softened but not browned. Stir in the pepper, sugar, tomatoes, coconut milk, and lime juice. Bring to a gentle simmer and cook, uncovered, for 15 minutes, adding a little water if it gets too thick. Add the drained cassava, and cook for 5 minutes longer. Season to taste, stir in the cilantro, and serve at once.

Cassava Fritters

SERVES 4

1 lb	cassava, peeled and grated	500 g
1-2	finger hot peppers, seeded and chopped finely	1-2
1/3 cup	sharp cheddar cheese	80 ml
1 Tbsp	melted butter	15 ml
3	eggs, beaten	3
1 tsp	mustard powder	5 ml
1/4 tsp	ground fennel	1 ml

This recipe is an old favourite. I could fritter away a few hours eating them all by myself.

1 tsp	salt	5 ml
1/2 tsp	sugar	2 ml
	vegetable oil for shallow-frying	

Combine the ingredients in a mixing bowl until blended. Form the mixture into small balls, and then flatten them into little patties. Heat an inch (2.5 cm) of vegetable oil in a skillet or deep frying pan, and shallow-fry the fritters in batches for a few minutes on each side, until golden. Drain on paper towel, and serve hot with salsa and sour cream.

Cauliflower

The cauliflower is a thing of beauty. Its snowy white florets, or curds, are packed tightly together in a heavy bouquet, surrounded by a cloak of curling green leaves. It used to be that, like the rest of us, a good-looking head of cauliflower couldn't rely on nature alone. In order to keep the florets pale and creamy, the outer leaves were gathered around the head and tied together to protect it from sunlight. (Some of us can really relate to this, no longer having much of a natural sunblock on our heads.) Nowadays there are varieties that can withstand sunlight, which means that cultivation is not so labour intensive, and cauliflower is less expensive than it once was. What a break! It has a delicious nutty-sweet flavour, and it can be eaten raw as well as steamed, stir-fried, braised, and baked.

Available year-round, cauliflower will cost less during peak local growing seasons. Choose clean, creamy heads composed of compact curds with a firm feel to them. Avoid any that are covered with grey or black patches, but, if the head is creamy-white overall with just a few grey spots, don't worry — these can be trimmed away using a sharp knife. More perishable than other members of the cabbage family, cauliflower will keep for up to five days if stored in a plastic bag in the refrigerator. But do use it as soon after buying as possible, as with age it acquires a strong, cabbagey flavour and smell that overpower its subtle taste.

To prepare cauliflower, remove the outer green leaves, if they've been left on, and trim away the very thick stalk at the bottom of the plant. Some people like to remove the entire stalk, others are happy to leave it in place, and many cooks in England leave the leaves in place and cook those as well. If you're not cooking the cauliflower whole, break off the florets, slicing larger ones in half to ensure even cooking. Steam cauliflower in an inch or two of boiling water, until it feels just tender when pricked with a fork. Florets will take 5-8 minutes, and a whole head can take up to 20 minutes. Drain and serve at once.

Because it's such a firm vegetable, cauliflower cooks very well in the microwave. To cook it whole, wrap the washed and trimmed head in plastic wrap pricked with a fork. Microwave for 3 minutes on high, turn the cauliflower over, and cook until almost tender, approximately 2-4 minutes more. To cook 2 cups (500 ml) of cauliflower florets, make sure they're even in size. Place in a microwave-safe dish with a tablespoon of water or stock,

EASY, DELICIOUS
CAULIFLOWER
Serve steamed or microwaved cauliflower with melted butter and salt and pepper, or with a sauce; cauliflower has a special affinity with Gruyère, old cheddar, and parmesan cheeses.

Florets can be added to any stir-fry.

Cauliflower is good raw, but if you're using it in a salad you may want to blanch the florets in boiling water for a minute and then drain well and refresh in cold running water. Adding a vinaigrette or dressing while the florets are still warm will help them absorb the flavour.

cover, and cook on high for 3-5 minutes to almost the desired degree of tenderness, stirring once. Whether you're cooking the whole head or florets, let the cauliflower stand for 3 minutes before serving to allow the stems to become as tender as the florets.

Balti-Style Cauliflower and Spinach

SERVES 4

Cauliflower is very popular in Indian vegetarian cooking. Balti-style refers to both the spices used and the pan in which such curries are cooked, traditionally a heavy steel wok. The trick to a good curry is to "cook out" the spices for 3-5 minutes before adding the other ingredients. Serve this on a bed of basmati rice.

2 Tbsp	vegetable oil	25 ml
1	onion, chopped finely	1
1	garlic clove, chopped finely	1
1/2 tsp	cumin seeds	2 ml
1 tsp	ground coriander	5 ml
1/2 tsp	ground cumin	2 ml
1/2 tsp	ground turmeric	2 ml
1 tsp	chili powder	5 ml
1 tsp	garam masala	5 ml
1	large cauliflower, trimmed and broken into small florets	1
1	large potato, peeled and cut in 1/2-inch (1-cm) cubes	1
5	plum tomatoes, seeded and chopped coarsely	5
2 Tbsp	tomato paste	25 ml
1/3 cup	water	80 ml
1 cup	packed shredded fresh spinach	250 ml
	salt and freshly ground black pepper	
1 Tbsp	freshly squeezed lemon juice	15 ml
2	finger hot peppers, seeded and sliced thinly, to garnish	2

Heat the oil in a wok or large skillet, and sauté the onion and garlic for 3 minutes. Add the spices, and cook for 3-4 minutes, stirring frequently. Stir in the cauliflower and potato, and cook for 2-3 minutes over a high heat, until they begin to brown. Add the tomatoes, tomato paste, and water, stir well, and bring to a simmer. Reduce the heat, cover, and simmer for 5 minutes. Stir in the spinach, season to taste with salt and pepper, and cook for 1 minute more, until the spinach wilts. Transfer to a serving bowl or onto a platter of freshly cooked rice, sprinkle with the lemon juice, and garnish with the sliced hot peppers.

Cauliflower and Green Bean Salad

SERVES 4-6

1	head cauliflower, trimmed and broken into small florets	1
1 lb	green beans, trimmed and cut in 2-inch (5-cm) pieces	500 g

For the vinaigrette:

1	small garlic clove	1
1/2 tsp	salt	2 ml
1	shallot, chopped finely	1
1/4 cup	freshly squeezed lemon juice	50 ml
1 cup	virgin olive oil	250 ml
1/2 tsp	toasted cumin seeds, crushed	2 ml
	freshly ground black pepper	

To prepare the vinaigrette: Crush the garlic and salt together until creamy. Then combine the garlic with the remaining vinaigrette ingredients in a small jar with a tightly fitting lid, and shake thoroughly.

Bring a large pan of lightly salted water to a boil, and add the cauliflower florets. Bring back to the boil, and then throw in the beans. Cook for 1 minute, drain, and rinse under cold running water. Drain again, and transfer to a large bowl. Pour the dressing over top, toss to coat, and refrigerate for at least 1 hour.

Roasted Cauliflower with Garlic and Almonds

SERVES 4

1	head cauliflower, trimmed and broken into large florets	1
2 Tbsp	butter	25 ml
1 Tbsp	olive oil	15 ml
3	strips bacon, chopped	3
2	shallots, chopped finely	2
2	garlic cloves, crushed	2
1/3 cup	slivered almonds	80 ml
2 Tbsp	chopped fresh parsley	25 ml

1/4 cup	freshly grated parmesan cheese	50 ml
	freshly ground black pepper	

TOASTED ALMONDS
Melt 2 tablespoons of butter in a shallow microwave-safe dish or pie plate. Stir in almonds, coating well with butter. Microwave on high for 3-6 minutes, until light brown, stirring several times. Let stand for 5 minutes, as the almonds will continue to brown.

Preheat the oven to 375°F (190°C).

Blanch the cauliflower in lightly salted boiling water for 2 minutes, and then drain well. Transfer to a shallow, ovenproof dish, and set aside.

Heat the butter and olive oil in a small saucepan over a medium heat. Stir in the chopped bacon, and cook for 3-4 minutes. Stir in the shallots and garlic, and cook for 5 minutes more, until softened. Add the almonds, sauté until golden, and then stir in the parsley.

Spoon the almond mixture on the cauliflower, scatter the parmesan evenly over top, and season with pepper. Bake for 12-15 minutes, until the cauliflower is just tender and the topping is golden.

Celeriac

If you're expecting celeriac to look anything like celery, you're in for a big surprise. A variety of celery that is grown for its bottom bits rather than for its branches, celeriac is a remarkably ugly vegetable. A round, bulbous creature, it looks a bit like a turnip, except that it's covered with lumps and bumps, with little rootlets squiggling out from one end and short stalks protruding from the other. Don't be turned off — it has a lovely personality. Beneath its ungainly exterior, celeriac hides mottled white flesh with a zesty yet subtle nutty flavour. It can be served raw in salads, turned into soups and purées, and braised or roasted. In fact, anything that you might do to a turnip will work equally well with celeriac.

SIMPLY CELERIAC
For a salad with real verve, shred, julienne, or grate raw celeriac, toss with a creamy vinaigrette, and let it improve overnight in the refrigerator.

Celeriac makes a wonderful soup or purée when combined with other root vegetables, adding a nutty base note to potatoes particularly.

Braised in butter and apple cider, celeriac is a delicious accompaniment to any roast meat.

Cook celeriac alongside a roast. It will absorb the flavour of the meat without losing its own identity.

Celeriac is slow to mature, so it doesn't arrive on the market until late fall. It does store well, so you can usually find it until early spring. Sometimes trimmed of its rootlets and stems, it can be hard to spot. Look for it where you normally find turnips and other roots, and follow your nose. Not surprisingly, it smells a lot like celery. Choose the smoothest root you can find; a small to medium-sized one that feels heavy for its size will have smoother, firmer flesh than a larger, older root, which might be spongy. If its stalk end is soft, reject it, as that's a good indication that the inside will be woody.

Trim any green stalks (they can be used to flavour soups and stocks). Store the root in a plastic bag in the refrigerator, where it will keep for at least a week. To prepare celeriac, scrub it thoroughly, cut away the rootlets, and trim both ends. Its gnarled skin can make peeling frustrating, so use a sharp knife to cut away the skin and ignore the waste. Chop or slice and submerge the pieces in cold water and lemon juice to prevent them from discolouring. You can boil or steam celeriac, but this tends to mute its flavour. It is better simply blanched for a few minutes and then either baked with a creamy sauce or sautéed until golden in a little butter.

Beauty is only skin-deep, so give this ugly fella a chance. I'm sure you'll be pleasantly surprised.

Celeriac Slaw with Creamy Dijon Dressing

SERVES 4

Celeriac is a fairly dense vegetable, so this slaw will taste even better when made the day before, allowing the flavours of the dressing to soak in.

1 lb	celeriac, peeled and shredded	500 g
1/4 cup	fresh chopped parsley	50 ml

For the dressing:

1/2 cup	mayonnaise	125 ml
2 Tbsp	freshly squeezed lemon juice	25 ml
2 Tbsp	Dijon mustard	25 ml
2 Tbsp	heavy cream	25 ml
	salt and freshly ground pepper	

Blanch the shredded celeriac in a large pan of boiling water for 1 minute. Drain, rinse with cold running water, and drain again. Pat dry.

Combine the dressing ingredients in a bowl, and whisk to blend. Stir in the celeriac and chopped parsley. Leave for 30 minutes, or refrigerate overnight, allowing the salad to come to room temperature before serving.

Celeriac, Apple, and Artichoke Salad

SERVES 4

1 lb	celeriac, peeled and julienned	500 g
2	large eating apples, cored and chopped	2
3/4 cup	canned artichoke hearts, quartered	175 g
1 Tbsp	freshly squeezed lemon juice	15 ml

For the dressing:

1	garlic clove	1
1 tsp	salt	5 ml
3 Tbsp	freshly squeezed lemon juice	40 ml
1/2 cup	olive oil	125 ml
1 tsp	mustard	5 ml
1 tsp	honey	5 ml
1 Tbsp	chopped fresh dill	15 ml

Combine the celeriac, apple, and artichoke hearts in a large bowl, and toss with the tablespoon of lemon juice.

To make the dressing: Crush the garlic and salt to a creamy paste. Then combine it with the remaining dressing ingredients in small jar with a tightly fitting lid, and shake thoroughly.

Pour the dressing over the salad, and toss well to coat. Leave for 15-30 minutes before serving.

Garlic Mashed Celeriac and Potatoes

SERVES 4-6

If you're lucky enough to have leftovers, fry them up the next morning with a couple of sausages. Delicious!

2 lb	celeriac, trimmed, peeled, and chopped coarsely	1 kg
1 lb	potatoes, peeled and chopped coarsely	500 g
3	large garlic cloves, peeled	3
3 Tbsp	butter	40 ml
1/4 cup	cream or milk	50 ml
	salt and freshly ground black pepper	

Combine the celeriac, potatoes, and garlic in a saucepan. Add enough water to cover, season with salt, and bring to a boil. Cook for 20-25 minutes, uncovered, until the vegetables are tender. Drain, reserving a little of the cooking water. Mash the vegetables as smooth as you desire, adding the butter, cream, and a little of the cooking water. Season to taste with salt and pepper, and serve at once.

Celery

Nutrionally speaking, celery doesn't offer much: a little potassium, calcium, some fibre. Dentists love it, since its stringy fibres act as a natural toothbrush.

As a greengrocer and a food lover, I don't have the heart to promote celery as a diet food. Don't get me wrong — I love celery. But I love it because it tastes great raw or cooked, it stores well, and it's beautiful to look at. I just can't love a vegetable for what it *doesn't* have, which is calories. And in any case, one of my favourite ways to eat celery is sautéed with salted butter, lots of it! I also like the smell of celery, which brings back memories of my days in Nottingham, learning the vegetable trade. I used to spend hours every day trimming and washing caseloads of celery, which would arrive covered in peaty black soil from the Lincolnshire fens. My fingers would be ready to drop off after opening and preparing a hundred cases of the stuff, but the sweet smell of celery stayed around long after the dirt came out from under my nails.

Celery has been around for several hundred years, bred in Italy from a small medicinal plant whose bitterness made it useless for eating. The modern celery retains some of that sharp and savoury flavour, which is why it goes so well with creamy cheeses and sweet apples. There are two main varieties of celery. White celery is blanched by earth as it grows to prevent the stalks from turning green in sunlight. It has pale yellow leaves and a slightly milder flavour. It tends to be available only during the winter months. Green celery, the more common variety, is available year-round, with no peak season.

When choosing celery, look for straight, tightly packed stalks with fresh-looking leaves. When stored in a plastic bag in the refrigerator, celery will stay fresh for up to two weeks.

Most grocers trim the celery at the store, so all you really need to do is break the ribs off as you need them, and rinse them well. If you aren't using a whole stalk at once, pare off the root end before you put it back in the refrigerator. There is very little waste in celery, as you can use the leaves in salads or soups. The outer ribs can be cooked, and the pale, inner heart is perhaps most enjoyed raw.

For some reason, North Americans shy away from cooking celery, perhaps because they grew up munching it raw, stuffed with peanut butter or Cheez Whiz. While raw celery is a treat in itself, do experiment with different cooking methods. Slice the ribs on the diagonal and add them to a stir-fry. Make some cream of celery soup — you'll never again be tempted to buy it in a can. Celery hearts braised in chicken stock and butter with a splash of vermouth is a dish fit for royalty and goes particularly well with roasted chicken.

However you cook it — or not — eat lots of it. Not because it has so few calories, but because it has so much taste.

CELERY REVIVAL
If your celery softens before you get around to using it, simply soak the stalks in ice-cold, salted water until they liven up. I don't recommend storing it this way, though, as its nutrients will leach into the water.

Cream of Celery Soup with Garlic and Parmesan Croutons

SERVES 6

2 Tbsp	butter	25 ml
1	onion, chopped finely	1
2	heads celery, cleaned, trimmed, and chopped finely	2
1 Tbsp	flour	15 ml
5 cups	chicken or vegetable stock	1.25 L
	salt and freshly ground black pepper	
2 oz	goat's cheese, chopped finely	50 g
1 Tbsp	chopped fresh dill	15 ml

For the croutons:

3	thick slices white bread, crusts removed	3
3 Tbsp	olive oil	40 ml

This soup is made thick and creamy by adding goat's cheese. If you prefer, simply substitute 1/4 cup (125 ml) cream.

In a microwave-safe casserole, mix the celery and onion together well, and add 2 Tbsp of water. Cover and cook on medium for 10-15 minutes until very soft, stirring twice. Purée and set aside.

Melt the butter in another large microwave-safe bowl. Stir in the flour, and cook on high for 15-20 seconds. Add the stock, mix well, and cook on high until hot, stirring several times. This will take 5-10 minutes.

Add the puréed vegetables, and season to taste with salt and pepper. Sprinkle with the goat's cheese and dill, and heat for another minute if necessary to melt the cheese.

1	garlic clove, crushed	1
2 tsp	freshly grated parmesan cheese	10 ml

Melt the butter in a large saucepan, and sauté the onion and celery for 5 minutes, until softened but not browned. Stir in the flour, and cook for 1 minute more. Pour in the stock, and bring to a simmer. Season to taste with salt and pepper, cover, and cook for about 45 minutes, until the celery is very soft. Transfer to a food processor or blender, and purée until smooth. Return to the saucepan, and reheat gently. Add the goat's cheese and dill, stirring until the cheese has melted.

To make the croutons: Preheat the oven to 400°F (200°C). Cut the bread in 1/2-inch (1-cm) cubes. Combine the olive oil and garlic on a plate, and place the grated parmesan on a second plate. Roll the bread cubes first in the oil and then in the cheese. Place them on a cooling rack set on a baking sheet, and bake for 10 minutes, until golden. Serve them in a bowl or scattered directly on the soup.

Celery, Pear and Walnut Salad with Blue Cheese Dressing

SERVES 4-6

8-10	celery stalks, trimmed and sliced thinly	8-10
2	large pears, cored and sliced	2
1/4 cup	walnut pieces	50 ml
3	strips bacon, chopped and fried until crisp (optional)	3

For the dressing:

1/2 cup	sour cream	125 ml
3 Tbsp	mayonnaise	40 ml
1 Tbsp	olive oil	15 ml
2 Tbsp	freshly squeezed lemon juice	25 ml
1	garlic clove, crushed	1
1 tsp	mustard powder	5 ml
2 oz	blue cheese, crumbled	50 g
2 Tbsp	fresh snipped chives	25 ml
	salt and freshly ground black pepper	

Combine the dressing ingredients in a large bowl, and beat well to combine. Add the celery, pears, and walnuts, and toss well. Sprinkle the bacon bits over top, if using, and serve at once.

Celery, Leek, and Apple Stuffing

MAKES ABOUT 4 CUPS

This stuffing is enough for a fairly large turkey; simply halve the quantities for a roast chicken. The stuffing will swell when cooking, so don't pack the bird's cavity too tightly.

6 Tbsp	butter	90 ml
1 cup	finely chopped celery	250 ml
1 cup	finely chopped leek	250 ml
2	large apples	2
1 Tbsp	freshly squeezed lemon juice	15 ml
1 1/2 cups	fresh white bread crumbs	375 ml
1/2 cup	chopped walnuts (optional)	125 ml
1/2 cup	chopped fresh parsley	125 ml
2	eggs, beaten	2
1 tsp	salt	5 ml
1/2 tsp	freshly ground black pepper	2 ml

Core and grate the apples, and toss them with the lemon juice. Melt the butter in a large skillet, and sauté the celery and leek over a low heat for 15 minutes. Stir in the grated apple, bread crumbs, walnuts (if using), parsley, beaten eggs, and salt and pepper. Refrigerate until you're ready to stuff the bird.

STUFFING IN THE MICROWAVE
You can use your microwave to good advantage for the cooked parts of this and other stuffings, since the vegetables become nice and soft with no danger of scorching.

Place the crumbs, walnuts, and parsley in a large bowl, and set aside. Beat the eggs in a small bowl. Melt the butter in a medium bowl in the microwave, add the celery and leek, and stir to coat. Cover and cook on high for 3-5 minutes, until soft, stirring twice.

Toss the vegetables with the grated appled, the bread crumb mixture, the eggs, and the salt and pepper. Refrigerate until using.

Collard Greens

Collard greens, which belong to the cabbage family, are the closest thing we've got to English "spring greens," with large, flat, deep green leaves and long, thick stalks. Their flavour is somewhere between cabbage and kale, earthy, sweet, and definitely peppery. They come to us from south of the equator. Originally cultivated in India, Africa, and South America, they were brought to the southern United States by African slaves and are integral to the cuisine known as "soul food." Think hominy grits, black-eyed peas, and cornbread, and you'll have the idea. Even so, collards are hardy, able to endure both hot and cold weather. They're available year-round, with supplies peaking in late winter and ebbing during spring.

When buying collards, look for fresh, springy leaves, deep green in colour. Avoid any with blemishes or those that have yellowed. As the stems are too tough to eat, choose collards with lots of relatively small leaves. You can wash them before storing them if they're dried thoroughly. Otherwise, refrigerate them in a plastic bag for up to 5 days. As they tend to have a lot of grit trapped in the leaves, rinse them well in a sink full of cool water, swishing them around to allow sand and dirt to settle to the bottom. Spin or pat dry, and cut out the stems. The generous size of the leaves allows you to stack them before chopping or shredding them, so preparation is fairly quick.

Collards are not good eaten raw, but you have a choice whether to cook them fast or slow. Traditionally, collards are slow-braised for hours with a smoked ham hock or slab of salt pork, producing a soft, chewy "mess of greens" with a mellow, kale-like flavour and velvety texture. Sautéing collards keeps the flavour strong and the texture more like cabbage. The assertive flavour can be mellowed by cooking with butter and cream, but collards can also withstand strong seasonings including hot peppers, garlic, and ginger, making this an ideal vegetable for curries.

Cheesy Bubble and Squeak

SERVES 4

5	potatoes	5
2 Tbsp	olive oil	25 ml
2	leeks, rinsed and shredded	2
3	sweet apples	3
2 tsp	brown sugar	10 ml
1	garlic clove, crushed	1
8 oz	collard greens, rinsed, trimmed and shredded	250 g
1/3 cup	chicken or vegetable stock	80 ml
	freshly squeezed juice of 1 orange	
1 Tbsp	chopped fresh thyme	15 ml
4 ounces	parmesan cheese, grated	125 g
	salt and freshly ground black pepper	

This is an old childhood favourite; my mum would use up leftover potatoes and make this for our tea. Normally made with cabbage, here it combines collard greens and leeks, and it's jazzed up with parmesan cheese. Serve this with crusty bread to soak up the juices.

Leave the skins on the potatoes, and cut them in bite-sized chunks. Boil them in lightly salted water for 5-8 minutes, until just tender. Drain and set aside. (Or be traditional and use leftovers.)

Heat the oil in a wok or large stir-fry pan over a high heat, and sauté the leeks and apples with the sugar, until golden brown. Add the cooked potatoes, garlic, and collards, and stir to coat. Pour in the stock and orange juice, season with thyme, salt, and pepper, and bring to a boil. Scatter the cheese over top, reduce the heat, and cover. Cook for 5 minutes, until the liquid has been absorbed and the greens are tender. Serve at once.

Slow-Simmered Collard Greens with Rice, Raisins, and Almonds

SERVES 4

3 Tbsp	butter	40 ml
2	shallots, peeled and chopped finely	2
1	garlic clove, peeled and chopped finely	1
2 tsp	grated fresh ginger	10 ml
1 lb	collard greens, rinsed, trimmed and shredded	500 g
1 cup	rice	250 ml
1/2 tsp	cardamom	2 ml
1/2 tsp	cinnamon	2 ml
1/4 tsp	freshly grated nutmeg	1 ml
1/2 tsp	salt	2 ml
1/4 cup	raisins	50 ml
2 cups	hot chicken stock	500 ml
1/4 cup	toasted slivered almonds	50 ml

This spicy-sweet dish is a variation of an Ethiopian recipe. You can substitute currants and pine nuts for the raisins and almonds.

Melt 2 tablespoons of the butter in a large casserole, and sauté the shallots for 4 minutes, until golden. Stir in the garlic and ginger, and cook for 1 minute more. Add the collards, and stir to coat. Cover and cook over a low heat for 15 minutes. Add the rice, spices, salt and raisins, and cook for 5 minutes more, stirring frequently. Pour in the hot stock, and bring to a boil. Cover and reduce the heat. Cook for 15-20 minutes, until the liquid is absorbed and the rice is almost tender. Remove from the heat, and stir in the remaining tablespoon of butter and the toasted almonds. Leave for 5 minutes, covered, before serving.

Corn

Fresh corn on the cob, dripping in butter, is one of summer's finest pleasures, and corn is probably the New World's single most important contribution to European diets. A cornfield truly is a field of dreams. In terms of acreage planted, corn is second only to wheat. Most of this corn reaches us indirectly, as it is primarily cultivated as a grain rather than a vegetable. It feeds the creatures who in turn provide us with meat and dairy products, as well as supplying the base material for everything from bourbon to acetone, cooking oil to varnish, syrup to shoe polish.

The corn grown as a vegetable is called sweet corn, and more often than not it arrives at the market still wrapped in its tight green husk. Few of us

An excellent source of carbohydrate, corn contains vitamins A and C, good amounts of the B-vitamins, and potassium, magnesium, and iron.

Soak the ears (in their husks) in cold water for an hour, and then bury them in a bed of coals. The husks will char and blacken, and the corn will take 10-15 minutes to cook.

Or husk the ears and rub them with butter. Wrap them individually in aluminum foil, and throw them on a closed grill. This method will take a little longer, up to 30 minutes.

can resist its tender, juicy sweetness. Although it is available year-round, fresh corn is at its best and cheapest during local growing seasons, which begin around June and peak in late summer.

In the past, kitchen lore demanded that you put the water on to boil before going out to pick the corn, as its natural sugars begin converting to starch as soon as the ears are plucked from their stalks. If you're cooking corn from the garden, this is still good advice. However, thanks to recent hybridization and innovations in harvesting technology, most of the corn we buy today will stay fresh and sweet for a matter of days rather than hours, provided you keep it in the refrigerator.

When choosing corn, go for heavy, sweet-smelling ears with tight green husks and fresh-looking golden silks. If you can peel back the husks, the kernels should be small but plump, shiny, and packed tightly. Small-kernel corn is usually sweeter and more tender than corn with large kernels, which can be a sign of age and therefore toughness. And avoid any ears with dimpled kernels, which indicates age and starchiness. To store, leave the husks in place and wrap the ears in damp paper towel. Store it in plastic bags in the refrigerator, and *please* cook it within at two days at the most.

Corn can be boiled, steamed, microwaved, roasted, or thrown on the barbecue. To boil, bring a large pot of *unsalted* water to a brisk boil, and husk the ears just before you drop them into the pot. You can trim the stem ends, but leave enough to serve as handles. If the ears are too large for your pot, simply chop them in half. Once the water returns to a boil, cover and cook for 5-8 minutes. Steaming corn will take a few minutes longer. Microwaving takes more cooking time, but you don't have to wait for the water to boil, and you don't have to wash the pot afterwards. Microwave no more than 4 unhusked ears at once. Cook on high for 3-5 minutes per ear, turning over and end-for-end once during the cooking time. Let stand for 5 minutes. Remove the husks carefully, using oven mitts or a towel.

However you cook it, corn cries out for lots of butter, salt, and pepper. By the end of a corn feast, you should be surrounded by shiny, happy faces.

Roasted Corn with Cilantro Butter

	fresh corn on the cob, husks and silks removed	
1/2 Tbsp	butter per ear of corn	8 ml
	finely chopped fresh cilantro	
	salt and freshly ground black pepper	

Preheat the oven to 375°F (190°C).

Mash together the butter and chopped cilantro with a pinch of salt and black pepper. Rub the butter over the corn, and wrap the ears individually in aluminum foil. Roast them near the top of the oven for 30 minutes. Serve the corn in its foil parcels to contain the delicious juices.

Spicy Corn Fritters with Sweet-Hot Sauce

SERVES 4

Lemon grass, cilantro, and chili powder give these corn fritters a Thai flavour.

2	eggs, separated	2
2 Tbsp	all-purpose flour	25 ml
2	stalks lemon grass, chopped finely	2
2 Tbsp	chopped fresh cilantro	25 ml
1/2 tsp	chili powder	2 ml
2 1/2 cups	fresh or frozen corn kernels	500 ml
	salt and freshly ground black pepper	
3-4 Tbsp	vegetable oil, for frying	40-60 ml

For the sauce:

1/4 cup	rice vinegar	50 ml
2 Tbsp	sugar	25 ml
1	garlic clove, chopped finely	1
1-2	small finger hot peppers, seeded and chopped finely	1-2
2 Tbsp	chopped fresh cilantro	25 ml
1 Tbsp	freshly squeezed lime juice	15 ml

Beat the egg yolks with the flour, lemon grass, cilantro, and chili powder. Stir in the corn, and leave to rest while you make the dipping sauce.

To make the sauce: Combine the vinegar, sugar, garlic, and hot pepper in a small saucepan. Bring to a boil and cook for 3 minutes. Remove from the heat and stir in the lime juice and cilantro. Pour into a shallow bowl and leave to cool.

Back to the fritters. In a clean bowl, whisk the egg whites until stiff but not dry, and then fold them into the corn mixture. Season with salt and pepper. Heat the oil in a wok or large skillet, until sizzling hot. Drop the batter in by spoonfuls, cook for 2-3 minutes, flip them over, and cook the other sides until golden brown. Drain on paper towel, and serve hot with the dipping sauce.

CUT YOUR OWN KERNELS
If you prefer eating your corn with a spoon or fork, or if you want fresh kernels for a recipe, place the husked ear upright on a damp cloth to keep it from slipping. Use a sharp knife and slice downwards, away from your body, as close to the ear as possible. A medium-sized ear of corn will yield approximately 1/2 cup of kernels.

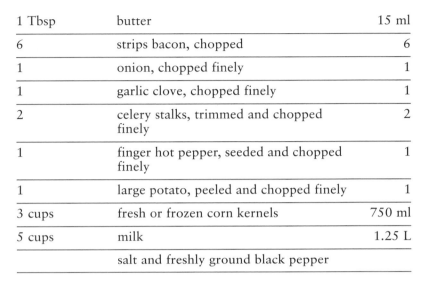

Corn Chowder with Red Pepper and Corn Salsa

SERVES 6

1 Tbsp	butter	15 ml
6	strips bacon, chopped	6
1	onion, chopped finely	1
1	garlic clove, chopped finely	1
2	celery stalks, trimmed and chopped finely	2
1	finger hot pepper, seeded and chopped finely	1
1	large potato, peeled and chopped finely	1
3 cups	fresh or frozen corn kernels	750 ml
5 cups	milk	1.25 L
	salt and freshly ground black pepper	

For the salsa:

1/2 cup	fresh or frozen corn kernels	125 ml
1/2	small red onion, chopped finely	1/2
1	large red sweet pepper, seeded and chopped finely	1
2	tomatoes, seeded and chopped finely	2
	freshly squeezed juice of 1/2 lime	
2 Tbsp	chopped fresh cilantro	25 ml
	a few drops of Tabasco sauce	
	salt and freshly ground black pepper	

Melt the butter in a large saucepan, and add the bacon, onion, garlic, and celery. Cook for 10 minutes over a medium heat, stirring frequently. Stir in the hot pepper, corn, and potato. Add the milk, and bring to a boil. Reduce the heat, and simmer, uncovered, for 15-20 minutes. Transfer to a blender or food processor in batches, and purée until smooth. Return to the saucepan, and thin with a little more milk if necessary. Season to taste with salt and pepper, and serve with a spoonful of salsa in each bowl.

To make the salsa: Combine the ingredients in a bowl and mix thoroughly. Refrigerate for at least 1 hour to allow the flavours to blend.

Corn and Tomatillo Frittata

SERVES 2

1 Tbsp	vegetable oil	15 ml
1	small onion, sliced thickly	1
4	tomatillos, husked and rinsed, with stems removed	4
1 cup	fresh or frozen corn kernels	250 ml
1	small finger hot pepper, seeded and chopped finely	1
3	eggs	3
	salt and freshly ground black pepper	
1/4 cup	grated cheddar cheese	50 ml
2 Tbsp	chopped fresh cilantro	25 ml

Preheat the broiler.

Heat the oil in a small frying pan with an ovenproof handle, and add the onion and tomatillos. Sauté for 3-4 minutes, until the tomatillos begin to brown. Stir in the corn and hot pepper, and cook for 1 minute more. Beat the eggs with a pinch of salt and pepper, and pour over the vegetables. Reduce the heat, and cook for about 5 minutes, until the bottom is set but the top is still slightly runny. Scatter the cheese over the eggs, and pop the pan under the broiler for about 1 minute, until cooked and golden brown. Sprinkle with the cilantro, and serve at once.

Cucumber

There is no other vegetable as cool as a cucumber. Literally. The inside of this squash-like fruit can be up to 20°F (8°C) cooler than its surface temperature, and its capacity to retain water makes the cucumber one of the most refreshing vegetables around, certainly my pick to carry on a trek through the desert. A plant native to the subcontinent, either India or Africa, the cucumber has been cultivated for at least 4000 years and was brought to Europe via the Middle East some thousand years ago. It suffered a bit of a bad patch in England, where, until the 18th century, it was considered a digestive hazard. It is true that garden cucumbers can be a bit "windy," but the English or "greenhouse" variety is supposedly burpless.

Until I arrived in North America in 1979, I didn't know that there was any type of cucumber other than the English variety, and I was a bit confused when I came across the more hefty garden cukes with skins like leather! However, these garden varieties are available year-round, with supplies peaking in summer with local crops. They range greatly in size, the best choice being small to medium ones with firm flesh and smooth, deep green skins. Very large ones will have tough skins and a preponderance of seeds,

Cucumbers are a very low-calorie source of dietary fibre and also contain small amounts of vitamin A and iron. A medium-sized cuke contains about 25 calories and is a good source of hydration on a hot summer day.

and you should also avoid those with a pale green or yellowish colour, which indicates over-maturity. English or greenhouse cucumbers are also available year-round, although during the winter months they can be expensive, as they are imported from Holland and Spain. They are long and slender, with thin green skins and fewer seeds. They are the cucumber of choice for most people (including myself) since they are sweeter and more tender than the garden variety. They should be well-shaped and feel very firm when pressed. Gherkins are tiny cucumbers used mostly for pickling, but they also make great salads.

An English cucumber should last for about a week when left in its plastic wrap and kept in the least cool part of the refrigerator. Garden cukes should not be wrapped even after they're cut; simply trim off the cut end before using. English cucumbers should be rinsed well but not peeled, while garden cucumbers generally need peeling, as their skins are sometimes coated in wax to promote longevity.

Although more commonly eaten raw, sliced cucumbers can be poached in a little water and vinegar, drained, tossed in melted butter, and sprinkled with fresh parsley.

Cucumbers are also tasty when sautéed. Drain the slices on paper towel, and then fry them in butter until heated through but still crisp. Stir in a splash of cream and teaspoon of Dijon mustard, season with salt and pepper, and sprinkle with fresh chopped dill.

Cucumbers are an excellent salad ingredient. Slice them very thinly and dress with a vinaigrette of cider vinegar mixed with a pinch each of dry mustard, sugar, salt, and black pepper. For a light, refreshing accompaniment to curried dishes, combine diced cucumbers with yogurt, lemon juice, and garlic.

Spicy-Sweet Cucumber and Peanut Salad

SERVES 4

2	English cucumbers, sliced lengthways and seeded	2
1 Tbsp	salt	15 ml

For the dressing:

1/3 cup	sugar	80 ml
1/2 cup	rice wine vinegar	125 ml
4	finger hot peppers, seeded and chopped finely	4
2 Tbsp	chopped fresh cilantro	25 ml
1/4 cup	roasted peanuts, chopped finely	50 ml

Salt the cucumbers, and set aside.

In a serving bowl, dissolve the sugar in the vinegar. Add the peppers and cilantro, and toss with the cucumbers. Refrigerate for 30 minutes before serving, garnished with the peanuts.

Minted Cucumber and Yogurt Soup

SERVES 6

3-4	medium-sized cucumbers	3-4
1 1/2 cups	plain yogurt	375 ml
3 cups	chicken stock	750 ml
1 1/2 cups	tomato juice	375 ml
1	garlic clove, crushed	1
2 Tbsp	chopped fresh mint	25 ml
2 tsp	chopped fresh parsley	10 ml
	Tabasco sauce, to taste	
	salt and freshly ground black pepper	

Peel and grate the cucumber into a large bowl, reserving 6 thin slices for a garnish. Stir in the remaining ingredients, including about 6 drops of Tabasco sauce, and salt and pepper to taste. Refrigerate for at least 4 hours, until chilled, and serve garnished with the reserved cucumber slices.

Cucumber and Mango Salad

SERVES 3-4

2	medium-sized cucumbers, peeled and sliced thinly	2
1	mango, peeled and sliced thinly	1
1	sweet red onion, sliced thinly	1
	freshly squeezed juice of 1 lime	
1/2 tsp	salt	2 ml
	a pinch of paprika	
2 Tbsp	chopped fresh basil	25 ml

Arrange the cucumber, mango, and onion slices in concentric circles on a serving platter. Sprinkle the lime juice over top, season with salt and paprika, and garnish with the fresh basil.

TO SALT CUCUMBERS
Salting sliced cucumbers and draining them before using reduces their water content, which is important if you don't want your dish to become watery. Salting also intensifies flavour.

Seed cucumbers, slice them thinly, and toss with about 1 1/2 teaspoons (8 ml) salt per cucumber. Set in a colander placed over a bowl, and allow to drain for 30 minutes. Rinse well under cold running water, drain again, and pat or squeeze dry.

Eggplant

TO PREPARE EGGPLANT
Rinse well and trim off the fuzzy top bit. Leave the skin on, slice or dice the flesh, and salt or not as you see fit. A simple but delicious method of cooking eggplant is to brush thick slices with olive oil, sprinkle with salt and pepper, and then either grill over a barbecue for 4-5 minutes on each side or roast in a hot oven for 20-30 minutes. Drizzle with a vinaigrette and serve warm or cold. Braise small cubes of eggplant — seasoned with crushed garlic, salt and pepper — in olive oil and a splash of balsamic vinegar for 30-40 minutes to create a great topping for bruschetta. I use thin slices of eggplant in lasagna, and I love it battered and deep-fried as well.

The glossy, deep-purple, elongated vegetable that most of us recognize as the eggplant seems strangely named. However, if you've been lucky enough to see the white variety, a plump, cream-coloured globe, you'll understand at once, and the spectrum of colours between this ivory goose-egg and the raven beauty is fantastic. Eggplant can be pale yellow, red, violet, and even striped, and it comes in any number of shapes and sizes: slender or full-figured, round or pear-shaped, and ranging from 2 to 10 inches (5-25 cm) in length.

A member of the nightshade family (and actually a berry rather than a fruit or vegetable), the eggplant is a native of India that made its way to Italy in the 15th century. It has a natural affinity with both Mediterranean and Far Eastern cooking, as its dense, spongy flesh can absorb intense, spicy flavours while retaining a mellow, buttery taste of its own. For the same reason, eggplant is notorious for being able to soak up several times its own weight in oil.

Eggplant is available year-round, although its long growing season means that local crops don't peak until late summer. When choosing an eggplant, regardless of the colour or shape, look for a smooth, shiny, taut skin with no pockmarks. The flesh should be firm and the eggplant heavy for its size. Try pressing it (gently, now!) with your finger. If the dent doesn't disappear, the eggplant is probably past its prime. The greenish-brown cap and stem should be clean, dry, and firmly attached.

Use eggplants as soon as possible after purchase. They don't really like the refrigerator, but if you've got no other cool, dark place available, they will keep there in a plastic bag for up to three days. The great thing about eggplant is that you can't overcook it. It may lose its shape if you slice it very thinly or chop it small, but it takes on a velvet, custard-like texture and an exquisite taste that has no equal in the vegetable world.

Eggplant and Sesame Dip
MAKES 2 CUPS (500 ML)

This variation of the Middle Eastern dip called baba ghanoush can be served with raw vegetables and warm pita bread. I like it tossed with fresh hot pasta as well.

3 medium or 2 large	eggplants	3 medium or 2 large
2 Tbsp	tahini paste	25 ml
1 Tbsp	olive oil	15 ml
2	garlic cloves, chopped finely	2
3-4 Tbsp	freshly squeezed lime juice	40-50 ml
2 Tbsp	chopped fresh cilantro	25 ml
	salt and freshly ground black pepper	

Preheat the oven to 400°F (200°C).

Lightly brush a roasting pan with olive oil, and place the whole eggplants on it. Pierce them with a fork to allow the steam to escape as they cook, and bake for 45-60 minutes, until they feel very soft when pressed. Remove from the oven, and allow to cool. Slice them in half, and scoop out the flesh into a bowl.

Combine the olive oil, tahini, garlic, lime juice, and half of the cilantro, and stir into the eggplant. Season to taste with salt and pepper, and garnish with the remaining cilantro.

Eggplant and Red Pepper Pasta

SERVES 4-6

2 Tbsp	olive oil	25 ml
1	large eggplant, cut in 1/2-inch (1-cm) cubes	1
1	onion, chopped finely	1
1	garlic clove, chopped finely	1
2	large sweet red peppers, seeded and chopped coarsely	2
1 lb	plum tomatoes, chopped coarsely	500 g
1 Tbsp	balsamic vinegar	15 ml
	salt and freshly ground black pepper	
1 lb	dried penne or farfalle	500 g
1/2 cup	chopped fresh basil	125 ml
1/2 cup	freshly grated pecorino Romano cheese	125 ml

Heat the olive oil in a large skillet over a high heat, and sauté the eggplant for 5-8 minutes, until it begins to brown. Reduce the heat, stir in the onion and garlic, and cook for 3-4 minutes more. Add the red pepper, tomatoes and balsamic vinegar, and bring to a simmer. Season with salt and pepper, and cook for 15 minutes, stirring occasionally, until the eggplant is tender.

Meanwhile, bring a large pot of salted water to the boil. Cook the pasta for 10-12 minutes, until *al dente*. Drain and toss with the sauce. Stir in the basil and cheese, and serve at once.

TO SALT EGGPLANT
Some people insist that eggplant needs salting before it's cooked to draw out the bitter juices. In fact, the bitterness disappears in cooking, but I do salt it before I fry it, as it's so porous it soaks up oil like a sponge. Salting makes it release a lot of liquid and close up its pores.

Place the sliced or diced eggplant in a colander over a bowl or in the sink, and sprinkle it liberally with salt. Lay a plate over top, and weight it with something heavy. Leave for 15-30 minutes, and then rinse the eggplant and pat it dry.

Roasted Eggplant with Sun-Dried Tomato Vinaigrette

SERVES 4

Eggplant is a good source of dietary fibre, with relatively small quantities of vitamins. Low in calories, it contains only 35 per 4-oz (120-g) serving.

Roasted or grilled eggplant is one of the simplest and most delicious things I know. You can serve it hot, warm, or chilled with any good vinaigrette.

2 medium or 1 large	eggplant	2 medium or 1 large
1 tsp	salt	5 ml
1-2 Tbsp	olive oil	15-25 ml

For the vinaigrette:

2	garlic cloves	2
1	shallot, peeled	1
8	sun-dried tomatoes preserved in oil, drained and chopped coarsely	8
8	black olives, pitted and halved	8
3 Tbsp	balsamic vinegar	40 ml
2/3 cup	olive oil	150 ml
2 Tbsp	chopped fresh basil	25 ml
	salt and freshly ground black pepper	

Preheat the oven to 400°F (200°C).

Cut the eggplant in 1/2-inch (1-cm) slices, and sprinkle them with the salt. Pour half the oil on a baking pan. Lay the slices on the pan, and brush them with the remaining oil. Bake in the centre of the oven for 10 minutes. Using a spatula, turn the slices over, and cook for 10-15 minutes longer, until browned and soft. Transfer to a serving platter, and drizzle with the vinaigrette. Serve warm or chilled.

To make the vinaigrette: Pulse the garlic, shallots, tomatoes, and olives in a food processor or blender to form a coarse paste. Pour in the vinegar and olive oil as you continue to pulse, until the mixture emulsifies. Transfer to a jar, stir in the basil, and season to taste with salt and pepper.

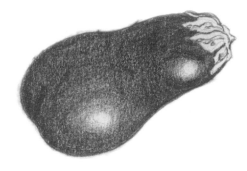

Belgian Endive, Curly Endive, and Escarole

BELGIAN ENDIVE

The Belgian endive (rhymes with on-leave) is actually the shoot of the common chicory root. This delicious vegetable was literally unearthed in the 19th century by a Belgian farmer. Having stored his fall harvest of chicory in the root cellar, in midwinter he discovered tender white leaves sprouting from them, ate them, and passed the word around. Thus was born the crunchy, delicate endive. It's still cultivated in forced beds, grown indoors to prevent the light from turning the leaves dark and excessively bitter. Belgium and Holland remain the number one producers, but this popular European vegetable has gained ascendancy in North America and is now available almost year-round.

Also called French endive or Witloof chicory, this tidy little vegetable has compact bundles of tightly wrapped, smooth white leaves ending in pale yellow tips. When choosing Belgian endive, look for firm, crisp, compact heads that give slightly when gently pressed. The leaves should be as white as possible with little or no colour. Wrap the bunches individually in paper towel and place in a plastic bag. They will keep well in the fridge for up to five days. Belgian endives are naturally clean creatures and require at most a quick wipe with a damp cloth.

Like its relative, the curly endive, the Belgian endive has a lovely, sharp tang that goes a long way. It contrasts beautifully with sweet flavours, making it a wow with apples or papaya. You don't need a lot: a mere handful of thinly sliced leaves will add zing and crunch to a ho-hum green salad, and you can add more coarsely sliced leaves to a stir-fry. It's lovely when braised very slowly in butter and cream, baked *au gratin* with chopped pancetta or bacon and parmesan, or sautéed and served with a vinaigrette.

CURLY ENDIVE AND ESCAROLE

Curly endive, like Belgian endive, is a chicory, and so is escarole. Curly endive and escarole are frequently mistaken for each other, which doesn't really matter as the two are pretty well interchangeable in terms of taste, if not appearance. Curly endive looks like a leaf lettuce with a bad perm, a frizzy mop of skinny green leaves with a pale yellow core; the baby-sized variety is called frisée. Escarole is a soft, broad-leaved green with flat, frilled leaves. Both curly endive and escarole are available year-round, the peak season being summer and early fall. Choose fresh-looking heads with crisp ribs and leaves. Wrapped loosely, both will keep in the refrigerator for several days. Rinse the leaves well and spin them dry before using.

In North America, we tend to use both curly endive and escarole raw, to add pungency and sparkle to salads. However, in Europe, both greens are often added to soups and casseroles or sautéed with olive oil. A good compromise is to dress the leaves with a warm vinaigrette, which gently wilts the leaf edges, bringing out the flavour while maintaining a bit of crunch.

Endive, both Belgian and curly, and escarole are not only great choices for taste appeal, but they're also excellent sources of folate and good sources of vitamin A and potassium.

BRAISED ENDIVE
WRAPPED IN PROSCIUTTO
page 65

JÍCAMA AND CITRUS SALAD
page 77

SCARPAZONNE (SPINACH PIE)
page 130

Endive Salad with Pears and Roquefort Dressing

3	Belgian endives, trimmed and separated into leaves	3
1	large pear, cored and sliced thinly	1
1/2 cup	walnut pieces	125 ml

For the dressing:

1/2 cup	sour cream	125 ml
3 Tbsp	mayonnaise	40 ml
1 Tbsp	olive oil	15 ml
2 Tbsp	freshly squeezed lemon juice	25 ml
1	shallot, chopped finely	1
1/2 tsp	Dijon mustard	2 ml
2 oz	Roquefort or any other blue cheese, crumbled	50 g
	salt and freshly ground black pepper	

To make the dressing: Blend all the ingredients except the cheese in a serving bowl. Add the cheese, folding gently so as not to break it up.

Now fold in the endive leaves, sliced pear, and walnuts. Serve at once.

Braised Endive Wrapped in Prosciutto

SERVES 4

Endive's sharpness is mellowed when it's braised in butter and baked with a creamy cheese sauce.

2 Tbsp	butter	25 ml
2	shallots, chopped finely	2
4	Belgian endives, trimmed and cored	4
1 cup	chicken stock	250 ml
1	sprig fresh thyme	1
1/3 cup	mascarpone or cream cheese	80 ml
1 Tbsp	freshly squeezed lemon juice	15 ml
4	slices prosciutto	4
1/4 cup	shredded Emmenthal cheese	50 ml
1 Tbsp	chopped fresh parsley, to garnish	15 ml

Melt the butter in an ovenproof casserole or skillet over a medium heat. Sauté the shallot for 3 minutes, until softened. Add the endives to the pan, and cook for 5 minutes, turning them frequently. Pour in the chicken stock, add the thyme sprig, and bring to a simmer. Reduce the heat, cover, and simmer for 5 minutes more, until the endive feels tender when pressed. Remove from the pan using a slotted spoon, and set aside to cool.

Preheat the oven to 350°F (180°C). While it heats, bring the stock to a gentle boil, and cook until reduced by half. Remove and discard the thyme. Turn off the heat, and stir in the mascarpone or cream cheese and lemon juice.

Wrap a slice of prosciutto around each endive, and place them back in the pan with the sauce, spooning some sauce over each one. Sprinkle with the grated cheese, and bake for 15 minutes, until golden and bubbling. Garnish with parsley, and serve at once.

ENDIVE HORS D'OEUVRES
For a perfect *hors d'oeuvre*, stuff satiny endive leaves with a soft cheese blended with something a little salty, such as anchovies.

Tangy Salad with Sweet Lemon-Poppy Seed Dressing

SERVES 4-6

This combination of escarole or curly endive, arugula, and radicchio with a sweetened dressing makes a sharp, refreshing salad, perfect for serving after a rich meal.

1	head escarole, rinsed, dried, and torn in bite-sized pieces	1
1	head radicchio, rinsed, dried, and torn in bite-sized pieces	1
2	bunches arugula, rinsed, dried, and torn in bite-sized pieces	2

For the dressing:

1	shallot, chopped finely	1
3 Tbsp	honey	40 ml
3 Tbsp	freshly squeezed lemon juice	40 ml
2 Tbsp	vegetable oil	25 ml
1 tsp	Dijon mustard	5 ml
1 tsp	poppy seeds	5 ml
	salt and freshly ground black pepper	

Combine the dressing ingredients in a jar with a tightly fitting lid, and shake well. Pour over the greens in a large bowl, and toss to coat. Serve at once.

Wilted Escarole Salad with Warm Camembert and Cider Dressing

Sharp greens such as escarole and endive react particularly well to warm dressings, added just before serving. Serve this with garlic croutons or thick slices of garlic toast.

1	head escarole, rinsed, dried, and torn in bite-sized pieces	1
1	tart eating apple, cored and sliced finely	1
1 tsp	freshly squeezed lemon juice	5 ml
1/4 cup	walnut or pecan pieces	50 ml
	garlic croutons (optional, see page 129)	

For the dressing:

8 oz	ripe Camembert cheese	250 g
2 Tbsp	sour cream	25 ml
1-2 Tbsp	apple cider	15-25 ml

Combine the salad ingredients in a bowl, sprinkling the lemon juice over the apples to prevent them from discolouring. Pour the dressing over the salad, and serve at once.

To make the dressing: Remove the rind from the cheese, and chop the cheese coarsely. Blend it with the sour cream, and heat gently, stirring until melted. Stir in enough cider to thin the dressing to pouring consistency.

Fennel

Fennel is very low in calories (only 25 a cup), so it's a flavourful treat for bored dieters. It is a good source of potassium and contains fair amounts of vitamins A and C.

Fennel looks a bit like fat celery; its thick, pale, broad stalks are braided together, forming a firm white bulb at the base with delicate, feathery greens sprouting from the top. Commonly used in both sweet and savoury Mediterranean dishes, fennel (*finocchio* in Italian) has a subtle licorice flavour and decided crunch. Although fennel is distinctive in appearance and flavour, there is some ambiguity over its name. Some believe that fennel and anise are the same creature, others insist that fennel is a vegetable and anise a herb, and still others think that the bulb is called fennel and its fern-like fronds are called anise. I'm sure that I'll get a few letters and phone calls on this one, but for the record: fennel — bulb and feathers included — is the vegetable. It is sometimes known as Florentine fennel, probably to distinguish it from common fennel, which has no bulb and is grown both as a fresh herb and for its anise-flavoured seeds. Anise is a different herb altogether, grown for its seed (aniseed), which is used to flavour Pernod, Sambuca, and ouzo. Its leaves are also edible, but the plant is not commonly cultivated for the market-place. Part of the confusion is that the English tend to call the vegetable, fennel, by the name of its flavour, anise.

To simplify things, the variety most often available in North America is the Florentine fennel, a delicious bulbous stalk weighing anything from 8 ounces to 2 pounds (250 g - 1 kg). Grown primarily in Italy, France, Greece, and California, until fairly recently fennel could be found only in Italian and specialty markets. Fortunately, it has become popular enough to make it available year-round in most major grocery stores. When choosing fennel, I find the smaller bulbs to be more tender. The stalks and fronds should be fresh and bright green in colour, and the bulbs a creamy white, with no cracks. Browning or yellowing usually indicates age, and fennel doesn't age particularly well.

Store fennel — with or without its tops — in a plastic bag in the crisper section of the refrigerator for no more than two or three days. Most recipes for fennel require only the bulb portion, but don't toss the fronds and stalks. They can be used — dare I say it — as a herb, for flavouring salads, broth, or stocks. Depending on the size and condition of the bulb, the outer layers can be peeled away like an onion. Before braising, sautéing, stir-frying, or roasting, halve or quarter the bulb and remove the tough inner core. Fennel's crisp texture makes it an ideal raw salad ingredient, and its subtle sweetness is complemented by salty foods, such as feta or goat's cheese. The stalks are more fibrous than celery, so dice or slice them finely for use in salads. Fennel can also be diced and substituted for onion or celery in any recipe. An Italian friend of mine makes a fennel-pork sausage that would make your knees grow weak.

Whatever you want to call it, give this lovely veg a try. There's no confusion over how good it tastes!

COOKED FENNEL IDEAS
Fennel braised in chicken broth and served with a creamy sauce is perfect with fish or poultry, and fennel soup with a splash of Pernod is a favourite at my house.

Braised Fennel and Leeks

SERVES 2

1 Tbsp	olive oil	15 ml
1 Tbsp	butter	15 ml
2	small leeks, rinsed, trimmed, and chopped coarsely	2
1	fennel bulb, trimmed and chopped coarsely	1
1/2 cup	chicken or vegetable stock	125 ml
1/2 cup	heavy cream	125 ml
1/3 cup	freshly grated parmesan cheese	80 ml
1/4 cup	pine nuts	50 ml
1 Tbsp	chopped fresh parsley	15 ml
	salt and freshly ground black pepper	

Heat the olive oil and butter in a small, ovenproof skillet or casserole over a medium-high heat. Sauté the leeks and fennel for 5 minutes. Add the stock,

IN THE MICROWAVE
In a microwave- and broiler-safe dish, melt the butter with the olive oil.

Add the leeks and fennel, and cook, covered, on high for 2-3 minutes, stirring twice. Add the stock, and cook for another 5 minutes. Stir in the cream, and cook 5 minutes more, until the fennel is tender and the sauce is reduced by half.

Then broil, as directed.

and bring to a boil. Reduce the heat, cover, and simmer for 10 minutes. Stir in the cream, and simmer for 10 minutes more, until the fennel is tender and the liquid has reduced by about half.

Preheat the broiler. Scatter the cheese and pine nuts over top of the fennel, and place the pan under the broiler for a few minutes, until bubbling and golden. Season with salt and pepper, garnish with parsley, and serve at once.

Roasted Fennel with Cherry Tomatoes and Sun-Dried Tomato Dressing

SERVES 4

This fennel-tomato combination goes particularly well with grilled fish.

2	fennel bulbs, trimmed	2
12	cherry tomatoes	12
2 Tbsp	olive oil	25 ml

For the dressing:

2	garlic cloves	2
1	shallot, peeled	1
8	sun-dried tomatoes preserved in oil, drained and chopped coarsely	8
8	black olives, pitted and halved	8
1/2 tsp	toasted fennel seeds, crushed	2 ml
1 tsp	toasted coriander seeds, crushed	5 ml
3 Tbsp	balsamic vinegar	40 ml
2/3 cup	olive oil	150 ml
	salt and freshly ground black pepper	

Bring a large pan of salted water to a boil, and add the whole fennel bulbs. Bring back to a boil, and cook for 8 minutes. Drain, and slice thinly lengthways.

Preheat the oven to 375°F (190°C), and brush half the olive oil on a baking pan. Arrange the fennel on the pan, and brush with the remaining oil. Season with salt and pepper, and bake for 15 minutes. Turn the fennel slices over, add the tomatoes, and bake for 15 minutes longer. Transfer to a serving platter, and pour the dressing over top. Allow to cool to room temperature before serving.

To make the dressing: Combine the garlic, shallots, sun-dried tomatoes, olives, and fennel and coriander seeds in a food processor or blender. Pulse to form a coarse paste. Gradually add the vinegar and olive oil, and pulse until smooth. Season to taste with salt and pepper.

Fennel Salad with Lime and Coriander Dressing

SERVES 2-4

1	fennel bulb, trimmed and sliced thinly	1
6-8	radishes, trimmed and sliced thinly	6-8
2 Tbsp	chopped fresh cilantro	25 ml
1 oz	fresh parmesan cheese, shaved finely	25 g

For the dressing:

1	garlic clove, crushed	1
1/4 cup	freshly squeezed lime juice	50 ml
1/2 cup	olive oil	125 ml
1 tsp	Dijon mustard	5 ml
1/2 tsp	toasted coriander seeds, crushed	2 ml
	a pinch each of salt and sugar	

Combine the dressing ingredients in a serving bowl, and blend well. Add the fennel, radishes, and cilantro, and toss to coat. Scatter the parmesan over top, and serve at once.

Fiddleheads

Fifteen years ago, when I opened my first fruit and veg stall in the Saint John City Market, two things happened that let me know spring was on its way. The first was that I was able to take off my fur hat and stop using a blow-dryer to keep the exotic fruits from taking a chill. The second was that more and more people started asking when the fiddleheads were due. It didn't take me long to figure out that they weren't talking about an itinerant string quartet. And when the fiddleheads did arrive, I couldn't unpack them fast enough.

In a world where the word "seasonal" no longer has any real meaning — with mandarin oranges available in June and asparagus on our Christmas menus — fiddleheads are one of the few vegetables that make us wait. Commercial cultivation of fiddleheads never got off the ground, which is where these delicacies grow. They're found in the wild along shady riverbanks and flood plains as far south as Virginia, and northwards to Newfoundland; they grow sparsely on the prairies and profusely in British Columbia. But the Maritimes are the true spiritual home of the fiddlehead, and it was surely a New Brunswick fiddler who coined the name.

Less commonly known as bracken or fern shoots, fiddleheads have a delicate, earthy flavour, reminiscent of asparagus, green beans, or artichokes.

Fat or thin, feast away. Fiddleheads have only 20 calories per 1 cup serving, and they're an excellent source of vitamin A and a fairly good source of vitamin C and dietary fibre.

Fiddleheads are a growth stage of the ostrich fern; it is the tightly coiled new-growth fronds or "crosiers" that are harvested. The season is short, because after only about two weeks the fern shoots unfurl into inedible plants. However, the season varies from region to region, as early as April in southern Maine and Vermont and as late as June or even July in the north. The first New Brunswick fiddleheads usually pop up towards the end of May.

As with most wild things, fiddleheads don't arrive clean, and they may need a few rinses to get rid of any sand or grit. Rub them gently between your hands to remove any fuzzy brown bits (scales), and snap or trim the ends off. Then swish them around in a sinkful of cold water, lift them out, and drain them well. Pat dry with a clean cloth or paper towel if you're not going to cook them right away. Fiddleheads will quickly lose their flavour, but you can store them for a few days in the refrigerator, ideally in perforated plastic vegetable storage bags.

Fiddlehead purists scoff at the idea of eating them any other way than simply steamed or boiled, with butter, salt and pepper, and a little vinegar — some say cider, some say white. If you're trying them for the first time, give your taste buds a treat and opt for fiddleheads *au naturel*. Boil the prepared fiddleheads in plenty of lightly salted boiling water for 5-7 minutes, or steam them in an inch of boiling water for 5-10 minutes, then drain and serve at once. Don't overcook them, as fiddleheads should be slightly *al dente*; however, undercooking will fail to bring out their delicate flavour.

Since the day I stopped looking out for the wandering fiddlers, I figure I've eaten enough fiddleheads to qualify as a true Maritimer.

HOW TO CHOOSE
FIDDLEHEADS
You want fiddleheads that are jade green in colour, with tightly coiled, springy heads no more than an inch (2.5 cm) or so in diameter. The stems should be short, as the flavour is in the heads, and you buy fiddleheads by weight.

Fiddleheads with Foamy Hollandaise Sauce

SERVES 4-6

Fiddleheads and hollandaise sauce are like peanut butter and jam, Fred Astaire and Ginger Rogers, champagne and moonlight — made for one another. Try the combination with grilled salmon fillets and new potatoes.

This version of the classic, rich hollandaise has been lightened up with stiffly beaten egg whites, so ladle it on freely. I like my hollandaise chilled, but it is equally tasty warm or even at room temperature.

REHEATING HOLLANDAISE
To reheat leftover hollandaise, microwave it on high for 10 seconds. Whisk rapidly, then heat for another 5-10 seconds if necessary, whisk again, and so on until it's the way you like it. If you overheat it and it curdles, try whisking in an ice cube. Remove what's left of the ice when the sauce is re-emulsified.

1 - 1 1/2 lb	fresh fiddleheads, cleaned and trimmed	500 - 750 g

For the sauce:

3	large eggs, separated	3
1 1/2 Tbsp	white wine vinegar	20 ml
1 1/2 Tbsp	freshly squeezed lemon juice	20 ml
1/2 cup	butter	125 ml
	salt and freshly ground black pepper	

Place the egg yolks in a food processor with a pinch of salt, and pulse until blended. Heat the lemon juice and vinegar until simmering, then pour the hot liquid in a steady stream into the food processor, pulsing continually. Melt the butter until it begins to foam, then add it to the food processor in the same steady stream, pulsing until the sauce is smooth and thickened. Transfer to a bowl.

Whip the egg whites in a clean bowl until they form soft peaks. Fold a spoonful of the whites into the yolk and butter mixture to loosen it. Gently fold in the remaining whites, and season to taste with salt and pepper. Cover and refrigerate until chilled, keep warm while you cook the fiddleheads, or simply set aside.

Bring a large pot of lightly salted water to a boil. Add the fiddleheads all at once and cook for 5 minutes. Drain well and serve on individual plates with a generous splash of hollandaise.

Fiddleheads Stir-Fried with Sesame and Garlic

SERVES 4

Although you can stir-fry fresh, raw fiddleheads, I think the flavour is brought out better if they are parboiled beforehand. These are a terrific accompaniment to grilled fish or chicken.

1 lb	fresh fiddleheads, cleaned and trimmed	500 g
2 Tbsp	soy sauce	25 ml
1 tsp	Oriental sesame paste or 2 tsp tahini	5/10 ml
1	small finger hot pepper, seeded and chopped very finely	1
1	garlic clove, crushed	1
3 Tbsp	peanut oil	40 ml
1	onion, halved and sliced	1

Parboil the fiddleheads a large pot of lightly salted boiling water for 3 minutes. Drain and plunge into a sinkful of ice water to halt the cooking process. Drain again, and pat dry.

In a small bowl, mix together the soy sauce, sesame paste, chili, and garlic, and thin with about 1 tablespoon of water. Set aside.

Heat the peanut oil in a wok or large frying-pan, until it sizzles when you flick a drop of water in it. Add the onions and fiddleheads all at once, and stir-fry for 3 minutes, adding a sprinkling of water if they appear to be drying out. Stir in the soy sauce mixture, and cook for 1 minute more. Transfer to a serving platter, and serve at once.

BEATING THE SEASON
If you're determined to have what you want when you want it, you can freeze fiddleheads and triumphantly produce them in midwinter. After rinsing and trimming, drop them into a large pot of lightly salted boiling water for 1 minute. Then quickly plunge them into ice water to halt the cooking process. Drain well and pat dry. Freeze in a single layer on a baking sheet, then transfer to an airtight freezer bag to store.

Linguine with Fiddleheads and Pine Nuts

Long, thin linguine noodles contrast nicely with coiled fiddleheads, but use whatever pasta you have on hand. Just make sure you don't overcook the fiddleheads!

2 lb	fresh fiddleheads, cleaned and trimmed	1 kg
2 cups	heavy or sour cream	500 ml
2 tsp	cornstarch	10 ml
1	garlic clove, crushed	1
1 Tbsp	freshly squeezed lemon juice	15 ml
3	strips prosciutto, chopped finely	3
1/4 cup	pine nuts, toasted	50 ml
1 1/2 lb	fresh linguini	750 g

Cook the fiddleheads for 5 minutes in a large pot of lightly salted boiling water, then drain. Purée half of them in a food processor until smooth, and set aside the rest in a warm oven.

Whisk together the cornstarch with a couple of tablespoons of cream until smooth, then blend with the remaining cream in a heavy-based saucepan over a low heat, stirring constantly, until thickened. Stir in the garlic, lemon juice, and fiddlehead purée.

Meanwhile, cook the pasta in a large pot of lightly salted boiling water for 3-5 minutes, just until *al dente*.

Drain and toss with the cream sauce. Fold in the prosciutto and toasted pine nuts. Serve on individual plates, dividing the reserved fiddleheads among them.

Garlic

Garlic is revered for its medicinal properties as well as its flavour. Although it may not actually ward off evil spirits, it definitely lowers blood cholesterol levels and thus may help to prevent heart disease. It has strong antibiotic compounds and may deter cancer, too.

Garlic is an onion, but, oh, such a significant onion. Affectionately known as the "stinking rose," garlic is something no self-respecting cook could live with without, as its aromatic — sometimes pungent, sometimes mild and sweet — flavour adds depth and perfume to so many dishes. There's a Frootique customer we call the Garlic King of Nova Scotia, since he buys (and eats) at least three pounds of garlic each week. He must be one of the lucky few who can consume it without suffering the antisocial after-effects. I find that even a single bite lingers with me for days, but that doesn't stop me from trying to compete with the king!

There are many garlic varieties, including stemmed and non-stemmed bulbs, and the general rule is that the smaller the cloves, the stronger the flavour. Elephant garlic (surprise, surprise) has giant cloves, mild enough to eat raw, but some say it has a peculiar flavour. Mexican garlic has pink or reddish skin and a juicy, powerful flavour. Available year-round, garlic is at its best during late spring and summer, when its flavour is sweet and mild. Keep your eye peeled in the spring for green garlic. This is the stem or shoot of immature bulbs that are just beginning to form. Green garlic is wonderfully delicate and can be used the way you would scallions or green onions, chopped in a salad, used as a garnish, or simmered in a clear soup or broth.

When buying garlic, choose tightly packed bulbs with relatively large cloves. They should be firm and clean, with no signs of sprouting or browning. Store them anywhere except the refrigerator, and preferably in a dry, dark place. (You can even buy ritzy garlic pots with holes in them to let the air circulate.) To peel a clove, break it away from the bulb, lay the flat blade of a wide knife over it, and give the blade a good whack with the heel of your hand. The peel will slip off easily, and you can slice off the root end. Garlic lovers love to debate the merits of chopping versus crushing, convinced that one or the other causes bitterness. I chop it, simply because I don't want to fiddle about with another utensil when I already have a knife in hand. To grind garlic to a paste, which is often called for in recipes using it raw, you can, of course, employ yet another utensil, a mortar and pestle (or the back of a spoon and a saucer). Or, still having the knife in hand, you can simply sprinkle a little coarse salt on the chopping board and use the flat side of the knife blade to mash the two together. The salt acts as a stabilizer, preventing the garlic from slipping about as well as soaking up its juices. Just use a little less salt in the recipe.

Whether you chop, slice, crush, or pulverize garlic, do it just before using it. Once cut, raw garlic begins to oxidize, rapidly becoming acrid and bitter. Olive oil will slow down this process, which is why it will keep its flavour in a vinaigrette, but you can taste the difference between a fresh dressing and one made the day before. Cook garlic gently to prevent it from browning. If you want just a suggestion of garlic in your dish, heat a whole, lightly crushed clove in your oil or butter, and remove it before it begins to brown. Or take a cut clove and rub it over bread for toasting or around the inside of the salad bowl. One of the best ways to enjoy garlic is baked or roasted, as after about 20 minutes it softens to a creamy pulp, mild enough in flavour to eat spread on toast. Peel just the outer skin from the top half of the bulb, and sprinkle with a little olive oil and salt. Place the bulb in a small, oven-proof dish, and add water to come about a quarter of the way up the bulb. Cover tightly and bake for 20-25 minutes at 375°F (180°C). Pull the cloves apart and squeeze them to release the flesh. Exquisite.

GARLIC ROASTED
IN THE MICROWAVE
Cut tips or tops off 4 bulbs of garlic. Place in a 4-cup (1-L) glass dish with 3 Tbsp olive oil and 1/3 cup (80 ml) chicken broth. Cover tightly and cook on high for 6-8 minutes or longer if bulbs are oversize. Let stand, covered, for 10 minutes before using.

Creamy Garlic and Eggplant Soup

SERVES 4-6

Both the garlic and the eggplant are brushed with olive oil and roasted, before being puréed with stock to make a light but creamy and full-flavoured soup.

1/2 cup	olive oil	125 ml
2	large eggplants	2
1	bulb garlic	1
4 cups	chicken or vegetable stock	1 L

1-2 Tbsp	freshly squeezed lemon juice	15-25 ml
2 Tbsp	chopped fresh tarragon	25 ml
	salt and freshly ground black pepper	

Preheat the oven to 375°F (180°C).

Pour half the oil into a shallow roasting pan. Trim and halve the eggplants lengthways, and place them, cut sides down, in the pan. Peel the outer leaves from the garlic bulb, and set it, root end down, in the roasting pan. Drizzle the vegetables with the remaining olive oil, and sprinkle with 1/2 cup of water. Cover and bake for 30-40 minutes, until both the garlic and the eggplant feel tender when pressed with your fingers.

Remove from the oven, and leave until cool enough to handle. Scoop the flesh from the eggplant into a food processor. Squeeze the garlic from its skin, and add to the food processor. Strain the cooking juices into the food processor, and purée until smooth.

Transfer to a large saucepan, and stir in the stock. Bring to a simmer, and season to taste with lemon juice, salt, and pepper. Sprinkle with the chopped tarragon before serving.

Pot-Roasted Chicken with Forty Cloves of Garlic

SERVES 4

This classic recipe tends to shock the uninitiated. Have no fear — the garlic becomes very mellow when roasted, infusing the bird with a sweet, nutty flavour. You can squeeze the flesh from some of the cloves to add to the sauce, mash some with potatoes, or pile the cloves around the chicken and let your guests do the popping.

6	strips bacon, chopped	6
3 1/2 - 4 lb	chicken, neck and giblets removed	1.5 - 1.75 kg
1	lemon	
5	bulbs of garlic, cloves separated but not peeled	5
1 1/2 cups	chicken stock	375 ml
1 cup	dry white wine	250 ml
1 Tbsp	chopped fresh thyme	25 ml
1 Tbsp	chopped fresh rosemary	25 ml
1 Tbsp	chopped fresh sage	25 ml
	salt and freshly ground black pepper	

Preheat the oven to 400°F (200°C).

In a large flameproof casserole dish or dutch oven, sauté the bacon until crisp. Remove and set aside, and pour excess fat if you wish.

Halve the lemon, pop it inside the chicken, and truss the chicken. Increase the heat under the casserole, and brown the chicken on all sides. Put the bacon back into the casserole along with the garlic cloves. Pour in the stock and wine, and scatter the herbs and seasoning on top. Bring to a simmer, remove from the heat, cover loosely, and place in the oven. Cook for 40-60 minutes, until the chicken juices run clear when you pierce the deepest part of the thigh.

Remove the chicken and garlic cloves from the casserole, and set aside on a serving platter to keep warm. If quite a bit of liquid remains in the casserole, place it over a high heat and boil until reduced to a nice glaze. Season to taste, and spoon the glaze over the bird.

Jícama

Every country has its potato, and jícama is standard fare in Mexico, where this nutty-sweet tuber originated. Unlike the potato, jícama is often eaten raw as well as cooked. Similar in flavour and texture to water chestnut, in Asia and the South Pacific it is a popular addition to everything from stir-fries to soups and is equally at home in a fruit salad.

Despite its role as the Mexican potato, jícama looks a bit more like a large turnip. Make that a very large turnip — it can range in weight from one to six pounds (.5-2.5 kg). It has thin brown skin and white, crunchy flesh, which, if you're lucky, can be as moist and crisp as an apple. Larger ones will be drier, and very large jícama can be too fibrous for my liking. Choose small to midsize, well-shaped tubers, and make sure their skin is smooth and unblemished. As with other tubers, weigh jícama in your hand — a good one will feel heavy for its size.

Available off and on all year, jícama is easiest to find between December and June. Most of our jícama comes from Mexico, where it is sold on every street corner and at beach stands along with melons and other snack food. In fact, my first taste of this delicious vegetable occurred when I was lying on a beach in Acapulco, and someone offered me a bag of jícama cut in neat shapes and sprinkled with lime juice and chili powder. Delicious! However, jícama does have a short shelf life, and you're best to use it ASAP, since it shrivels and grows mouldy in the cupboard and turns slimy when kept too long in the refrigerator. I wouldn't keep it chilled for more than two or three days at most. If you don't plan to use peeled jícama right away, you should submerge it in cold water with a little lemon juice to keep it from discolouring.

Jícama is a truly versatile vegetable and very user-friendly. Just peel it and you're ready to go. You can slice it, dice it, or cube it, and then throw it in a stir-fry with some peanut sauce, where it will remain crisp even when cooked. Or toss it with slices of red onion and papaya and dress it with fresh lime juice, olive oil, and cilantro. Salads made with jícama taste even better the next day because the vegetable soaks up flavours like a sponge. Jícama can take fiery seasoning, so it's commonly used in Oriental as well as Latin cooking. Think garlic, ginger, and hot peppers, and give your taste buds a treat.

Jícama is a good source of potassium and vitamin C. Low in sodium and calories, this vegetable is one of nature's finest snack foods.

Stir-Fried Jícama and Snow Peas

SERVES 4

Jícama cooks quickly and absorbs flavours well, so it makes an ideal stir-fry ingredient. The snow peas add a sweet, fresh taste.

3 Tbsp	soy sauce	40 ml
1	garlic clove, chopped finely	1
1 Tbsp	finely chopped fresh ginger	15 ml
2 tsp	sesame oil	10 ml
1 tsp	chili sauce	5 ml
1/2 tsp	sugar	2 ml
1 Tbsp	vegetable oil	25 ml
1 lb	jícama, peeled and sliced thinly	500 g
1 lb	snow peas, trimmed	500 g
2 Tbsp	chopped fresh cilantro	25 ml

Combine the soy sauce, garlic, ginger, sesame oil, and sugar in a small bowl, and set aside. Heat the vegetable oil in a wok or large stir-fry pan, and stir-fry the jícama for 3 minutes. Add the snow peas and the chili sauce at the same time, and cook for 2 minutes more. Stir in the chopped cilantro, and serve at once.

Jícama and Citrus Salad

SERVES 4-6

The slightly sweet taste of jícama is enhanced by the sweet and tart flavours of orange and grapefruit. This salad is great on its own or with barbecued fish or meat.

1 lb	jícama, peeled and cut in 1/2-inch (1-cm) cubes	500 g
1	red onion, chopped coarsely	1
1	large grapefruit, peeled	1
1	large orange, peeled	1
1	finger hot pepper, seeded and chopped finely	1
1/4 cup	chopped fresh cilantro	50 ml
1 Tbsp	freshly squeezed lime juice	15 ml
1/2 tsp	chili powder	2 ml
1/2 tsp	salt	2 ml

Combine the jícama and onion in a bowl. Separate the grapefruit and orange into segments, using a sharp knife to slice the segments away from the membranes and catching the juices in a bowl. Chop the segments in 1/2-inch (1-cm) pieces, and combine with the jícama. Stir in the hot pepper and cilantro, and squeeze the lime juice over top. Sprinkle with chili powder and salt to taste, and stir well. Refrigerate until chilled.

Kale

Kale is a member of the cabbage family, but like collards (see pages 52-54), it is a loose-leafed variety. Also called "curly kale," it looks like a genetically enhanced bunch of parsley. Its large, frilly leaves can vary in colour from apple to ivy to bluish green, as well as pink, purple and silvery-white. It is not unusual to find flowering kale (also called salad Savoy) in flowerbeds, but although this showy plant is edible, you won't be thanked for filching it for your supper.

This hardy green is best known in northern climates, from Scandinavia to Scotland. The Scots are particular fans, and being "invited to cail" is still an invitation to dinner. Traditionally kale is cooked long and slow. While some people appreciate the soft, mild results, I prefer it crisp and with a bit of kick, which it has in a stir-fry or sautéed in a bit of bacon fat or butter.

Available year-round, kale is at its best once it's been nipped by frost, and your best bet is to buy it from December through April. Choose a smallish bunch with vibrant colour and moist, crisp leaves. Stay away from kale that is turning yellow — a sign of age — or has wilted stems and tired-looking greens. Although it is prized for its endurance in the ground, once harvested and home, kale should be used as soon as possible. It will keep in the refrigerator in a perforated plastic bag for about two days.

You should wash kale thoroughly, as sand and grit are common guests among its curly leaves. Rinse it several times in a sink full of cold water, swishing it about with your hands. Lift out, drain, and give the leaves a shake to get rid of excess water. Very small stems can be left on, but most of the leaves should be stripped and sliced or shredded. You can steam kale as you would spinach, with just the water left clinging to its leaves. Bear in mind that it will take longer to cook and should be left until it's quite soft. Try blanching kale and then sautéing it for a few minutes in butter or olive oil flavoured with garlic. You can add a splash of cream to the sauté pan, which will neutralize the kale's acidic qualities. I like to fry up a bit of chopped bacon and onions, and then add the kale, which absorbs the lovely salt of the bacon and the sweetness of the onions. Kale can also be braised in chicken stock or added to soups and stews.

Kale is an excellent source of vitamins A and C as well as folate. You'll also get appreciable quantities of iron and calcium but only 40 calories in each cup of cooked greens.

MELLOW KALE
If you're sautéing kale but would like a fairly mild flavour, blanch it in boiling salted water for 3-5 minutes first, and then drain well.

Kale, Potato, and Kielbasa Soup

SERVES 6

1 lb	kale, rinsed	500 g
2 Tbsp	olive oil	25 ml
1	onion, chopped finely	1
2	garlic cloves, chopped finely	2
1 lb	small potatoes, peeled and sliced thinly	500 g
1 lb	kielbasa sausage, sliced thinly	500 g

Kale can hold its own with the robust flavour of garlic sausage. Use small potatoes so that the slices are bite-sized, similar to the sausage rounds. This soup tastes even better the next day.

6 cups	hot beef stock	1.5 L
	salt and freshly ground black pepper	
2 Tbsp	freshly squeezed lemon juice	25 ml

Remove the stalks from the kale, and shred the leaves. Heat the olive oil in a large saucepan, and sauté the onion and garlic for 5 minutes, until softened. Stir in the potatoes, cover, reduce the heat, and cook for 15 minutes, until softened. Add the sliced sausage and the kale, stirring to coat. Pour in the stock, and bring to a simmer. Cook for 10 minutes, until the kale is softened, and then season to taste with salt and pepper. Stir in the lemon juice just before serving.

Kale and Bacon Quiche

SERVES 4-6

1 lb	kale, rinsed	500 g
1 Tbsp	olive oil	15 ml
6	slices bacon, chopped finely	6
1	red onion, chopped finely	1
	freshly ground black pepper	
3	eggs	3
1/3 cup	heavy cream	80 ml
1/2 cup	grated fresh parmesan cheese	125 ml

For the pastry:

2 cups	all-purpose flour	250 ml
1/2 tsp	salt	2 ml
1 Tbsp	finely chopped fresh oregano	15 ml
1/2 cup	water	125 ml
1/2 cup	olive oil	125 ml

To make the pasty: Sift the flour with the salt in mixing bowl or food processor. Stir in the oregano, and add the water and olive oil all at once, stirring well or pulsing until it forms a moist dough. Press the dough evenly into an 11-inch (28-cm) flan pan with a removable bottom, and refrigerate for 1 hour.

Preheat the oven to 350°F (180°C). Remove the stalks from the kale, and shred the leaves. Heat the olive oil in a skillet, and sauté the bacon and onion for 5 minutes. Stir in the kale, and cook for 10 minutes, until softened. Season with pepper, remove from the heat, and allow to cool. Beat together the eggs, cream, and parmesan, and stir into the kale. Transfer the mixture into the chilled pastry case, and bake in the centre of the oven for 40 minutes, until firm and golden brown. Cool to room temperature before removing the sides of the pan and serving.

Kale with Parmesan

SERVES 4

1 lb	kale, rinsed	500g
3 Tbsp	olive oil	40 ml
2	garlic cloves, chopped finely	2
2	shallots, chopped finely	2
1/3 cup	water	80 ml
1/4 cup	grated fresh parmesan cheese	50 ml
	salt and freshly ground black pepper	

Remove the stalks from the kale, and shred the leaves. Heat the oil in a wok or large skillet, and sauté the garlic and shallots for 3-4 minutes, until softened. Add the kale, stirring well to coat, and then stir in the water. Bring to a boil, reduce the heat, and cover and simmer for 20 minutes, or until the kale is tender. Remove the cover, raise the heat, and cook until the liquid has evaporated. Stir in the parmesan cheese, season with salt and pepper, and serve at once.

IN THE MICROWAVE
In a microwave-safe casserole, combine the olive oil, garlic, and shallots. Cook on high for 1 minute, stirring once. Add the kale, toss to coat well, and pour water over all. Cover with plastic wrap with one edge turned back a bit, and microwave on high for 10-12 minutes, stirring several times. Stir in the parmesan, season with salt and pepper, and serve.

Kohlrabi

Kohlrabi is a bit of an oddity in the world of greens because it looks more like a root vegetable, and it is grown primarily for its bulbous stalk rather than its leaves. However, it does grow above ground and is in fact a member of the cabbage family, despite the second part of its name, *rabi*, which means turnip in German. This "cabbage-turnip" looks a bit extraterrestrial, with long, leafy tentacles sprouting from pale green or purple bulbs that can range in size from golf ball to baseball. No doubt its appearance has helped to convince North Americans that this is a strange if not exotic vegetable, but in Europe, Israel, and South East Asia, kohlrabi is as common as cabbage. But don't be misled by all this talk of cabbage; kohlrabi actually tastes more like broccoli, with perhaps a hint of radish.

You can find kohlrabi in most supermarkets from late May through November, although its peak season is in early summer. The tops may be removed, but keep your eye out for bulbs with their leafy greens still attached, as you can use the leaves as a garnish or add them to soups and stews. Either way, choose small bulbs, which will be more tender, unless you wish to stuff and bake them, in which case go for the larger variety. They should have smooth, unblemished skin, with no visible cracks or fibres.

Kohlrabi is an excellent source of vitamin C and potassium. High in fibre and low in calories, it is nutritious as well as delicious.

To store kohlrabi, trim away any leaf stems (and use them within a day or two), and refrigerate the bulbs in a plastic bag for up to a week. Peel the bulbs before using, whether raw or cooked.

Sautéed Kohlrabi with Caraway and Mustard

SERVES 4

2 lb	small kohlrabi, trimmed and peeled	1 kg
2 Tbsp	butter	25 ml
1 Tbsp	olive oil	15 ml
2 Tbsp	coarse-grained prepared mustard	25 ml
1 Tbsp	freshly squeezed lemon juice	15 ml
2 tsp	caraway seeds	10 ml

Halve the kohlrabi bulbs, and shred coarsely. Heat the butter and olive oil in a wok or large skillet over a medium-high heat, and sauté the kohlrabi for 2-3 minutes. Stir in the mustard, lemon juice, and caraway seeds, and cook for a minute or so. Serve at once.

IN THE MICROWAVE
Cooking this dish in the microwave will give a slightly different texture but an equally delicious taste. Simply cook the shredded kohlrabi on high, covered, for 2-3 minutes, stirring after 1 minute. Add the mustard, lemon juice, and caraway seeds, cook for 1 minute longer, and serve.

Kohlrabi and Watercress Salad with Ginger-Soy Vinaigrette

SERVES 4

2 lb	small kohlrabi, trimmed, peeled, and shredded or julienned	1 kg
1	bunch watercress, trimmed and chopped coarsely	1

For the vinaigrette:

1	garlic clove, peeled	1
2	shallots, peeled	2
2 Tbsp	chopped fresh ginger	25 ml
1/4 tsp	salt	1 ml
1 Tbsp	soy sauce	15 ml
1/4 cup	rice vinegar	50 ml
1/2 cup	vegetable oil	125 ml
	freshly ground black pepper	

I like to chop kohlrabi in matchsticks or grate it coarsely, and then sauté it in butter until tender. Squeeze a bit of lemon juice over top, season with salt and pepper, and you have a terrific side dish. Or you can boil or steam whole or sliced bulbs until barely tender, dressing them with a vinaigrette, and serve hot or chilled.

To make the vinaigrette: Combine the garlic, shallots, chopped ginger, and salt in a food processor or blender, and pulse to form a paste. Add the soy sauce and vinegar, and pulse to combine. Gradually pour in the vegetable oil while continuing to pulse, until the mixture emulsifies. Season to taste with pepper.

Toss the kohlrabi and watercress with the dressing, and serve at once. Alternatively, leave out the watercress, and refrigerate the dressed kohlrabi for an hour or so to allow the flavours to soak in. Toss in the watercress before serving.

An excellent crudité, raw kohlrabi has a special affinity for citrus dips and dressing. It's a wonderful salad ingredient, grated and dressed as for coleslaw.

Leeks

Depending on where you live in the world, the leek is cherished as prince of the onions or disparaged as the poor man's asparagus. This probably says more about relative cost than flavour, which to my mind is very little like asparagus, although both are members of the lily family. However, leeks have a sweet, earthy, succulent flavour of their own, and I'm quite willing to throw my lot in with the first description: leeks deserve to wear a royal crown.

Leeks are available year-round, although they will be best value from late fall through early spring. They can be as small as your finger or as large as a bowling pin, but the average leek is about the size of a celery stalk. Very large leeks tend to be woody, but otherwise you should choose leeks by the length of their whites and the fresh, crisp greenness of their tops. Store them in the refrigerator, wrapped well, as their odour will be absorbed by any other nearby foods. They will keep for several days; store them any longer and the greens will begin to dry out.

The two complaints I hear most about leeks is that they are difficult to clean and there is a lot of waste, since so many recipes call for just their white stems. Leeks are blanched with earth as they grow, so it's not surprising that they contain a lot of grit and mud. However, as most of us can boast running water in our kitchens, this should not be a real deterrent. As for the waste, simply trim the base and remove the first layer of leaves. You'll probably find that the white part extends further than you realized, so that you have less green than you expected to trim away. Slice off the coarser tops, leaving several inches of the tender green leaves on the stem. And don't throw away the top bits — they are a beautiful addition to stocks, soups, and stews.

To clean leeks, trim them individually, and then cut through the centre lengthways. Rinse under cold running water, separating the leaves so that the water gets right between the layers. Or you can slice the leek crossways in rings, as you would an onion, and submerge the slices in a sink full of water. Use your fingers to separate the rings, and the grit will settle to the bottom. Lift out the rings, rinse again in a colander, and *voila*! Clean leeks.

Small trimmed leeks can be steamed whole, braised in butter, or brushed with olive oil and grilled. Larger leeks should be sliced and stir-fried, but don't treat them like onions and allow them to brown, since they will toughen. Leek soups are a winter mainstay in my house, and I've included a recipe that will satisfy those who can't bear to throw anything away. Prince or pauper, treat yourself to a bunch of leeks next time you're at the market, and rediscover their royal taste.

Roasted Leeks with Blue Cheese

SERVES 4-8

Leeks are an excellent source of vitamin C and folate and contain fair amounts of potassium and iron.

Serve these leeks as a main course for 4, with a light soup and a tangy green salad, or as a starter for 8.

8	leeks	8
1/4 cup	olive oil	50 ml
2 oz	blue cheese, such as Roquefort or Stilton, crumbled	50 g
	freshly ground black pepper	

Preheat the oven to 375°F (190°C), and lightly oil a shallow baking dish.

Clean and trim the leeks, leaving 2 inches (5-cm) of green, and halve them lengthways. Place the leeks in the dish, cut sides up. Drizzle with the olive oil, and scatter the cheese over top. Bake for 30 minutes, basting with the oil at least twice during cooking. Season with pepper, and serve at once.

Leek, Potato, and Parsley Soup

SERVES 4-6

4	large leeks	4
1 cup	parsley, packed	250 ml
3 Tbsp	butter	40 ml
2	potatoes, peeled and chopped finely	2
3 cups	chicken or vegetable stock	750 ml
1 1/2 cups	milk or light cream	375 ml
	salt and freshly ground black pepper	

Trim off the root ends and the coarsest green parts of the leeks, cut them crossways in thin slices, and clean them. Strip off the parsley leaves and reserve, and chop the stems.

Melt the butter in a large saucepan over a low heat. Stir in the leeks, potato, and parsley stems, and season with salt and pepper. Cover and cook for 15 minutes, stirring occasionally. Pour in the stock and milk or light cream, and bring to a gentle simmer. Partially cover, and cook for 20 minutes, until the vegetables are very soft. Transfer to a food processor in batches, adding the parsley leaves, and purée until smooth. Return to the saucepan, and heat through until you're ready to serve.

Stir-Fried Leeks and Chinese Cabbage

SERVES 2

Serve this stir-fry on a bed of steaming hot egg noodles or fragrant rice.

2 Tbsp	Chinese black vinegar, balsamic vinegar, or dry sherry	25 ml
1 Tbsp	soy sauce	15 ml
2 Tbsp	water	25 ml
1 tsp	cornstarch	5 ml
2 Tbsp	peanut or vegetable oil	25 ml
1	garlic clove, chopped finely	1
1/2 Tbsp	grated fresh ginger	7 ml
2	leeks, cleaned, trimmed, and cut in 1 1/2-inch (4-cm) diagonal slices	2
2 cups	shredded napa or Chinese cabbage	500 ml
2	spring onions, chopped coarsely on the diagonal	2

In a small bowl, mix together the vinegar or sherry, soy sauce, water, and cornstarch, until smooth. Set aside. Heat the oil in a wok or frying pan, and stir in the garlic and ginger. Cook for about 30 seconds, and add the leeks and cabbage. Stir-fry for 1 minute more, and then pour in the vinegar mixture and stir in the spring onions. Cook for 2-3 minutes, until the vegetables are just wilted, and serve at once.

Lettuce

Back in my salad days (when I was still green behind the ears), I somehow talked my way into a job as a sous-chef in a posh hotel restaurant in the Channel Islands. One of my first assignments was preparing the salads. Easy peasy, I thought — a bit of Boston lettuce, a slice of tomato, and a dollop of salad cream. Lucky for me a generous galley slave saw my creation before my boss did, which probably saved me my job.

While back then even up-market London restaurants couldn't boast the variety of salad greens available today, I was amongst the many who thought that Boston lettuce *was* lettuce. Iceberg is the North American equivalent, and it remains one of the top sellers for a good reason. Crisp and juicy, with a sweet if somewhat bland flavour, iceberg lettuce is refreshing and enjoyable. It also stores and travels well, which is why it tends to be cheaper than other greens. Another familiar favourite, of course, is romaine. This lettuce has firm, elongated leaves and a somewhat nutty-sweet taste, and it commonly plays a starring role in Caesar salads.

Aside from iceberg and romaine lettuces, there are many other terrific salad greens. Bibb or Boston lettuce has a small head and tightly packed furled leaves surrounding a firm heart. Butterhead lettuce is also generally quite small but has floppy, butter-tender leaves and a pale heart. Then there are the looseleaf lettuces, which have no hearts but plenty of flavour. Their tender but meaty leaves can be green, red, or a combination, and broad, curly, or oak-leaf shaped.

There are still other salad greens that do not properly belong to the lettuce family but *do* belong in your salad bowls. Lamb's lettuce, or mâche, has small, dark-green, spoon-shaped leaves on short stems and an intense, nutty flavour. Arugula, radicchio, endive, escarole, and frisée, all add a sharp, peppery, or bitter element to ho-hum green salads. You can also buy mixes of baby salad-green leaves, called mesclun, either packaged or in bulk. Mesclun generally includes some or all of baby leaf lettuces, bitter greens, chicories, mustard greens (including the delicately flavoured mizuna), dandelion greens, and frisée, and sometimes leafy herbs such as chervil. Mesclun is good value for money if you only want a small amount of salad; otherwise try creating your own mixtures.

Whatever lettuces or salad greens you buy, choose fresh heads or bunches with crisp leaves. Avoid any that are already wilted or show holes or spotting. Use salad greens as soon as possible; if storing, first remove any rubber bands or twist-ties binding them together. Refrigerate unwashed greens in the crisper section in a perforated plastic vegetable storage bag to prevent moisture from building up. Very tender lettuces will last for two or three days at the most, while firmer heads such as romaine or iceberg will stay crisp for a few days longer. Separate the leaves before rinsing them well in a sink full of cold water. Drain and spin dry in a salad spinner, or gently shake them in a colander before patting them dry with paper towel. I like to chill washed greens for an hour before using to crisp them up again. Iceberg lettuce can be popped into the freezer for 5-10 minutes after washing to really crisp it up.

To prolong the life of iceberg lettuce, cut out the core, and run water into the cavity until the leaves start to separate. Then turn over, and drain thoroughly in a colander. Wrap in a tea towel, and store in a plastic bag in the crisper. The lettuce will keep well for at least a week, and the leaves will separate nicely, too. This tea towel method also works well with rinsed, well-drained leaf lettuce.

Generally speaking, salad greens should be dressed just before serving to prevent them from getting soggy. However, don't reserve greens for cold salads. Try using a warm dressing, which will cause the leaves to wilt. Or braise lettuce hearts in a little butter and cream and serve them hot or warm. Some of the sturdier greens, especially bitter varieties such as radicchio or arugula, make a terrific last-minute addition to stir-fries or pasta sauces.

The next time you're shopping for the salad bowl, use your imagination. Steer your way clear of the iceberg, and you might just run into a different kind of adventure.

Crunchy Caesar Salad

SERVES 6

1	small head romaine lettuce, rinsed, dried, and torn in bite-sized pieces	1
1	small head iceberg lettuce, rinsed, dried, and torn in bite-sized pieces	1
1	small head curly endive, rinsed, dried, and torn in bite-sized pieces	1
1/4 cup	grated fresh parmesan cheese	50 ml

For the dressing:

1	large egg	1
1	large garlic clove, peeled	1
1 tsp	dry mustard	5 ml
8	canned anchovy fillets, drained and chopped, with oil reserved	8
2 Tbsp	freshly squeezed lime juice	25 ml
1/2 tsp	Worcestershire sauce	2 ml
2/3 cup	virgin olive oil	150 ml
	freshly ground black pepper	

For the croutons:

1	garlic clove, chopped	1
1/4 tsp	salt	1 ml
2 Tbsp	olive oil	25 ml
2 Tbsp	finely grated parmesan cheese	25 ml
4	thick slices white bread, crusts removed, cut in 1/2-inch (1-cm) cubes	4

Created in the 1920s by Caesar Cardini at his famous restaurant in Tijuana, this salad remains a favourite. You can turn it into a main course by adding grilled chicken or shrimp, and vegetarians beware — you can't really call it a Caesar salad without the addition of anchovies, which are fundamental to the piquant dressing. This version uses a variety of crisp greens, as soft-leaf lettuces can't stand up to the heavy dressing.

To make the croutons: Preheat the oven to 350°F (180°C). Mash the garlic with the salt to form a paste, and stir in the olive oil and parmesan. Roll the bread cubes in the oil mixture to coat well, and then place them on a baking pan. Bake for 8-10 minutes on the highest oven shelf, remove from the oven, and allow to cool.

To make the dressing: Combine the egg, garlic clove, mustard, a few pieces of anchovy, the lime juice, and the Worcestershire sauce in a food processor or blender. Pulse to form a smooth paste, and then slowly drizzle in the olive oil until the mixture emulsifies. Add some of the reserved anchovy oil, along with freshly ground black pepper, to taste.

Combine the lettuce leaves with the remaining chopped anchovies, and pour the dressing over top. Toss well to combine, and then sprinkle with the parmesan cheese and croutons. Toss again, and serve at once.

Lettuce and Fresh Pea Soup with Minted Cream

SERVES 4

Although we normally don't think of cooking lettuce, it makes a delicious and delicate soup. If you don't have any leftover potatoes on hand to thicken the soup, boil potatoes in lightly salted water until tender, and use the cooking water as part of the vegetable stock.

4 cups	vegetable stock	1 L
3	small heads Bibb lettuce, rinsed, dried, and shredded	3
1 lb	shelled fresh peas	500 g
3-4	new potatoes, cooked, peeled, and cubed	3-4
	salt and freshly ground black pepper	
1/2 cup	whipping cream	125 ml
1 Tbsp	chopped fresh mint	15 ml

Bring the stock to a boil in a saucepan, and stir in the lettuce, peas, and cooked potatoes. Season with salt and pepper, and simmer for 3-4 minutes, until the peas are tender. Transfer to a blender or food processor, and purée until smooth. Return to the saucepan, and reheat. Meanwhile, whip the cream, and stir the mint into it. Serve the soup hot, with a dollop of whipped cream floating in each bowl.

Warm Potato and Mesclun Salad

SERVES 4-6

Instead of this mixture of mild and sharp leaves, you can make up your own combination or use premixed mesclun.

1 lb	small new potatoes, scrubbed	500 g
1	butterhead lettuce, rinsed, dried, and torn in bite-sized pieces	1
1	bunch baby mizuna leaves, rinsed, dried, and torn in bite-sized pieces	1
1	bunch arugula, rinsed, dried, and torn in bite-sized pieces	1
1 cup	mixed fresh leafy herbs such as chervil, parsley, basil, and/or oregano	250 g

For the dressing:

1/4 cup	cider vinegar	50 ml
1/3 cup	sour cream	80 ml
1/4 cup	buttermilk	50 ml
3 Tbsp	honey	25 ml
1 Tbsp	Dijon mustard	15 ml
1	small garlic clove, chopped finely	1
1	spring onion, chopped finely	1
1/2 cup	olive oil	125 ml
	salt and freshly ground black pepper	

Bring a large pot of lightly salted water to a boil, and cook the potatoes for 15-20 minutes, until tender. Drain and cut in bite-sized pieces. Combine the salad greens and herbs on a large platter.

To make the dressing: Blend together the dressing ingredients, except for the olive oil, in a large mixing bowl. Add the oil last, whisking it in until the mixture emulsifies. Fold the warm potatoes into the dressing, and then spoon the potatoes onto the salad greens, drizzling any remaining dressing over top. Serve at once.

Mushrooms

BUTTON MUSHROOMS

Mushrooms are a regular item on most shopping lists. But we've come a long way from the days of buying white button mushrooms sweating in a cellophane packet, forgetting them in the bottom of the vegetable crisper, then tossing them into a stew or tomato sauce to disguise their less-than-fresh appearance. With the wide variety of cultivated and wild mushrooms available in today's markets, fungi have come into their own.

But let's not throw the baby out with the bath water. The small, white button mushroom, with its smooth, rounded cap and creamy, mild taste, still deserves a place in your shopping basket. Available year-round, button mushrooms are usually sold loose, allowing you to bag your own. Choose firm, plump mushrooms, with dry skins and tightly closed caps. Avoid any with wrinkled skins, blemishes, or a moist, slimy texture. Mushrooms have a short life and should be used as soon as possible. If you must keep them for a day or two, refrigerate them in a paper bag or wrapped loosely in a slightly moistened paper towel. Humidity accelerates spoilage, so store them on a shelf with lots of space around them, rather than in the vegetable crisper, smothered under a giant daikon or eggplant.

Because their high water content causes them to shrink considerably when cooked, leave small mushrooms whole. The stems of larger mushrooms can be trimmed or peeled, if you have the patience. Because button mush-

INSTANT MUSHROOMS
Button mushrooms are good raw, sliced in a salad or left whole and eaten with a dip.

Sauté mushrooms in butter with some garlic, and sprinkle with parsley or cilantro. I like to add a splash of cream to the pan before spooning the whole lot onto a piece of toast. Delicious!

rooms have a subtle taste, they are an economical way to bulk up a dish made with the wild or exotic varieties.

HOW TO CLEAN MUSHROOMS

Cultivated mushrooms are grown in sterilized compost, which, believe it or not, is very sanitary. So all you need to do to clean them is brush or wipe them gently. And because these delicate creatures absorb moisture very easily, I *never* put them near water. They need to be kept as dry as possible, especially if you want to sauté or dry-fry them.

EXOTIC AND WILD MUSHROOMS

Chanterelles are the pretty, flower-like mushrooms that grow wild on both coasts; they're gathered from late summer into the fall. Ranging in colour from pale gold to rich apricot, these trumpet-shaped fungi have a mild, nutty flavour that goes well with poultry or creamy pasta dishes. As they cannot be cultivated, fresh chanterelles are considered a real delicacy. They are also available tinned or dried, usually imported from Europe, although ironically most of these are originally exported for processing from North America. When buying fresh chanterelles, choose plump, firm mushrooms with a spongy texture and dry, unblemished skin. They keep better than other varieties and can be stored in the refrigerator for several days if placed in a single layer under a barely damp cloth.

Cremini mushrooms are a larger variety of the button mushroom. Grown outdoors, they have pale brown caps and a slightly more intense flavour. Portobellos, the largest variety of cremini, can be up to 6 inches (15 cm) wide, a real man-sized mushroom. Their robust flavour and large, flat caps make them ideal for grilling or stuffing and broiling, either whole or sliced thickly. This is the one vegetable that could convert me to vegetarianism!

Enoki look more like sea creatures than mushrooms, with long, slender stems joined at the base and topped with tiny ivory caps. Their faintly fruity taste and delicate appearance make them ideal for serving raw in salads or sandwiches, much like sprouts. They can also be added to clear soups or broths just before serving. Usually sold in cellophane packets, enoki should appear firm and springy. The spongy base should be pale and dry; avoid any that look watery or brown. To prepare, simply trim away the base and gently separate the stems.

Oyster mushrooms are a commercially cultivated wild fungus. Mild in flavour, these "oysters of the woods" are creamy-beige or pale grey in colour, with silky, deep-gilled caps and short stems. As with most other mushrooms, avoid any that appear wet or slippery. To prepare, simply wipe gently and trim the clustered stems before slicing thickly. Don't overpower the delicate flavour with strong seasonings or too much butter or oil.

Shiitake mushrooms appear naturally in the woods, but the variety we find in produce markets is cultivated in artificial logs. Shiitakes have a distinct garlicky-woodsy scent and a robust, earthy flavour. Look for large, plump, dry caps with a wholesome fragrance. Unlike other mushroom varieties, shiitakes should be cooked through, and they are not overwhelmed by strong seasonings or red meats. Their stems can be quite tough and should be removed and cooked separately or saved and added to stews or stocks. Shiitake mushrooms will last for several days when stored in the refrigerator in a single layer under a barely damp cloth.

Other wild mushrooms, including porcini or ceps, morels, and wood or cloud ears, are more commonly available dried in small packets. These can add superb flavour and depth to stews, soups, and other mushroom recipes. Rehydrate by soaking in warm water until softened, then drain and chop, reserving the soaking liquid, which can be added to most dishes.

Oven-Baked Wild Mushroom Risotto

SERVES 6

This is truly a cheat's recipe — it produces a dish that will make your guests think you spent the day foraging in the woods and the evening slaving over the stove. The creamy sauce that clings to each al dente *grain of rice in an authentic risotto is created by slow, stovetop cooking, with the gradual addition of hot liquid to the special short-grained rice and constant stirring, stirring, stirring. After a little preparation, this version lets you kick back with a gin and tonic while the oven does the work.*

Mushrooms are mostly water, so 4 ounces (120 g) of raw mushrooms contain only 35 calories. However, this also means that they shrink in cooking; a pound (500 g) of raw mushrooms will serve 3-4 people.

1 oz	dried porcini or other wild mushrooms	15 ml
4 cups	boiling water	1 L
1 lb	assorted fresh mushrooms, chopped coarsely	500 g
4 Tbsp	butter	60 ml
1 Tbsp	olive oil	15 ml
1	large onion, chopped finely	1
1 1/2 cups	risotto rice (arborio or carnaroli)	375 ml
1 cup	Marsala wine or dry sherry	250 ml
1 1/2 tsp	salt	7 ml
	freshly ground black pepper	
1/2 cup	freshly grated or shaved parmesan	125 ml
1/4 cup	finely chopped fresh parsley	50 ml

Place the dried mushrooms in a heatproof bowl, and pour the boiling water over top. Leave to soak for half an hour, or until the mushrooms are softened. Line a sieve with a double thickness of paper towel, and set it over another bowl. Strain the mushrooms, squeezing out any excess moisture, and reserve the soaking liquid. Chop the mushrooms finely.

Preheat the oven to 300°F (150°C), and place a large, shallow baking dish in it to warm.

Melt the butter and olive oil in a large saucepan over a gentle heat, and sauté the onion for about 5 minutes. Stir in both the fresh chopped mushrooms and the dried mushrooms. Cook over a low heat for about 20 minutes, stirring occasionally. Stir in the rice, wine, reserved mushroom liquid, salt, and pepper, and bring to a gentle simmer.

Remove the baking dish from the oven, and transfer the contents of the saucepan to the dish. Stir once, and set it back in the oven. Bake for 25 minutes, and then gently stir in all but a handful of the parmesan. Bake for another 15-20 minutes, until all the liquid has been absorbed. Remove from the oven, and cover with a tea towel, which will absorb some steam. Leave to rest for 5 minutes before sprinkling with the parsley and remaining parmesan.

Marinated Mushrooms

SERVES 4-6

You can serve these tasty morsels as a salad or as party nibbles: double (or triple) the recipe and place a basket of toothpicks beside the bowl.

1 lb	button mushrooms, wiped and trimmed	500 g
	zest of 1 lime	
1/4 cup	chopped fresh cilantro	50 ml

For the dressing:

2 Tbsp	toasted coriander seeds, crushed	25 ml
	freshly squeezed juice of 1 lime	
1 Tbsp	water	15 ml
6 Tbsp	olive oil	90 ml
2 tsp	coarse-grained prepared mustard	10 ml
1/2 tsp	sugar	2 ml
	salt and freshly ground black pepper	

Combine the dressing ingredients in a large bowl, and mix well. Stir in the prepared mushrooms and half of the lime zest and cilantro. Sprinkle the remaining zest and cilantro over top. Refrigerate for at least 1 hour, and bring back to room temperature before serving.

Soufflé Omelette with Creamy Mushroom Filling

SERVES 2

For the filling:

4	strips bacon, chopped finely	4
2	shallots, chopped finely	2
1/2 lb	fresh mushrooms, chopped coarsely	250 g
1/4 cup	heavy cream	50 ml
	freshly ground black pepper	

For the omelette:

3	eggs, separated	3
1 Tbsp	water	15 ml
	salt and freshly ground black pepper	
1 Tbsp	butter	15 ml
2 Tbsp	snipped fresh chives	25 ml

To make the filling: Fry the bacon in a small skillet until the fat begins to run. Add the chopped shallots, and sauté for a few minutes. Stir in the mushrooms, and cook for 3-4 minutes over a medium heat. Add the cream, season with pepper, and cook until the liquid has reduced, stirring occasionally.

Preheat the broiler. In a large bowl, beat the egg yolks with the water, and season with salt and pepper. In a separate bowl, whip the egg whites until stiff, and carefully fold the whites into the yolks. Melt the butter in a large frying pan over a low heat. Pour the egg mixture into the pan, and cook for 2-3 minutes, until the omelette begins to set. Transfer the pan to the top oven shelf, and broil for 3 minutes, or until the omelette is puffy and golden brown. Remove from the oven, pour the mushroom sauce over one side, and gently fold the other side over it. Slide the omelette onto a serving plate, and cut it in half, sprinkling the chives over top.

Okra

The world is divided into those who love okra, those who hate it, and the vast majority who have never even tried it. Its champions revel in its tender, viscous texture and sweet, fresh taste; its detractors can't get past its exceptional slickness (they say sliminess). I'm a huge fan myself, and I especially love okra breaded with cornflour and pan-fried in butter.

Okra is native to Africa and was brought to the New World by slave traders in the 16th century. Integral to Creole cuisine, okra is the ingredient that lends gumbos their characteristically thick consistency. It is also widely used in the Middle East, the Balkan states, India, and Asia, where contrast in texture is as important to a meal as yin-yang flavours.

With a peak growing season of mid to late summer, okra is generally available year-round. If you're not familiar with the vegetable, ask for it, or look around for ridged green bullet-shaped pods. They're pretty easy to spot. The smaller ones are your best bet, no bigger than your index finger (unless you've very small hands), as larger, mature pods may be dry and woody. Think of snap peas when checking for firmness, and avoid any limp or blemished ones. Okra will keep fresh for up to 4 days when kept in a plastic bag in the refrigerator.

There are two basic methods of cooking okra, whole and cut. When cut, the pods release their mucilaginous (gummy) substance, thickening and flavouring whatever they are cooked with. For this reason, if you're cooking okra to eat as is, whether steamed, boiled, or stir-fried, leave the pods whole. Rinse them and carefully trim the caps, making sure not to cut into the pods themselves. Steam over boiling water until just tender, 3-5 minutes for small pods and up to 7 minutes for larger ones. Toss with butter, a squeeze of lemon juice, salt, and pepper, and serve at once. They are also good with any sauce or dressing that you might serve with asparagus. Try hollandaise or aïoli. Raw sliced okra can be added to soups or stewed dishes during the last 8-12 minutes of cooking. Okra has a natural affinity with tomatoes, eggplants, sweet peppers, and garlic, making it a good addition to Mediterranean-style dishes. But it also stands up to the spicy-sweet flavours of Asian and Caribbean cooking, so experiment with ginger, hot peppers, peanut sauce, and coconut.

If you've never tried okra, get into the game and give it a shot. I'll be interested to hear which camp you fall into.

STIR-FRIED OKRA
To stir-fry okra, first blanch the pods in boiling water for 1 minute. Drain and pat dry, then slice in rounds. Sauté in olive or peanut oil for 5 minutes or until bright green, and then stir in some finely chopped garlic and finger hot pepper. Cook for another few minutes, and season to taste.

Okra with Sun-Dried and Cherry Tomatoes

SERVES 4

2 Tbsp	olive oil	25 ml
3	strips bacon, chopped	3
1	small red onion, sliced thinly	1
1	garlic clove, chopped finely	1
1/2 tsp	coriander seeds, crushed	2 ml
1 lb	small okra, trimmed and cut in 1/2-inch (2.5-cm) slices	500 g
1/2 lb	cherry tomatoes	250 g
6	sun-dried tomatoes in oil, drained and chopped	6
2 Tbsp	freshly squeezed lemon juice	25 ml
1/3 cup	water	80 ml
	salt and freshly ground black pepper	
2 Tbsp	chopped fresh cilantro	25 ml

Heat the olive oil in a skillet, and fry the chopped bacon with the onion and garlic for 5 minutes. Stir in the coriander seeds, and cook for 1 minute. Add the okra, cherry and sun-dried tomatoes, lemon juice, and water, and bring to a simmer. Cook for 10-12 minutes, until the okra is just tender. Season to taste with salt and pepper, and stir in the cilantro. Serve at once.

Onions

Onions are an excellent source of vitamin C and are thought to be a powerful antioxidant.

Onions are the single most important cooking ingredient in the world and perhaps the least appreciated. Maybe it's because we use them so often that we take them for granted — almost every other recipe seems to start with "Chop an onion. . . ." But nobody ever stops to ooh and ahh over a display of onions, and although it's true that even the most gorgeous red onion doesn't inspire me to grab it and take a bite, just try and imagine life without onions. Now *that's* something worth crying over.

The onion belongs to the *allium* family. There are dozens of varieties, but all of them have in common, to lesser and greater degrees, a characteristically pungent odour. This onion smell is due to volatile chemical compounds that lie just beneath the skin, which also explains why chopping onions can bring you to tears. However, the sharp odour and taste of onions is quickly transformed when they are cooked, which is why a mess of fried onions is about the tastiest, sweetest treat around.

The most frequently used onions are the yellow cooking onion, the sweet "eating onion," the shallot, and green onions and scallions. The yellow onion is an all-purpose cooking variety. The papery outside skin is golden brown, while the flesh inside graduates from yellow to white as you peel away the layers. Too strong to eat raw, it takes on a mellow, sweet flavour when fried, boiled, or baked, and is usually used as a base for other ingredients. The smallest ones are also good when braised whole in butter and white wine or added to casseroles. The little baby, button, or pearl onions, which look like miniature yellow onions except for their white skins, are frequently used for pickling.

Sweet onions have thinner skin and higher moisture content. Mild and juicy, they are great for eating raw, sliced thinly and added to sandwiches and salads. However, their size makes them ideal for stuffing and baking whole or slicing in rings and deep-frying. Sweet onions are generally grown in mild climates. Two of the most popular varieties are the Spanish and the Vidalia, which is grown in Georgia and considered the Dom Perignon of onions. Red onions, mild and tender, add a splash of colour to any dish, whether raw or cooked.

Despite their appearance, shallots are not simply baby cooking onions but a distinct variety. Like garlic cloves, shallots grow together in small clusters, so you may find more than one bulb attached to a single root. Their intense yet delicate flavour and fine flesh make them a required ingredient in many sauces and dressings. They can also be used when you want just a small amount of onion.

Green onions and scallions are different creatures, but they taste very similar and are generally used interchangeably. Green onions are any immature onions harvested with their greens still attached, and their bulbs can range from almost non-existent to large. True scallions, or spring onions, are the shoots of a special variety of white onion that does not form enlarged bulbs. Both green onions and scallions have a mild flavour, and the slender white bulbs as well as the green shoots can be used. Chopped finely, they make a zesty addition to an omelette, salad, or stir-fry.

All onions are available year-round, although green and some sweet varieties will have a local peak season from late spring to early fall. When buying dried onions, choose firm, well-shaped specimens with narrow necks and unblemished skins. Avoid any that have already sprouted. Dried onions store very well for over a month in a cool, dry place. Sweet onions should be used as soon as possible to make the most of their flavour. Green onions and scallions should look fresh, clean, and sprightly. They should be kept in a plastic bag in the refrigerator for no longer than five days. Once any onion has been cut, wrap it tightly to prevent it from flavouring everything else in the refrigerator, and use it as soon as possible.

ONIONS IN THE MICROWAVE
The microwave might have been invented for cooking onions. Microwaving "sweats" them a little, helping them to yield their full flavour, and they cook quickly, with little chance of unwanted browning.

To soften chopped onions: Place 1/4 cup of onion with 2 tablespoons of fat in a shallow dish. Cover and cook on high for 2 minutes. Adjust amounts and times accordingly for any amount of onion.

Green onions are wonderful when brushed with olive oil or melted butter and grilled until brown and tender.

French Onion Soup with Gruyère and Garlic Croutons

SERVES 6

I love this soup. The croutons ooze with melted smoky cheese, which contrasts beautifully with the sweet, mellow flavour of the soup.

3 Tbsp	olive oil	40 ml
1 Tbsp	butter	15 ml
2 lb	red onions, sliced thinly	1 kg
3	garlic cloves, chopped finely	3
1 tsp	sugar	5 ml
5 cups	beef stock	1.5 L
1 1/4 cups	dry white wine	300 ml
2 Tbsp	brandy (optional)	25 ml
1 Tbsp	fresh thyme leaves	15 ml
	salt and freshly ground black pepper	

For the croutons:

2 Tbsp	olive oil	25 ml
1	garlic clove, chopped finely	1
12	1/2-inch (1-cm) baguette slices	12
1 cup	grated Gruyère cheese	250 ml

TO BLANCH ONIONS
IN THE MICROWAVE
Arrange pearl onions in a single layer in an uncovered oval dish; for each 1/2 pound (250 g), use 1 tablespoon (15 ml) of water, and cook on high for 1 minute.

For whole small white onions (12 per pound), peel, arrange in a 10-inch (23-cm) round dish, add a cup of water or sauce per pound, and cook on high for 5 minutes. For larger peeled yellow onions, cook 1/2 pound (250 g) in a 4-cup (1-L) glass dish with 6-8 Tbsp (75-125 ml) water for 8 minutes; if you're cooking a larger quantity, stir once or twice during the cooking period.

Melt the olive oil and butter in a large saucepan, and stir in the onions, garlic, and sugar. Cook for 5 minutes over a high heat, until the onion begins to turn brown at the edges. Reduce the heat to low, and cook for 30 minutes more, stirring occasionally. Pour in the stock and wine, bring to a simmer, and season to taste with salt and pepper. Half cover, and leave to simmer gently for 1 hour.

To make the croutons: Preheat the oven to 350°F (180°C). Drizzle the olive oil and sprinkle the garlic on a large baking pan. Press both sides of each baguette slice in the oil, and then bake for 20 minutes, until crisp. Remove from the oven, and set aside.

When you're ready to serve the soup, add the brandy, if using, and the fresh thyme. If your soup bowls are ovenproof, ladle the soup into the bowls, top each with two croutons, and scatter a handful of grated cheese on each serving. Pop the bowls under the broiler until the cheese melts, and serve at once. Otherwise, divide the cheese among the croutons while they are still on the baking pan, broil until melted, and place 2 croutons in the bottom of each bowl. Pour the soup over top, and serve at once.

Sweet and Sour Green Onions

SERVES 4

1 Tbsp	olive oil	15 ml
2 oz	sliced pancetta	50 g
1 lb	small green onions, with stems trimmed to 1/2 inch (1 cm)	500 g
2 Tbsp	sugar	25 ml
2/3 cup	white wine vinegar	150 ml
	salt and freshly ground black pepper	

This classic Italian antipasto makes a great accompaniment to grilled fish or chicken. Look for green onions with bulbs about 1 inch (2.5 cm) in diameter, and don't use scallions, as the bulb is necessary. You can, however, substitute shallots or baby onions.

Heat the olive oil in a large skillet, and sauté the pancetta over a medium-high heat for 2 minutes. Stir in the onions, and sprinkle with the sugar. Cook for 2 minutes more, and then pour in the vinegar. Reduce the heat, cover, and cook for 30-35 minutes, or until the onions are tender. Remove the lid, and increase the heat to reduce the liquid to a syrup. Season to taste with salt and pepper.

Roasted Onion and Bacon Dip

MAKES ABOUT 2 CUPS (500 ML)

This delicious dip for vegetable crudités or potato chips tastes ten thousand times better than the commercial variety.

4	large onions	4
1 Tbsp	olive oil	15 ml
	salt and freshly ground black pepper	
4-6	strips bacon	4-6
1 1/2 cups	sour cream	375 ml
1 1/2 tsp	Worcestershire sauce	7 ml
1/2 tsp	Dijon mustard	2 ml
2 Tbsp	snipped fresh chives	25 ml

Preheat the oven to 400°F (200°C) and move the oven rack to its lowest position.

Halve the onions across the middle, and place them, cut sides down, on a foil-lined baking sheet greased with the olive oil. Cut a small X in the top of each onion, and bake for 30 minutes, until tender. Remove from the oven, cool, and then peel and chop finely. Meanwhile, fry the bacon until crisp, drain, and crumble. Mix the onion and bacon with the remaining ingredients, and refrigerate until chilled.

Japanese Noodle (Udon) Soup with Scallions

SERVES 6

This savoury broth is seasoned with shichimi, *a Japanese 7-spice mix, but you can substitute Chinese 5-spice seasoning if you prefer.*

8 cups	chicken stock	2 L
3 Tbsp	soy sauce	40 ml
2 Tbsp	sugar	25 ml
1/2 Tbsp	salt	15 ml
	shichimi or Chinese 5-spice powder, to taste	
1 lb	dried udon noodles, cooked according to package directions and drained	500 g
2	large bunches scallions, trimmed and chopped	2

Bring the stock to a boil, and stir in the soy sauce, sugar, salt, and seasoning to taste. Stir in the drained udon noodles and chopped scallions, and heat through. Serve at once.

Parsnips

Before Columbus brought potatoes to Europe from the New World, parsnips were the main source of vegetable starch for ordinary souls like you and me. While they weren't exactly banished in favour of the potato, they did take a back seat. Then they became as widely used in sweet dishes as they were in soups and stews, not to mention the country folks' wine. We still think of parsnips as a humble sort of root, despite the fact that they are turning up in fashionable restaurants in the form of croquettes, purées, and chips.

Although these roots are available year-round, we still think of them as a winter veg, as many insist that they need to be nipped by frost before they develop their characteristic sweetness. I happen to like tender new-crop parsnips, braised in a little butter and sprinkled with lots of parsley and a bit of parmesan. I also shred them into salads and eat them raw. When choosing parsnips, look for the smaller and mid-sized roots, as the very large ones can be a bit woody. Make sure they are firm and unblemished, and avoid any that seem limp or have rootlets sprouting from them.

Parsnips will keep well for up to two weeks in a perforated plastic bag in the refrigerator. The smallest ones don't need to be peeled; just scrub them and trim the ends. Larger ones may need to be peeled thinly, and very large parsnips should be peeled and halved and their woody cores removed. You can slice, chop, or shred parsnips and cook them any way you would a carrot or potato.

THE COOK'S TEARS

There are many bits of kitchen lore on how to prepare onions without tears: peeling them under running water; holding a crust of bread between your teeth; simultaneously wiggling your bottom and singing Christmas carols. All cooks have their own tricks, and probably none of them works. If you're cooking for a crowd, you may find it worth your while to get out the food processor, but otherwise I'd just grin and bear it.

Parsnips are an excellent source of potassium when munched raw, and the cooked roots still provide a good amount of vitamin C and folate. They are relatively low in calories for a starchy vegetable, only 80 in 1/2 cup.

Curried Parsnip and Apple Soup

SERVES 6

This lovely, thick, and creamy soup has a hint of curry beneath the sweet parsnips and apple.

2 Tbsp	butter	25 ml
1 Tbsp	olive oil	15 ml
1	onion, chopped finely	1
1	garlic clove, chopped finely	1
2 lb	parsnips, scrubbed and chopped	1 kg
2	potatoes, peeled and chopped	2
2	apples, peeled, cored, and chopped	2
1 Tbsp	curry powder	15 ml
4 cups	chicken stock	1 L
1/2 cup	heavy cream	125 ml
	salt and freshly ground black pepper	
2 Tbsp	snipped fresh chives, to garnish	25 ml

Melt the butter and oil in a large saucepan, and stir in the onion, garlic, parsnips, potatoes, and apple. Cover and cook for 15 minutes over a low heat, stirring occasionally, until the vegetables are softened. Stir in the curry powder, and cook for 1 minute. Add the stock, bring to a boil, and then reduce the heat. Season with salt and pepper, and simmer for 30 minutes, until the vegetables are very tender. Transfer to a food processor or blender, and purée until smooth. Return to the saucepan, and add the cream. Reheat gently, check the seasoning, and serve, garnished with fresh snipped chives.

IN THE MICROWAVE
In a large microwave-safe casserole, combine the butter, olive oil, onion, and garlic. Cover and cook on high for 2 minutes, stirring once, until the onion is limp. Add the parsnips and potatoes, stirring well to coat, and cook on high for 5-7 minutes, stirring once. Add the apples, curry powder, and hot chicken stock. Cook on high for 6-8 minutes, until the vegetables are soft. Purée until smooth. Return to the casserole, add the cream, and reheat to serving temperature, about 1-2 minutes. Salt and pepper to taste, sprinkle with the chives, and serve.

Roasted Parsnips with Maple Syrup and Mustard Glaze

SERVES 6

Maple syrup and mustard make a beautifully sweet-tangy glaze for naturally sweet roots such as parsnips and carrots.

3 lb	parsnips, scrubbed and trimmed	1.5 kg
3 Tbsp	vegetable oil	40 ml
3 Tbsp	maple syrup	40 ml
2 Tbsp	prepared mustard	25 ml

1 tsp	caraway seeds	5 ml
	salt and freshly ground black pepper	

PARSNIPS EVERY WHICH WAY
Boil or steam parsnips until very soft, and mash them with butter and pinch of nutmeg, on their own or with potatoes.

Shred and stir-fry parsnips with beets, and season with lemon juice and fresh dill.

Roasted parsnips are delicious, as are parsnip french fries and parsnip fritters.

Preheat the oven to 475°F (240°C) and move the oven rack to its highest position.

Halve the parsnips, removing the cores if necessary, and cut them into even-sized pieces. Parboil them in lightly salted water for 5 minutes, and drain.

Meanwhile, pour the oil into a shallow roasting pan, and heat in the oven until the oil is sizzling hot. Remove from the oven, and transfer the parsnips to the pan, giving it a shake to coat the vegetables. Season with salt and pepper, and roast for 25 minutes, until golden brown and crisp. Mix together the maple syrup, mustard, and caraway seeds, and brush the glaze over the parsnips. Roast for 10 minutes more, and serve at once.

Oven-Braised Parsnips and Shallots with Sherry and Tarragon Butter

SERVES 4

1 1/2 lb	parsnips, peeled and trimmed	750 g
12	shallots, peeled	12
3/4 cup	vegetable stock	175 ml
2 Tbsp	medium-dry sherry	25 ml
2 Tbsp	soft butter	25 ml
1 Tbsp	chopped fresh tarragon	15 ml
	salt and freshly ground black pepper	

Preheat the oven to 375°F (190°C) and lightly butter a shallow baking dish.

Halve the parsnips, removing the cores if necessary, and cut in even-sized pieces. Toss them with the shallots in the baking pan, and add the stock and sherry. Mix the butter and tarragon together, and dot over the vegetables. Season with salt and pepper, cover, and bake for 45 minutes. Uncover, give the pan a shake, and bake for 10 minutes more, until the vegetables are tender and begin to colour.

Peas

GARDEN PEAS

Garden peas are one of the few vegetables still marked by local growing seasons. Although you can find imports occasionally throughout the year, peas are a labour-intensive harvest, they don't travel well, and they have to be fresh to be good. In Canada, this means that, as a rule, garden peas are something to celebrate from July through August. Until recently, garden peas were grown purely for commercial processing, and fresh peas were the guarded treasure of home gardeners. Their growing popularity over the past half decade has led to more producers turning over some of their fields to fresh market development.

Garden peas begin to deteriorate as soon as they are picked, as their sugar converts to starch. When buying them, choose fresh, bright green, lively-looking pods. They should be firm and fat, filled to bursting with plump peas. Store them in a plastic bag in the refrigerator for a few days only, using them as soon as possible. To prepare them, first rinse the pods under running water. Shell them by pressing open the pods with your fingers and using your thumb to push out the peas. If you don't fancy sitting on the front porch with a shelling basket on your knees, you can even find fresh shelled garden peas at some supermarkets.

Fresh peas are best served by simply boiling them in a little salted water for 4-8 minutes, depending on their age and size. I like to add a few pods to the cooking water to sweeten it. Peas can also be steamed or braised, and they take naturally to the microwave: Cook 2 cups (500 ml) of fresh peas with 1/4 cup (50 ml) of water, covered, on high for 3-5 minutes on high. For frozen peas, add a pat of butter and leave out the water. Salt only after cooking. Peas love fresh herbs and cream, as well as onions, carrots, and potatoes.

SUGAR SNAP AND SNOW PEAS

Unlike garden peas, sugar snap and snow peas are eaten in their pods. Sugar snap peas are something between garden peas and snow peas. Like the former, they are plump and full of good-sized peas, but their pods are as sweet and tender as those of snow peas. Snow peas are grown entirely for their tender pods; their peas are immature and usually minute. Sugar snap peas are available off and on throughout the year, but snow peas can be found all year long. Both are imported from California and Guatemala during our winter months. Their popularity has increased along with Asian cooking, and they are a favourite stir-fry ingredient.

Both sugar snap and snow peas are very perishable. Stored in a plastic bag, they will keep for 2-3 days in the refrigerator. They should be rinsed before cooking, and larger, older pods may need to have their strings removed. Both sugar snap and snow peas can be eaten raw, steamed lightly, or stir-fried.

HOW MUCH TO BUY
One pound (500 g) of garden peas in their pods will yield approximately 1 cup (250 ml) of shelled peas.

Garden Peas and Baby Onions Braised in Cream

SERVES 4

3 Tbsp	butter	40 ml
12	pearl onions or tiny yellow onions, peeled	12
2 cups	shelled fresh peas	500 ml
1/4 cup	water	50 ml
1/2 cup	cream	125 ml
	salt and freshly ground black pepper	
1 Tbsp	freshly squeezed lemon juice	15 ml
1 Tbsp	chopped fresh mint	15 ml

IN THE MICROWAVE
Put the onions and 1/4 cup (50 ml) of water into a microwave-safe casserole. Cover and microwave on high for 6-8 minutes, until tender, stirring once. Drain, add the butter and peas, and cook, covered, for 2-3 minutes, stirring once. Add the cream, and reheat on medium for about 1 minute. Stir in the lemon juice and chopped mint, and serve.

Cut the onions in half if they seem large. Melt the butter in a skillet or casserole over a medium heat, and sauté the onions for 5 minutes. Stir in the peas, and cook for 2 minutes more. Add the water, and bring to a simmer. Cover and cook for 8-10 minutes, until the onions and peas are almost tender. Stir in the cream, season with salt and pepper, and cook for 3 minutes more, until the liquid has reduced. Stir in the lemon juice and mint, and serve at once.

Stir-Fried Snow Peas and Red Pepper

SERVES 2

1 Tbsp	vegetable or peanut oil	15 ml
1	onion, sliced thinly	1
1 Tbsp	finely chopped fresh ginger	15 ml
1	large sweet red pepper, seeded and sliced in strips	1
1 Tbsp	soy sauce	15 ml
1 lb	snow peas	500 g
1 tsp	toasted sesame seeds	5 ml
1/2 tsp	lemon pepper (optional)	2 ml

Serve this colourful dish on a bed of fragrant rice. Don't stir-fry snow peas for too long; you just want to "show them the pan" in order to heat them through.

Heat the oil in a wok or frying pan over a high heat, and stir-fry the onion for 2 minutes. Add the ginger and sweet pepper, and cook for 3-4 minutes more. Stir in the soy sauce and snow peas, and stir-fry for 1 minute. Sprinkle with the sesame seeds and lemon pepper, if using, and serve at once.

Fresh Pea Pilaf

SERVES 4-6

Fresh peas make a great addition to a rice pilaf. If you prefer a stronger-tasting curry, substitute your favourite curry paste for the powder.

1 Tbsp	vegetable oil	15 ml
1	onion, chopped coarsely	1
2	garlic cloves, chopped finely	2
2-3 tsp	curry powder	10-15 ml
1/2 tsp	ground cinnamon	2 ml
1 1/2 cups	long-grain rice	375 ml
3 cups	vegetable stock	750 ml
2 cups	shelled fresh peas	500 ml
	salt and freshly ground black pepper	
1 Tbsp	chopped fresh basil	15 ml

Heat the oil in a skillet over a medium heat, and sauté the onion, garlic, and curry powder for 5 minutes. Stir in the cinnamon and rice. Add the stock, and bring to a boil. Reduce the heat, cover, and simmer for 15 minutes. Stir in the peas, and cook, uncovered, for 5-10 minutes more, until the peas are tender. Stir in a little extra stock or water if necessary. Season with salt and pepper, and garnish with the chopped basil. Serve hot.

IN THE MICROWAVE
In a 3-quart (3-L) microwave-safe casserole, combine the oil, onion, and garlic. Stir to coat, and cook on high for 1 minute. Stir in curry powder, cinnamon, rice, and stock. Cover with plastic wrap, rolling back one edge, and cook on high for 7 minutes. Reduce heat to medium (50%), and cook 5 minutes more. Fluff the rice with a fork, add peas, and cook at medium until done, 5-7 minutes. Season, garnish, and serve.

Hot Peppers

Hot, hotter, and hottest. That's the way I like my peppers. And to straighten out a point of general confusion right off the bat, hot peppers and chilies are the same thing. They are *capsicums*, members of the same botanical family as sweet peppers, which they resemble in miniature, with their brightly coloured glossy skins and interior pith and seeds. But the resemblance ends there. Most hot peppers possess a fiery heat that makes them good for flavouring dishes rather than for eating whole. The range of heat and the variety of peppers is bewildering to the unsuspecting, but thanks to Wilbur Scoville — a man of some courage and a sense of adventure — we now have a scale to rate the heat of peppers. On the Scoville scale, a 1 is very mild, while a 10 can take the roof off your mouth.

It used to be that if you wanted hot peppers you had to buy them dried, powdered, or in a can. Now we have such an ever-increasing variety of fresh hot peppers available that it is impossible to list them all. Like sweet peppers, all hot peppers begin life green. Those left to ripen on the vine at length can become red, yellow, purple, orange, or a range of colours in between. Green

Whatever you do when preparing hot peppers, don't rub your face. I've been careless in the past and ended up with stinging, blinded eyes. If you do get a pepper burn, try rubbing it with the inside of a banana peel — eat the banana for consolation!

Touch your tongue to a cut pepper before you decide how much you want to add. Even if you've used a specific variety in the past, each pepper will be different, and you may get a fiery surprise.

peppers have a fresh, grassy undertone, while red peppers may have a slightly sweet flavour. Generally speaking, the larger the pepper the milder it is. Anaheim peppers, which are usually red or green, are a 3 on the Scoville scale. Often roasted, peeled, and puréed for soups or sauces, or diced and added to cooked dishes, they can also be stuffed and baked. Similar in size to the Anaheim is the poblano, a name for a number of different hot peppers that are all used when green.

Two hot peppers that break the larger-is-milder rule — and break it with a bang! — are the Scotch bonnet and the habanero. Both come in a variety of colours and both rate a 10 on the Scoville heat scale. Similar in shape — resembling miniature squashed sweet peppers — the habanero is widely used in Mexican salsas and sauces, while the more aromatic Scotch bonnet features in Caribbean food.

The term "finger hot pepper" is used to describe a wide range of medium-sized and medium-hot varieties (3-6), including the popular serrano and cayenne. Serranos, popularly known as green chilies, are usually found in the ingredient list for salsa verde. Jalapeños, red or green, are juicy and fresh-tasting, a favourite for use in raw salsas and stirred into soups and stews. Serranos and jalapeños are the two varieties commonly used to make chipotles, which are smoked and dried hot peppers. I love the flavour of chipotles and use them a lot in sauces, soups, and stews to give that smoky, hot, Latin flavour. The very tiniest of hot peppers, including Thai and bird's eye peppers, can be fiercely hot (9-10). These often feature in Southeast Asian cooking.

If you're not used to cooking with hot peppers, by all means experiment, but begin cautiously. The heat in hot peppers is concentrated in their seeds and inner ribs, and most recipes call for seeded peppers. Either wear plastic gloves, or be sure to wash your hands thoroughly afterwards. There are several tricks to controlling the heat of your cooking, but once you've gone too far there's no turning back. Rather than adding diced peppers, cut a slit in one and add it whole to your dish while cooking. Keep tasting, and when the dish is hot enough for your liking, remove and discard the pepper.

Roasting peppers and skinning them before use may not lessen the heat, but it can improve the flavour and increase digestibility. Place under the broiler for a few minutes, turning to toast all sides, until the skins are charred. Pop them into a plastic bag until cool, and slip the skins right off. If you have a gas stove, you can blacken them directly in the flame, skewered on a fork. In the microwave, cook in a small covered dish or, better, in a microwave-safe plastic bag, for 4-6 minutes on high. Cool, then skin. Remember that if you open the bag while the peppers are hot, the steam will carry some of the oil, so be careful.

Follow your own taste buds when using hot peppers. As with other ingredients, don't feel as if you're bound to follow someone's recipe to the letter. In a pinch, a teaspoon of sugar added to a too-hot dish will help a little to cool it down. Use a little, use a lot. If you're like me, you'll like it hot.

Thai-Style Sweet Red Chili Sauce

MAKES ABOUT 1 CUP

8-10	red finger hot peppers, chopped	8-10
6	garlic cloves, chopped	6
1/2 cup	water	125 ml
1/2 tsp	salt	2 ml
2 tsp	sugar	10 ml
1-2 Tbsp	freshly squeezed lime juice	15-25 ml
1 Tbsp	fish sauce	15 ml
1 Tbsp	peanut oil	15 ml

This sweet and simple chili sauce will keep for two weeks in the refrigerator.

Combine all the ingredients in a saucepan, and bring to a boil. Cover, reduce the heat, and simmer for 5 minutes. Transfer to a food processor or blender, and purée until smooth. Adjust the seasonings to taste, and refrigerate until needed.

Red Hot Pepper, Cilantro, and Coconut Soup

SERVES 4

3 cups	chicken stock	750 ml
4	red finger hot peppers, seeded and chopped finely	4
1 Tbsp	chopped fresh ginger	15 ml
6-inch	length of lemon grass, peeled and chopped	4-cm
1	garlic clove, chopped finely	1
4	scallions, chopped finely	4
1/2 cup	chopped fresh cilantro	125 ml
1-2 Tbsp	freshly squeezed lime juice	15-25 ml
2 Tbsp	fish sauce	25 ml
1 cup	unsweetened coconut milk	250 ml

Heat the chicken stock in a saucepan with the peppers, ginger, lemon grass, garlic, and scallions. Bring to a boil, and then reduce the heat and simmer for at least 30 minutes. Transfer to a food processor or blender, add the cilantro, and pulse until smooth. Pour back into the saucepan, stir in the lime juice, fish sauce, and coconut milk, and heat through. Serve hot.

Fast and Fresh Black Bean Chili

SERVES 6-8

Serve this vegetarian chili with Avocado Salsa (see page 22) and a dollop of sour cream.

2 Tbsp	olive oil	25 ml
1	large onion, chopped	1
2	garlic cloves, chopped finely	2
1 Tbsp	ground cumin	15 ml
1 Tbsp	coriander seeds, crushed	15 ml
3	finger hot peppers, seeded and chopped finely	3
3 cups	chopped fresh or canned tomatoes	750 ml
2 Tbsp	tomato paste	25 ml
2	red or green sweet peppers, seeded and chopped	2
1/2 cup	water	125 ml
2 cups	fresh or frozen corn kernels	500 ml
3 cups	cooked or canned black beans	750 ml
	Tabasco sauce, to taste	
	salt and freshly ground black pepper	
1/2 cup	chopped fresh cilantro	125 ml

Heat the olive oil in a large saucepan or deep skillet, and sauté the onion, garlic, cumin, coriander seeds, and hot peppers for 5 minutes. Add the tomatoes, tomato paste, sweet peppers, and water, and bring to a boil. Simmer for 10 minutes, stirring occasionally. Add the corn, black beans, Tabasco sauce, and salt and pepper to taste, and cook for 10 minutes more. Stir in the cilantro just before serving.

Sweet Peppers

One medium-sized sweet red pepper has a mere 30 calories and makes a delicious snack. Peppers are chock-full of vitamins A and C and contain valuable antioxidant compounds and a fair amount of potassium.

I'm sweet on peppers, especially sweet peppers. With their vibrant colours and snappy taste, these gorgeous creatures make my mouth water. Sweet peppers are closely related to hot peppers, or chilies, which derive their fieriness from capsaicin, not to be confused with *capsicum*, which is the botanical name for all pepper varieties, but which the Brits tend to use to describe sweet peppers. Confused? Don't be. In North America we simply call them sweet peppers, although people with Yankee tendencies might say "bell pepper."

Believed to have originated in South America, the sweet pepper was taken to Europe by the earliest Spanish and Portuguese explorers. Today, it's grown year-round (often in greenhouses during the winter months) everywhere from Canada to Spain; the world leader is Holland. In the past few years, Mexican growers have brought winter prices down, and in late summer and early fall, you can gorge yourself on perfect, beautiful-looking, locally grown sweet peppers and even freeze some to enjoy through the winter.

The common green pepper is one picked before it ripens to the orange, yellow, red, purple, or even black shade it would become if left on the vine. The longer peppers are allowed to ripen, the sweeter and juicier they become. Green peppers have a fresh, raw flavour, while red and other brightly coloured peppers are decidedly sweeter and more pungent. When buying sweet peppers, look for firm ones with brightly coloured, smooth and shiny skins. Avoid any that are soft or blemished. Store them in a plastic bag in the refrigerator for up to a week. Sweet peppers are delicious raw, served with dip, sliced into a salad, or even munched as you would an apple. And you'll never run out of ways to cook sweet peppers. Stuff pepper halves with just about anything you can think of, and bake until the flesh is soft and tender. Sauté pepper slices with onion and garlic, and then braise with tomatoes and herbs for an easy ratatouille. Roasting or grilling sweet peppers adds a whole other dimension to their flavour and texture, which becomes velvety smooth and luxurious.

HOW TO PREPARE
SWEET PEPPERS
Cut around the stem with a sharp knife, and then slice the pepper lengthways. Pull the halves apart and remove and discard the seeds and pith. *Voila!*

If you wish to remove the skins, grill whole peppers 5-6 inches (13-15 cm) below the broiler or hold them on a toasting fork above the flame of a gas stove until they turn black, then toss them into a plastic bag and leave until cool to the touch. The skins will slip off easily.

Roasted Sweet Red Pepper Soup
SERVES 6

2 lb	sweet red peppers	1 kg
1 lb	plum tomatoes	500 g
2	onions	2
4-6	garlic cloves	4-6
3 Tbsp	olive oil	40 ml
1 1/2 cups	hot chicken or vegetable stock	375 ml
	salt and freshly ground black pepper	
	chopped fresh basil leaves, to garnish	

Serve this healthy Mediterranean-style soup with thin slices of toasted baguette spread with tapenade.

Preheat the oven to 400°F (200°C).

Arrange the whole peppers and tomatoes in an oiled roasting pan. Slice the onions in half, leaving the skins on, and place them, cut sides down, in the pan. Scatter the unpeeled garlic cloves between the other vegetables. Drizzle with the olive oil, and roast for 45-60 minutes, turning and basting the vegetables halfway through.

When the vegetables are cool enough to handle, peel away the blackened skins from the peppers, tomatoes, and onion. Cut the peppers in half, and scrape out and discard the pith and seeds. Squeeze the creamy flesh from the garlic cloves, and transfer all the vegetables to a food processor or blender. Purée until smooth, adding the hot stock gradually. If you like, you can strain the soup to remove any seeds or stray bits of skin. Transfer to a saucepan, heat through, and season to taste with salt and pepper. Garnish with basil just before serving.

Roasted Sweet Peppers Stuffed with Tomatoes, Anchovies, and Goat's Cheese

SERVES 6

Zesty cilantro balances the salty intensity of the anchovies, and you can substitute grated parmesan for goat's cheese if you like. Adjust this great starter for a pasta dinner as much as you like: allow 1 pepper, 1 tomato, and 2 anchovies per person. In the microwave version, the flavours remain more distinct.

6	large sweet peppers	6
6	plum tomatoes, skinned and halved	6
12	canned anchovies, drained and chopped	12
3	garlic cloves, chopped finely	3
4 oz	goat's cheese, chopped coarsely	125 g
1/2 cup	olive oil	125 ml
	freshly ground black pepper	
2 Tbsp	chopped fresh cilantro	25 ml

Preheat the oven to 350°F (180°C).

Slice the peppers lengthways, leaving the stems intact. Remove and discard the pith and seeds. Arrange the peppers in an oiled shallow roasting pan, cut sides up. Stuff each with half a tomato, and then divide the anchovies, chopped garlic, and goat's cheese among them. Drizzle with the olive oil, and season with pepper. Place the pan on the second-highest oven rack, and cook for 45-60 minutes. The peppers should be soft and their edges slightly blackened. Transfer to a serving platter, and pour the pan juices over top. Garnish with cilantro and serve warm.

MICROWAVE VERSION (SERVES 1)

Lay 4 pepper halves, cut sides down, in a baking dish, and cover with vented plastic wrap. Cook on high for 5-6 minutes, until slightly tender. drain and set aside.

For the stuffing: In a microwave-safe casserole, combine 2 chopped and skinned tomatoes, 4 drained and chopped anchovies, 1 finely chopped garlic clove, and 1/4 cup (50 ml) olive oil. Cook 3-4 minutes on high, stirring twice, until bubbling.

Preheat the broiler. Spoon the stuffing into the pepper halves, and sprinkle with goat's cheese and pepper. Broil for 1-2 minutes, until cheese is light brown and bubbly. Garnish with cilantro, and serve.

Crostini with Sweet Peppers, Olives, and Mozzarella

MAKES 20

Crostini are miniature bruschetta: thick slices of Italian bread rubbed with cut garlic and drizzled with olive oil. Prepare them ahead of time, and then assemble and pop into the oven just before serving.

4	large red, orange, and/or yellow sweet peppers	4
3	garlic cloves	3
1 Tbsp	olive oil	15 ml
12	black olives, chopped coarsely	12

For the crostini:

1	thin baguette, cut in 1/2-inch (1-cm) slices	1
2 Tbsp	olive oil	25 ml
5-6 oz	mozzarella, sliced thinly	150-175 g
	freshly ground black pepper	
	chopped fresh basil or arugula, to garnish	

Preheat the oven to 400°F (200°C).

Arrange the whole peppers in an oiled roasting pan. Tuck the unpeeled garlic cloves between the peppers. Drizzle with 1 tablespoon of olive oil, and roast for 45 minutes, until the peppers are soft. Place the peppers in a plastic bag until cool enough to handle, and then slip off the skins. Halve the peppers, and remove the pith and seeds. Chop the flesh coarsely, and place in a bowl. Squeeze the garlic flesh into the bowl, and add the chopped olives. Season with pepper, and toss to combine. Set aside.

To make the crostini: Brush the bread slices with 2 tablespoons of olive oil, and bake for 10 minutes. Set aside to cool. When ready to serve, place a slice of mozzarella on each, and top with a spoonful of the pepper mixture. Heat through for 5-10 minutes, until the cheese is melted. Garnish with chopped basil or arugula.

Plantain

If you've ever seen a pile of very green, bruised, or blackened bananas in a supermarket and thought that the produce manager wasn't doing his job, chances are that you were looking at plantain. This is the "cooking banana" so popular in Latin American, Asian, and Caribbean kitchens. While closely related to the more familiar banana we pack in our lunch boxes, the plantain is far more versatile, as it can be used at almost every stage of ripeness. When green, the plantain's flesh is very firm and rather tasteless, and it can be sliced and cooked pretty much like a potato. As it ripens and turns yellow, the flesh becomes creamier in texture and takes on the sweeter fragrance and subtle flavour of bananas. But unlike bananas, even when plantains are bruised and blackened, their flesh remains firm when cooked.

Plantains are available year-round, and are imported mostly from Central and South America. Choosing plantains depends on how or when you want to cook them. Green plantains will ripen at home over time, provided they are not refrigerated, while mottled or black plantains should be slightly soft when purchased; avoid any black plantains that are still hard. Green plantains can be peeled, chopped, and boiled, and then served with a spicy salsa, added to soups or casseroles, or roasted on their own, with root vegetables or around a roast. They are also good when mashed with sweet potatoes or winter squash and plenty of butter and salt. Sliced thinly, plantains can be sautéed in butter or oil or deep-fried like french fries. Riper plantains, yellow or black, can be cooked the same ways, although I tend to leave their skins on when boiling, as this helps them to keep their shape.

To peel a plantain, score the skin from end to end with a sharp knife and pull it away from the flesh. Ripe plantains are excellent when peeled, halved lengthways, and grilled, basted frequently with oil or a honey-mustard barbecue sauce. Also try baking whole ripe plantains. Leave the skins on, but slit them along their length, and bake for 45 minutes at 350°F (180°C). You can season them with something spicy or sweet.

SWEET BAKED PLANTAINS
Cut a slit down the length of a plantain, and bake for 30 minutes in a 375° F (190° C) oven. Dot with butter and crushed pineapple, sprinkle with brown sugar, and bake for 10 minutes more. Serve hot, with a scoop of vanilla ice cream.

Oven-Baked Plantain Crisps

SERVES 4

Serve these very thin baked crisps with salsa or sour cream seasoned with lime juice and chopped cilantro.

4	plantains, peeled and sliced very thinly	4
2 Tbsp	olive oil	25 ml
1 Tbsp	butter	15 ml
	salt and paprika or chili powder	

Preheat the oven to 400°F (200°C).
Place the oil and butter in a large, shallow roasting pan, and set in the hot

oven for 5 minutes. Toss the plantain slices in the hot oil, and season liberally with salt and paprika or chili powder. Bake for 10 minutes, and then give them a stir and bake for 5 minutes more, until crisp. Drain on paper towel, and serve hot.

Eating plantain is an excellent way to get a dose of vitamin C and potassium. Like bananas, plantains are high in carbohydrates.

Plantains in Sweet and Spicy Coconut Sauce

SERVES 4

2 Tbsp	peanut oil	25 ml
1	garlic clove, chopped finely	1
2 tsp	grated fresh ginger	10 ml
1	red finger hot pepper, seeded and chopped finely	1
1 Tbsp	curry powder	15 ml
1 tsp	sugar	5 ml
3	large ripe plantains, peeled and sliced in 1 1/2-inch (3-cm) chunks	3
1/2 cup	unsweetened coconut milk	125 ml
1/4 cup	freshly squeezed lime juice	50 ml
	salt and freshly ground black pepper	
2 Tbsp	chopped fresh cilantro	25 ml

Heat the oil in a skillet, and sauté the garlic for 2-3 minutes, until softened. Add the ginger, hot pepper, curry powder, and sugar, and cook for 2 minutes more, stirring frequently. Stir in the plantain chunks, and cook for 2 minutes. Pour in the coconut milk and lime juice, and bring to a boil. Reduce the heat, cover, and simmer for 40 minutes, until the plantain is tender and the liquid has reduced to a creamy sauce. Season to taste with salt and pepper, and stir in the cilantro. Serve at once.

Potatoes

One potato, two potatoes, three potatoes . . . and more. There are lots of different varieties around, and a good thing too, since we eat a tremendous amount of potatoes. Until very recently, New Brunswick school children were given a two-week school break each autumn to help bring in the province's potato harvest. Mechanization — and the fact that more kids were turning up in shopping malls than in potato fields — has put an end to that charming tradition. However, this cash crop is no small potatoes for the Maritime provinces, especially Prince Edward Island, which produces a third of Canada's potatoes.

Potatoes are a rich source of complex carbohydrates, vitamins A and C, iron and calcium.

POTATO HINTS
Bake potatoes at a medium oven temperature (350°F/ 180°C) to give them a crisp skin and fluffy flesh.

When boiling potatoes, cut them in even-sized pieces, salt the water, and don't boil them too furiously, as they tend to fall apart. Adding a sprig of mint to the water lends a lovely hint of flavour, especially to new potatoes.

For crunchier roasted potatoes, parboil them and bash them around a bit before tossing them in the hot fat.

IN THE MICROWAVE
To microwave potatoes for use in salads and other recipes: Put 2 1/2 pounds (1 kg) new potatoes in a covered microwave-safe dish with 1/2 cup water (125 ml) and 1/2 tsp (2 ml) salt, and cook on high power for 7-8 minutes, or until barely tender. Let stand for 3 minutes, and drain. Stored potatoes and cut potatoes will need less cooking time, as will potatoes being only partially precooked.

Traditionally, potatoes have been categorized as bakers, boilers, and all-purpose. Bakers have a lot of starch and little moisture, which means they are fluffy and dry when baked. Because of their starchiness, these potatoes are also ideal for frying or for using in rosti, potato pancakes, or baked goods. Boilers have a higher moisture content and less starch; they can be more easily chopped or sliced once boiled, and they have that creamy texture that is so good in potato salads. All-purpose potatoes fall somewhere between the mealiness of bakers and the creaminess of boilers, containing moderate levels of starch and moisture.

While these categories are useful, there are no hard and fast rules. Bakers are also good for boiling, but only if you're going to mash them or cook them in soup, because when cooked in liquid they tend to fall apart. They will also boil faster and produce a drier, fluffier mash than boilers. On the other hand, boilers are delicious when baked or roasted, as their skins become crisp and their waxy flesh absorbs the flavour of whatever oils or butter they are cooked in.

There are four general types of potatoes, each of which has any number of varieties. Russets, elongated potatoes with thick skins and mealy flesh, are considered to be the best choice for baking or french-frying. Round, white-fleshed potatoes have a slightly floury texture that makes for a good all-purpose spud. Round, yellow-fleshed potatoes have a somewhat more creamy texture but can still be treated as all-purpose. Red-skinned potatoes are valued for their smooth, thin skins and creamy, moist flesh. These are my personal favourite.

New potatoes are in a category of their own. While they have long been prized in Europe, it is only recently that North American commercial producers began to value them as premium potatoes rather than rejecting them as unsaleable. New potatoes are simply immature; almost skinless, they are harvested early and marketed immediately rather than stored. They have a limited shelf life, and local crops peak in July and August. Any later and they begin to develop a skin. New potatoes can be any type or variety, but most commonly we see round, white-fleshed potatoes harvested when immature. New potatoes are available year-round, as they are imported from the south once local crops are finished. Load up on them when you see them; whether you like them simply steamed and served with melted butter, or roasted in olive oil and thyme, these little gems move in and out of the stores like hot potatoes!

When buying potatoes, choose ones that are firm and heavy for their size, with smooth, clear skins. Avoid any that are cracked, bruised, or have a greenish tinge. Regular potatoes will keep for up to several months when stored in a cool, dark, dry place. New potatoes may be kept in the refrigerator for no more than a week; any longer and they will begin to grow mouldy.

Since most of the vitamins and minerals found in potatoes are contained in or just beneath the skin, it is best to eat them skins and all. New potatoes can simply be rinsed under cold running water, while you may need to scrub potatoes with thicker skins. If you prefer to peel potatoes, try to peel them very thinly, or else peel them after boiling.

Oven-Baked Potato and Pear Rosti

SERVES 4

3/4 lb	medium-sized potatoes, scrubbed	300 g
2	firm but ripe pears	2
1 Tbsp	freshly squeezed lemon juice	15 ml
	freshly grated nutmeg	
	salt and freshly ground black pepper	
1 Tbsp	all-purpose flour	15 ml
3 Tbsp	melted butter	40 ml

Use stored potatoes to make rosti, as new potatoes don't have enough starch to hold them together. You can substitute apples for the pears in this recipe if you prefer.

Parboil the whole, unpeeled potatoes in lightly salted water for 8 minutes, drain, and set aside.

Preheat the oven to 425°F (220°C), and set an oven rack at the highest level. Peel, core, and coarsely grate the pears, tossing them with the lemon juice in a mixing bowl. Peel the cooled potatoes, and shred them coarsely into the pears. Drain well, squeezing out any excess liquid with your hands. Season to taste with nutmeg, salt, and pepper.

Shape the mixture into 8 balls, flattening them into patties. Place the flour on a plate, and press each patty into the flour to coat both sides. Brush a baking pan with 1 tablespoon of the melted butter, arrange the patties on the pan, and brush the tops with another tablespoon of butter. Bake for 10 minutes, flip them over, brush with the remaining butter, and bake for 10-12 minutes longer, until crisp and golden brown. Serve at once.

Pesto Mashed Potatoes

SERVES 4

2 lb	potatoes, peeled and cut into chunks	1 kg
1/3 cup	pesto sauce	80 ml
1/2 cup	cream (optional)	125 ml
	salt and freshly ground black pepper, to taste	
	fresh basil leaves, chopped	

Boil the potatoes in salted water until tender, and then drain, reserving about 1/2 cup of the cooking water. Mash with the pesto, cream (if using), and enough of the cooking water to loosen the mixture. Stir in some chopped basil, and season to taste with salt and pepper. Serve at once.

RED HOT PEPPER, CILANTRO
AND COCONUT SOUP
page104

WARM RADICCHIO, CHICKEN,
AND ORANGE SALAD
page 117

SZECHUAN-STYLE RED-HOT RAPINI
page 123

Pete's Potato Temptation

SERVES 4

This rich, satisfying dish can be served as a main course, along with a crisp salad of tangy greens.

2 lb	potatoes, peeled and sliced thinly	1 kg
1/2 lb	salmon trimmings	250 g
	salt and freshly ground black pepper	
3 Tbsp	chopped fresh dill	40 ml
1 cup	heavy cream	250 ml
3/4 cup	fish or vegetable stock	175 ml
1	lemon, quartered, to garnish	1

IN THE MICROWAVE
Layer ingredients in a 2-quart (2-L) microwave-safe casserole, and set aside. In a Pyrex measuring cup, heat the stock for about 2 minutes on high. Stir in the cream, and pour over the casserole. Cover with a lid or vented plastic wrap, and cook on high for 15-20 minutes, until the potatoes are tender, stirring 2-3 times during cooking. Garnish and serve at once.

Preheat the oven to 400°F (200°C), and butter a large casserole dish.

Arrange a layer of potatoes on the bottom of the dish, followed by a layer of salmon pieces. Season lightly with salt and generously with pepper. Sprinkle with dill. Repeat the layers, finishing with a layer of potatoes. Pour the cream and fish stock over top, and bake for about 1 hour, until golden brown and tender. Check the dish after about 40 minutes, and cover with foil if it is browning too quickly. Allow to cool for 5 minutes before serving with lemon wedges.

Potatoes Steamed in Parchment with Garlic, Tomatoes, and Olives

SERVES 4

12	small red potatoes, quartered	12
12	pearl onions, peeled and quartered	12
12	garlic cloves, peeled	12
4	plum tomatoes, quartered	4
8	large green olives, pitted and quartered	8
1 Tbsp	olive oil	15 ml
2	sprigs fresh rosemary	2
4	sprigs fresh thyme	4
	salt and freshly ground pepper	

Preheat oven to 400°F (200°C).

Combine the potatoes, onions, garlic, tomatoes, and olives in a bowl. Drizzle the olive oil over top, season well with salt and pepper, and toss to coat the vegetables. Arrange the vegetables on one side of a long, doubled length of parchment paper. Place the rosemary and thyme on top, and then fold the paper over the vegetables, making small, overlapping folds along the open edge to create a tightly sealed half-moon-shaped packet.

Place the packet on a baking sheet, and bake for 30 minutes. Remove from the oven, open the packet, and remove the rosemary and thyme sprigs. Pull the leaves from the sprigs, and crumble them over the vegetables. Serve at once on a platter or cutting board.

Pumpkin

Never has a vegetable provided so much fun and been eaten so rarely. Pumpkins are considered one of our most seasonal vegetables, since most people don't think about them until October rolls around and the supermarket aisles get clogged with giant bins of the beautiful orange globes. At this point they are merely a pleasing and festive sight for most of us, although in rural areas pumpkins take on great importance — especially the enormous ones. Towards Thanksgiving, dedicated bakers and pie lovers will pick one up, knowing that the canned purée doesn't taste nearly as good. But by the end of the month, everyone and their mothers rush off to choose the fattest, brightest pumpkin possible, and the slaughter begins.

Let's put aside the fun. Pumpkin is a vegetable to be eaten. Pumpkin is a generic name for any winter squash that is round in shape, usually ridged, and bright orange in colour. Generally speaking, excessively large pumpkins won't be very sweet (although don't buy the tiny, palm-sized variety for anything other than decoration). It's a good idea to take weight into consideration — choose one that feels heavy for its size. It should have firm, smooth skin, with no blemishes or mouldy patches. A fresh pumpkin will keep for up to a month when stored in a cool, dry place, so it's worth picking up a few during the Halloween mania. Once cut, the pieces should be wrapped in plastic and refrigerated for no longer than a week.

Like other orange vegetables, pumpkins are high in vitamin A and other carotenoids, which have antioxidant properties. They also contain vitamin C, potassium, and fibre.

You can cook pumpkin any way that you would cook other winter squash, *au naturel* to best savour its delicate sweetness or combined with other foods and seasonings. Pumpkin loves strong, spicy flavours, and it is a useful ingredient in Indian and Asian cooking, especially in curried dishes, where it has time to absorb the seasonings. To prepare, split the pumpkin open lengthways, and scrape out the seeds and fibrous bits. Add cubes of pumpkin to soups or stews, or slice it very thinly and stir-fry it in olive oil and garlic.

I think it's time we realized that pumpkins mean more than pie, more than jack-o'-lanterns, and more than blue ribbons at the county fair. Beat the October rush and buy a pumpkin for your supper. I'll bet you'll be back for more.

TOASTED PUMPKIN SEEDS
Spread pumpkin seeds on a baking sheet in a single layer, drizzle with a little sesame oil, salt well, and toast in a 350°F (180°C) oven for 3-4 minutes, until golden brown. Or toss them for a few minutes in a frying-pan over medium heat.

Pumpkin Soup with Parmesan Croutons

MICROWAVE PUMPKIN PURÉE
Cut the pumpkin in half
lengthways, scrape out
seeds and fibre, and place
one half, cut side down,
in a shallow baking dish.
Add 2 Tbsp (25 ml) of water,
and cover with plastic wrap,
venting one side. Cook on
high for 12-15 minutes, until
tender. Let stand, covered,
for 5 minutes. Remove the
plastic, cool, scrape out
pumpkin, and purée in a
blender or food processor.
Repeat with the other half
of the pumpkin.

This soup adds to pumpkin the autumnal flavours of apples and leeks, seasoned with nutmeg and coriander. The parmesan croutons give a decided crunch to the velvety-smooth texture of the soup, or use toasted pumpkin seeds.

2 Tbsp	olive oil	25 ml
4	strips bacon, chopped (optional)	4
1	large onion, chopped	1
3	large garlic cloves, crushed	3
2 lb	pumpkin, peeled, seeded, and chopped	1 kg
1	large carrot, peeled and chopped	1
1	leek, white part only, chopped	1
2	ribs celery, chopped	2
2	apples, peeled, cored, and chopped	2
5	cups chicken or vegetable stock	1.5 L
1/2 cup	heavy cream (optional)	125 ml
2 Tbsp	chopped fresh cilantro	25 ml
	freshly grated nutmeg	
	salt and freshly ground black pepper	

For the croutons:

1	garlic clove, chopped	1
1/4 tsp	salt	1 ml
2 Tbsp	olive oil	25 ml
2 Tbsp	finely grated parmesan cheese	25 ml
4	thick slices white bread, crusts removed, cut in 1/2-inch (1-cm) cubes	4

Heat the olive oil in a large saucepan and sauté the chopped bacon (if using), onion, and garlic, until softened but not browned. Stir in the chopped vegetables and apples. Lower the heat, cover, and cook, stirring occasionally, until the vegetables are "sweating" and slightly softened. Add the stock, and bring to a gentle simmer. Leave to cook, uncovered, for about 40 minutes, or until all the vegetables are very tender.

To make the croutons: Preheat the oven to 350°F (180°C). Mash the garlic with the salt to form a paste, and stir in the olive oil and parmesan. Roll the bread cubes in the oil mixture to coat well, and then place them on a baking sheet. Bake for 8-10 minutes on the highest oven shelf, remove from the oven, and allow to cool.

Purée the soup until smooth in a blender or food processor, and return it to the saucepan. Season to taste with salt, pepper, and nutmeg, and then reheat gently, adding the cream (if using). Sprinkle with cilantro, and scatter each serving with a handful of croutons or toasted pumpkin seeds.

Penne with Pumpkin Sauce

SERVES 4

2 Tbsp	olive oil	25 ml
1	onion, chopped finely	1
1	garlic clove, chopped finely	1
1 lb	pumpkin, peeled, seeded, and chopped coarsely	500 g
2 Tbsp	dry white wine	25 ml
	salt and freshly ground black pepper	
3 Tbsp	chopped fresh parsley	40 ml
3 Tbsp	grated fresh parmesan	40 ml
1 lb	dried penne pasta	500 g

Heat the olive oil in a large saucepan, and sauté the onion and garlic for 3 minutes. Stir in the chopped pumpkin and the wine, reduce the heat, cover, and cook for 30-40 minutes, until the pumpkin is very soft. Mash well, adding a little extra wine if very thick. Season with salt and pepper.

Meanwhile, boil the pasta in plenty of salted water for 12–14 minutes, until *al dente*. Drain and toss with the pumpkin, parsley, and cheese. Serve at once.

TO COOK PUMPKIN
To roast pumpkin, cut the flesh into large pieces and place, cut sides down, on an oiled baking sheet. Cook in a 350°F (160°C) oven for 25-40 minutes, until tender.

Scoop out the flesh, and mash it (on its own or with potatoes or other baked roots) with butter, cream, salt, pepper, and nutmeg.

You can roast pumpkin whole, but first pierce it in several places to allow the steam to escape and avoid having it blow up in your oven.

Radicchio

It's almost impossible to find an up-market restaurant which doesn't feature radicchio on its menu. Closely related to endive and escarole (see page 64), this red-leafed chicory has surged in popularity in North America, and it has long had a prized place in the salad bowls of Europe. Its bittersweet flavour is somewhere between lettuce and radish, adding warmth and bite to almost any salad.

Radicchio originates in Italy, and its name is literally translated as red chicory, of which there are dozens of varieties. The one commonly available, rossa di Verona, resembles a soft red cabbage about the size of a Bibb lettuce. Its colour can be anything from a deep purple-burgundy to a more coppery red. Sometimes you can find a loose-leaf radicchio called rosso di Treviso,

Like its cousins endive and escarole, radicchio is an excellent source of vitamins A and C, and it's high in fibre to boot.

A soft cheese such as Camembert, melted and thinned with a little cream and cider vinegar, makes a beautiful dressing for radicchio leaves and sliced apples.

The cup-shaped leaves of rossa di Verona serve as edible bowls for salads, soft cheeses, or other fillings.

which has pinkish-red leaves ranging in size from endive to romaine; it is especially meaty and chewy and perhaps a bit sweeter than the Verona variety. My pal Loris, who grows wonderful radicchio here in Nova Scotia, is probably responsible for my recent conversion to this super leaf vegetable. Available year-round, most of our radicchio comes from California, Mexico, Chile, and Italy.

When choosing radicchio, look for a clean, white bottom and a firm head with tightly wrapped bright, crisp leaves. The heads contain more leaves — and flavour — than a similarly sized lettuce, so one head is usually ample for a large mixed salad. To prepare, trim away the base, and separate the leaves. Rinse under cold running water and spin or pat dry. In a plastic bag, radicchio will stay fresh in the refrigerator for up to a week, and it will last longer if you core it, run water through it, drain it, wrap it in a tea towel, and then put it in a plastic bag. If the outer leaves turn a bit brownish, simply peel them back to reveal the fresh, red leaves.

Try mixing radicchio leaves with a few of its endive cousins for a quick, vervy salad. It responds beautifully to warmed vinaigrettes, which will gently wilt the leaf edges while the thicker rib sections stay wonderfully crunchy. Radicchio can also be sautéed, grilled, or baked with a little butter, although its robust colour will darken when cooked.

Warm Radicchio, Chicken, and Orange Salad

SERVES 2

Try this recipe with boneless duck breasts, which will take longer to cook than the chicken. You can substitute blood oranges when they are available.

2	boneless, skinless chicken breasts	2
	zest and freshly squeezed juice of 1 lime	
3 Tbsp	olive oil	40 ml
1	garlic clove, chopped finely	1
	salt and freshly ground black pepper	
1	head radicchio	1
2	oranges, peeled	2
2 Tbsp	sherry	25 ml
1 tsp	soy sauce	5 ml

Combine the lime juice and zest, 1 tablespoon of olive oil, the chopped garlic, and a pinch of salt and pepper, and pour over the chicken breasts in a shallow dish. Leave to marinate for at least 15 minutes while you prepare the radicchio and orange.

Separate the radicchio leaves, and tear them in large pieces, dividing them between two serving plates. Peel the oranges. Using a sharp knife, remove the segments, slicing between the membranes and catching the juices in a bowl. Divide the segments between the plates, and set the juices aside.

Heat the remaining oil in a skillet over a high heat, and pan-fry the chicken for about 4 minutes on each side. Remove from the pan, and set aside until cool enough to handle. Meanwhile, add the remaining olive oil to the pan, along with the sherry, soy sauce, and reserved juice from the oranges. Bring to a boil, scraping the pan juices into the sauce. Slice the chicken thickly, and arrange on the plates. Pour the warm dressing over top, and serve at once.

Sautéed Radicchio with Prosciutto on Ciabatta

SERVES 2

1 Tbsp	olive oil	15 ml
1	garlic clove, chopped finely	1
1/2	head radicchio, rinsed, dried, and shredded	1/2
6-8	slices prosciutto	6-8
4	thick slices ciabatta	4
	freshly ground black pepper, to taste	

These open-faced sandwiches are so good you may not want to share. Italian ciabatta is my bread of choice, with its floury crust and chewy texture, but any good bread will do.

Combine the olive oil and garlic in a bowl, and toss the radicchio and prosciutto in it to coat well. Throw the lot into a hot frying pan, and sauté very briefly, until the radicchio barely wilts. Pile it on the bread, seasoning well with pepper. Eat and enjoy.

Radicchio and Escarole Salad with Warm Bacon and Mushroom Dressing

SERVES 4

You can use any salad greens you like, but this lovely, tart combination stands up to the saltiness of the dressing.

1	head radicchio, rinsed and dried	1
1	head escarole, rinsed and dried	1
	freshly ground black pepper	

For the dressing:

1 Tbsp	olive oil	15 ml
1	shallot, chopped finely	1
4	strips bacon, chopped	4

1/2 lb	small button mushrooms, halved	250 g
1 tsp	coriander seeds, crushed	5 ml
1/2 tsp	Dijon mustard	2 ml
2 Tbsp	white wine vinegar	25 ml

Tear the radicchio and escarole leaves in bite-sized pieces into a large bowl. Heat the olive oil in a frying pan over a high heat, and sauté the shallot for 3 minutes. Stir in the bacon, and cook for 3-5 minutes more. Add the mushrooms, coriander seeds, and mustard, and sauté until the mushrooms begin to brown. Stir in the wine vinegar, and bring to a boil. Pour over the lettuce greens, and toss well. Season with pepper, and serve at once.

Radishes

Both varieties of radish are a good source of vitamin C and dietary fibre. Their calorie count is negligible, so crunch away to your heart's content!

Radishes come in all shapes and sizes, including the prairie black radish, which is about the size of an orange but otherwise similar to the more familiar red radish. The garden variety produces tiny scarlet jewels, round or elongated, and the lovely bicolour French breakfast radishes are variegated red and white. Both have firm white flesh, a mild to eye-watering peppery flavour, and decided crunch. Too good raw and too fiddly to bother cooking, their pungent flavour clears the palate, so they make a simple and effective appetizer. Although they are available most of the year pre-packaged in cellophane, the best radishes are grown in the cool spring and autumn months; common radishes are one of the earliest spring crops. Look for fresh bunches of uniformly sized radishes, preferably with their crisp green tops still attached. Rinse in cool water and scrape away any blemishes before eating. Radishes should last for up to two weeks when stored, wrapped, in the refrigerator. If you're faced with a limp bunch of radishes, soak them in a bowl of ice water for an hour to perk them up.

The daikon or mooli radish, also known as the Oriental radish, is another matter altogether. Shaped like a carrot, with smooth white skin, this beauty usually weighs between 1 and 2 pounds (500 g - 1 kg), although the record-breakers weigh in at over 50 pounds (23 kg)! Despite their size, daikons are mild in comparison to common red or French breakfast radishes. They tend to be most mild and flavourful in fall and winter, growing hotter and less appealing during the spring and summer months. Choose smooth, un-blemished daikons with slightly shiny skins. As their flavour is not affected by size, you can choose one to fit your refrigerator. Don't be shy about asking your greengrocer to cut a section for you if the entire root looks too daunting. Unlike red radishes, daikons are quite perishable, turning dry, spongy, and loosing flavour; use them raw within 2-3 days of purchase. Grate some into a coleslaw, or add diced raw daikon to a creamy chicken or tuna salad. Daikons also add crunch and texture to soups and stir-fries; for cooking purposes, they will last for up to a week, wrapped in plastic and refrigerated.

Radish and Endive Salad with Feta Dressing

SERVES 4

The slight bitterness of endives beautifully complements the peppery flavour and crunch of radishes. You can substitute any mild, crumbly cheese for the feta if you like.

10	radishes	10
6	small Belgian endives	6
2	green onions	2

For the dressing:

1/2 cup	virgin olive oil	125 ml
3 Tbsp	sour cream	40 ml
1/2 cup	feta cheese, crumbled	125 ml
1 1/2 Tbsp	balsamic vinegar	20 ml
1 Tbsp	finely chopped fresh thyme	15 ml

Combine the dressing ingredients in a jar with a tightly fitting lid, shaking well to combine.

Trim and slice the radishes. Discard the tough outer leaves of the endives, core them, and slice them thinly. Arrange the radish and endive slices on a serving plate, then drizzle the dressing evenly over top. Scatter with thinly sliced green onions, and refrigerate until slightly chilled.

Creamy Radish, Beet, and Apple Salad

SERVES 4

Serve this salad with black olives and a dense, dark bread such as pumpernickel or rye. Plain yogurt can be substituted for the sour cream, but drain it through a cheesecloth-lined sieve beforehand so it's not runny.

15	red radishes, trimmed and sliced thinly	15
1	tart eating apple, cored, halved, and sliced thinly	1
2	celery ribs, chopped coarsely	2
1 cup	cooked beets, sliced thinly	250 ml

For the dressing

1/2 cup	sour cream	125 ml
2 tsp	horseradish sauce	10 ml
2 Tbsp	chopped fresh dill	25 ml
1/2 tsp	salt	2 ml

Combine the dressing ingredients in a large bowl, mixing well. Gently fold in the sliced radishes, apples, celery, and beets. Transfer to a serving bowl, and refrigerate for 1 hour, to allow the flavours to meld.

A SENSATIONAL SNACK
Radishes are a real treat served simply with sea salt, butter, and dark bread. The trick is to butter the radish rather than the bread, then sprinkle it with salt before popping it in your mouth.

Crunchy Daikon and Snow Pea Salad

SERVES 4

The key to this salad is to marinate the vegetables for at least an hour to allow the flavours to develop. The creamy dressing makes a nice contrast to the crisp texture of the vegetables. Because daikons range widely in size, it is easier to measure them by weight.

1 Tbsp	sugar	15 ml
1 Tbsp	Dijon mustard	15 ml
1/2 tsp	salt	2 ml
1/2 cup	rice or white wine vinegar	125 ml
1 lb	daikon, grated coarsely	500 g
1/2 lb	carrots, grated coarsely	250 g
1/4 lb	snow peas, trimmed and halved	125 g

For the dressing:

1/2 cup	sour cream or plain yogurt (drained)	125 ml
2 tsp	prepared horseradish	10 ml
3	green onions, sliced thinly	3
	salt and freshly ground black pepper	

In a non-metallic bowl, mix together the sugar, mustard, salt, and vinegar. Stir in the vegetables and toss well. Cover and refrigerate for at least 1 hour.

Combine the dressing ingredients in a large serving bowl, reserving a tablespoon of green onion. Drain the marinated vegetables, squeezing them gently to remove the liquid. Fold them into the dressing, and garnish with the reserved green onion.

Rapini (Broccoli Raab, Flowering Calabrese)

Rapini is a fairly new vegetable to most North Americans, although until a few years ago it was better known in Europe — especially in Italy — than our more common broccoli, to which it is closely related. It makes a magnificent table centrepiece, with its tiny buds of broccoli bunched in with large, spiky leaves and the occasional yellow flower. However, for my money, I'd rather eat it. It packs a wallop of flavour, its aggressive bitter taste being so well suited to both spicy and sweet seasoning that it's a favourite with Italian and Asian cooks.

Since the bulk of our rapini comes from California, it is usually available throughout the year, but its peak season is in the cooler months, from late fall to early spring. Look for deep green leaves, firm slim stems, and just a few small, tightly closed buds. The heads can be purple, green, or white. Avoid those with limp stems or wilted, tired leaves.

You can store well-wrapped rapini in the refrigerator for up to 3 days. To prepare, rinse thoroughly under cold, running water, shake dry, and trim away any coarse stems. If you're trying rapini for the first time, simply steam the whole head in an inch or so of lightly salted boiling water for about 5 minutes, then drain it well and serve it with a vinaigrette. It can also be chopped and sautéed in olive oil with crushed garlic and a splash of soy sauce. Rapini does have a tendency to overwhelm the uninitiated palate, and if you find the flavour a bit too strong, I suggest blanching it for a few minutes in boiling salted water and then draining it well before combining it in a recipe with other assertive flavours. Spicy Italian sausage is an excellent partner, and a red-hot Asian stir-fry is a good bet. Alternatively, you can mellow the flavour by braising rapini in cream, as you might cook spinach.

Rapini is an excellent source of potassium and is low in sodium.

Rapini and Cannellini Beans

SERVES 4

This makes a lovely quick pasta sauce, or you can spoon it over thick slices of crusty white bread or focaccia.

1 Tbsp	olive oil	15 ml
1	onion, chopped	1
2	garlic cloves, chopped finely	2
5	plum tomatoes, peeled and chopped coarsely	5
1 Tbsp	balsamic vinegar	15 ml
1	large bunch rapini, rinsed, trimmed, and chopped coarsely	1

1	19-oz (540 ml) can cannellini beans, drained	1
	a pinch of paprika	
	salt and freshly ground black pepper	

Heat the olive oil in a saucepan, and sauté the onion and garlic for 3-4 minutes, until softened but not browned. Stir in the tomatoes and balsamic vinegar, and bring to a gentle simmer. Cook for 10 minutes, and stir in the rapini and beans. Cook for 3-5 minutes, and then season to taste with paprika, salt, and pepper.

Szechuan-Style Red-Hot Rapini
SERVES 4

This is not for those with timid taste buds. If you prefer a milder flavour, blanch the rapini in boiling water for 1 minute, rinse in cold water, drain, and pat dry. You can also omit the hot pepper.

1 Tbsp	peanut oil	15 ml
1 Tbsp	sesame oil	15 ml
1	garlic clove, peeled and lightly crushed	1
1	red onion, peeled and sliced thinly	1
1	finger hot pepper, seeded and chopped finely	1
1/2 tsp	peppercorns, crushed	2 ml
1/2 tsp	sugar	2 ml
1	large bunch rapini, rinsed and trimmed	1
2 Tbsp	rice vinegar	25 ml
1 Tbsp	honey	15 ml
1 Tbsp	soy sauce	15 ml
2 tsp	sesame seeds	10 ml

IN THE MICROWAVE
In a large microwave-safe casserole, heat the oil and garlic on high for 1 minute. Remove and discard the garlic. Add the onion, pepper, crushed peppercorns, and sugar to the oil, cover, and microwave on high for 2 minutes, stirring after 1 minute. Stir in the rapini, cook covered for 2-3 minutes, stirring once, and let stand for 3 minutes. Combine the vinegar, honey, and soy sauce in a small bowl, and heat for 30 seconds on high. Stir into the rapini, sprinkle with sesame seeds, and serve.

Heat the oils in a wok or large frying pan, and sauté the whole garlic clove for 2-3 minutes, until golden. Remove and discard. Add the onion, stir-fry for 3 minutes, and then stir in the chopped pepper, peppercorns, and sugar. Cook for 1 minute. Stir in the rapini, and cook for 3-5 minutes, until wilted. Combine the rice vinegar, honey, and soy sauce in a small bowl and stir into the rapini. Sprinkle the sesame seeds over top, and serve at once.

Italian-Style Rapini

SERVES 4

2 Tbsp	olive oil	25 ml
1	red onion, peeled and sliced thinly	1
2	garlic cloves, chopped finely	2
1	large bunch rapini, rinsed, trimmed, and chopped coarsely	1
8	canned anchovies, drained and chopped	8
1/2 cup	pitted black olives, halved	125 ml
	freshly ground black pepper	
2 Tbsp	grated fresh parmesan cheese	25 ml

Heat the olive oil in a wok or large skillet, and sauté the onion and garlic for 4-5 minutes, until softened but not browned. Increase the heat, and stir in the rapini, anchovies, and olives, and cook for 3-5 minutes, stirring constantly. Season to taste with pepper, sprinkle with parmesan cheese, and serve at once.

Serve this side dish with warm focaccia bread.

Rutabaga

Rutabaga is one of those vegetables that gets lost in the shuffle, both in terms of its name and also amongst the other roots at the supermarket. Commonly mistaken for a turnip (which it is not; see page 149-151), it is sometimes called a swede or a neep. A member of the cabbage family, the rutabaga was known in England as turnip-rooted cabbage until early in the 19th century, when Sweden began exporting them. Thus they became swedes. The Scots insisted on thinking of them as turnips and so called them neeps. Both names have stuck.

Rutabaga, swede, or neep, this root is fatter than the turnip and has a thick golden skin tinged reddish-brown at the top. Its flesh is creamy yellow in colour and firmer and sweeter than the white flesh of the turnip. Like other root vegetables, rutabagas are available year-round, although the peak season is between November and March, when they've been nipped by cold weather, turning them sweet. Most are large in size, but you can sometimes find smaller ones, which will be sweeter and more tender. In any case, make sure the root feels heavy for its size and has a smooth and unblemished skin. Especially in the winter, rutabagas may be waxed to keep them fresh.

If you have a cool, dark, dry place for vegetable storage, you can keep a rutabaga for a couple of months. In a plastic bag in the refrigerator, it will stay fresh for about a week. Scrub and peel it using a sharp knife; any wax will come off with the skin. Then slice or chop it according to how it will be cooked.

SUPERB MASHED RUTABAGA
Boil rutabaga with a few
potatoes. Add a peeled, cored,
and quartered apple halfway
through, and then mash the
whole lot with butter, salt,
pepper, and a sprinkling of
nutmeg.

In typical fashion, because the rutabaga was a staple vegetable during the Depression, it is often passed over as "poor people's food" or relegated to the stewpot. And while it is both economical and a great addition to stews and soups, this vegetable also happens to be delicious and versatile. Its pleasant, nutty-sweet flavour and firm, dry flesh make it an ideal roasting and baking vegetable, and it's a flavourful addition to any stir-fry.

Now that you know that the rutabaga is not a turnip, I'll put your mind at ease. If you've been mistaking one for the other all your life, don't worry. You can use them interchangeably and no one will know the difference except you. And me.

Braised Rutabaga with Shallots, Mushrooms, and Cream

SERVES 4

You can add a variety of other root vegetables to this dish. Serve it with garlic bread and a large salad of sharp greens.

2 Tbsp	butter	25 ml
1 Tbsp	olive oil	15 ml
1	bay leaf	1
1	garlic clove, peeled	1
12	shallots, peeled	12
1 cup	thickly sliced mushrooms	250 ml
1/2 cup	dry white wine	125 ml
1 1/2 lb	rutabaga, peeled and cubed	750 g
1/2 tsp	salt	2 ml
1/2 tsp	freshly ground black pepper	2 ml
1 Tbsp	all-purpose flour	15 ml
1 1/2	cups chicken or vegetable stock	375 ml
1/4 cup	heavy cream	50 ml
1 Tbsp	Dijon mustard	15 ml
1/4 cup	fresh chopped parsley or thyme	50 ml

Melt the butter and olive oil in a large skillet over a medium heat. Stir in the bay leaf, garlic clove, and shallots. Cook for 8-10 minutes, stirring frequently, until the shallots and garlic are browned. Remove and discard the bay leaf and garlic clove. Add the mushrooms, and sauté for 3-4 minutes. Pour in the wine, increase the heat, and cook for 4-5 minutes, until the liquid has reduced by half. Stir in the cubed rutabaga, and season with salt and pepper. Stir in the flour, and add the stock. Bring to a boil, reduce the heat, cover, and simmer for 20-25 minutes, until the rutabaga is tender and most of the liquid is absorbed. Stir in the cream, mustard, and chopped herbs. Heat through, and serve at once.

Rutabaga Puffs

MAKES 12

This crackerjack combination of creamy mashed rutabaga and Yorkshire pudding makes a perfect accompaniment to a Sunday roast.

1 lb	rutabaga, peeled and chopped	500 g
2	large potatoes, peeled and chopped	2
1 1/2 cups	milk	375 ml
4 Tbsp	butter	60 ml
1 Tbsp	chopped fresh thyme	15 ml
6 tsp	vegetable oil	30 ml
2	eggs	2
3/4 cup	all-purpose flour	175 ml
	salt and freshly ground black pepper	

Boil the rutabaga and potatoes in a large pot of lightly salted boiling water for about 15-20 minutes, until tender. Drain and mash with 1/2 cup milk, the butter, thyme, and salt and pepper to taste. Set aside.

Preheat the oven to 400°F (200°C). Spoon 1/2 tsp vegetable oil into each of 12 muffin cups, and place the muffin pan in the oven to heat.

Beat together the remaining cup of milk with the eggs, flour, and a little salt, until smooth. When the oil in the muffin pan is very hot, remove from the oven, and divide half the batter among the cups. Now spoon in the rutabaga mash, divided equally among the cups, and top with the remaining batter. Bake for 15-20 minutes, until puffy and golden brown. Remove from the oven, and turn the puffs out onto a warm serving dish. Serve at once.

MICROWAVED RUTABAGA
Combine 1 pound (500 g) peeled, cubed rutabaga with 1/2 cup (125 ml) water in a 1-quart (1-L) microwave-safe casserole. Cover, cook 7-10 minutes on high, and let stand for 3 minutes. Drain, and use in a recipe or add butter, salt, and pepper, mash, and serve.

Salsify and Scorzonera

This pair of roots is relatively new in the scheme of things, having arrived on the European scene only in the 17th century. While sources disagree over whether they are botanically related, they share a host of similarities. Both are carrot-shaped, with creamy white flesh and a distinct flavour that some say is a cross between asparagus and artichokes, while others insist it is reminiscent of parsnip. Still others claim to detect a faint oyster taste; although in England salsify was once known as "the poor man's oyster" and is still called "oyster plant," my taste buds have never picked up on this subtlety. Despite their similarities, at first glance salsify and scorzonera are startlingly different. Salsify is beige, like a parsnip, while scorzonera has dark, almost black skin and is often sold as "black salsify."

Both roots are usually available from late fall through spring, although you may find them off and on through the rest of the year. Salsify is often twisted and unruly, with tiny rootlets springing unchecked in every direction. It is sometimes sold with its grassy green tops still attached; these can be picked through, the nicest ones used in salads, and the rest thrown into a stock or soup. Scorzonera roots should be straight and even, and they may be sold whole or in pieces. Either way, look for firm roots, slightly softer than a fresh carrot. Medium-sized roots are your best bet, as large ones can be woody and the smaller ones end up minuscule once peeled.

Salsify, white or black, will keep for about two weeks when wrapped in plastic and stored in the refrigerator. I recommend peeling these roots after they are cooked, for several reasons. Most of the flavour resides in the skin and is absorbed by the flesh as it cooks; the raw flesh will begin to mottle and darken as soon as it is exposed to air; and white salsify, with its wild rootlets and twisted body, is frustrating to peel when raw, although when it's cooked the skin should slip off fairly easily.

You can use both types of salsify in any recipe that calls for parsnips, and it makes a nice change from potatoes as well. I like to steam rather than boil salsify because, unlike hardier root vegetables, it has a tendency to break. Steam for about 10 minutes over 2 inches (5 cm) of boiling water; it is ready when tender, overdone once it feels mushy. Blanch in cold water and slip off the skin. Reheat by sautéing in a little butter, or mash with butter and a splash of cream, and season with salt, pepper, and a grating of fresh nutmeg.

KEEPING SALSIFY WHITE
If a recipe calls for salsify in its raw state, peel it before you get the other ingredients ready and submerge it in acidulated water to keep it from discolouring.

Salsify with Parmesan

SERVES 4-6

Serve this on thick slices of toasted Italian bread that have been rubbed with a cut garlic clove and drizzled with olive oil.

2 lb	salsify, scrubbed and trimmed	1 kg
2 Tbsp	butter	25 ml
1 Tbsp	olive oil	15 ml
1/4 cup	grated fresh parmesan cheese	50 ml
	salt and a pinch of cayenne pepper	

Place the whole, unpeeled salsify roots in a steamer basket over 2 inches (5 cm) of boiling water. Cover and steam for about 10-12 minutes, until barely tender. Drain and rinse under cold running water, and then peel and slice in 4-inch (10-cm) lengths.

Heat the butter and olive oil in a frying pan, and sauté the salsify for 3-4 minutes, until golden brown. Transfer to a plate, sprinkle with the parmesan cheese, and season with salt and cayenne pepper, or serve atop bruschetta.

Salsify and Leeks Braised in Cream

SERVES 4-6

1 lb	salsify, peeled and cut in 2-inch (5-cm) lengths	500 g
1 Tbsp	freshly squeezed lemon juice	15 ml
1 lb	leeks, rinsed, trimmed, and sliced thinly	500 g
1 cup	vegetable stock	250 ml
1 cup	heavy cream	250 ml
	salt, freshly grated black pepper, and freshly grated nutmeg, to taste	

Preheat the oven to 325°F (170°C), and generously butter a shallow, ovenproof dish.

Bring a large pot of lightly salted water to a boil, and add the lemon juice and salsify. Simmer for 8 minutes, until barely tender. Drain and transfer to the baking dish, along with the leeks. Heat the stock and cream gently, seasoning with salt, pepper, and nutmeg. Pour over the vegetables, and bake for 1 hour, until bubbling and golden brown.

Cream is a natural partner for both salsify and leeks. Remember to place the chopped salsify in water with a little lemon juice if you're not using it right away, as it will discolour if exposed to the air.

Spinach

In spite of Popeye's enduring efforts to popularize spinach, it continues to provoke groans of disgust from some children. Perhaps this is because many parents still force overcooked, soggy green mush down their offsprings' gullets, in the hopes of counteracting a diet of chips and chocolate bars. What a crime! Spinach has got to be one of the tastiest, most versatile greens going. Raw, stir-fried, steamed, or baked, spinach can be every cook's dream vegetable.

Spinach is available year-round, although local crops peak from mid-April through early June. Fresh from the market, spinach usually requires several washings in a sink full of cold water, to remove the silt and sand that gets trapped between the leaves. Use your hands to swish around the loose leaves, allowing the grit to settle to the bottom of the sink. Lift out the spinach, drain the sink, and repeat the process until the water runs clear. Drain in a colander or spin dry. Remove any long or tough stems by holding the leaf at its base and stripping away the stems. Spinach can usually be purchased rinsed and ready to use in tidy cellophane packets, but I don't mind having to clean my own, especially when there's the added bonus of enjoying young spinach, with tender leaves and few coarse and fibrous stalks to remove. Curly spinach, with its thicker, ruffled leaves, is what you'll usually get at restaurants, since its bulky appearance lets the chef get away with putting less on your plate.

When buying loose spinach, use your nose as well as your fingers and eyes. Fresh spinach has a raw, earthy scent, intense green colour, and crisp,

Popeye's bulging biceps were more likely the result of bench-pressing Olive Oyl than of his formidable spinach consumption. Although spinach is extremely high in iron, it is bound up with oxalic acid, which prevents its absorption. However, spinach is an excellent source of vitamins C and A. It also contains a high level of potassium.

Simply shake off the excess water from the final rinse, and cook covered, in the moisture left clinging to the leaves, until just wilted; this will take only a few minutes. Drain well, dab a knob of butter on top — and perhaps add a squeeze of lemon juice — and serve at once.

resilient leaves. If it smells like cabbage or appears tired or wilted, it's past its prime. When choosing cellophane-wrapped spinach, go for the package with the most spring to it. As this delicate green is extremely perishable, use it as soon as possible, and don't expect either loose or packaged spinach to last more than 2-3 days in the refrigerator.

With its subtle but assertive flavour, spinach is especially complemented by cheese, eggs, and fish. The Italians love their spinach, and any recipe containing the words *alla Fiorentina* or Florentine includes spinach. Young, leaf, or baby spinach is best served raw in salads. More robust varieties take well to steaming or stir-frying. I usually don't bother pre-cooking spinach for use in baked dishes such as lasagna, unless the recipe specifies cooking and draining or squeezing it dry. Eggs and spinach taste great together — I like to fold fresh chopped spinach into my scrambled eggs at breakfast. Spinach has a high water content, so using raw leaves may add too much liquid to your dish. Water adds bulk to raw spinach; 2-3 pounds (1 kg) of raw spinach will produce only around 2 cups (500 ml) when cooked.

Spinach Salad with Creamy Blue Cheese Dressing and Garlic Croutons

SERVES 4-6

1 lb	fresh spinach, trimmed, rinsed well, and spun dry	500 g
2	scallions, chopped finely	2
1	small red onion, sliced thinly	1
1/2 lb	fresh button mushrooms, sliced	250 g
6	strips bacon, cooked until crisp and then crumbled	6

For the dressing:

1	garlic clove	1
1/2 tsp	salt	2 ml
2/3 cup	sour cream	150 ml
2 Tbsp	mayonnaise	25 ml
1 tsp	Dijon mustard	5 ml
1 Tbsp	virgin olive oil	15 ml
1 Tbsp	white wine vinegar	15 ml
1 Tbsp	freshly squeezed lemon juice	15 ml
2 oz	blue cheese, crumbled	50 g
	freshly ground black pepper	

2-3	thick slices of hearty white bread, crusts removed	2-3
1 Tbsp	virgin olive oil	15 ml
1 Tbsp	finely grated fresh parmesan	15 ml
1	garlic clove, crushed	1

To make the croutons: Preheat the oven to 350°F (180°C). Cut the bread in 1/2-inch (1-cm) cubes, and toss them with the olive oil, parmesan, and crushed garlic. Spread them evenly on a baking sheet, and bake them on the highest oven rack for 7-8 minutes. Watch carefully to make sure they don't burn. Remove them from the oven, and set aside to cool.

To make the dressing: Crush the garlic with the salt to form a paste. In a small bowl, combine the garlic with the sour cream, mayonnaise, mustard, olive oil, vinegar, and lemon juice. Fold in the cheese, and season to taste with pepper. Set aside.

Tear the spinach into bite-sized pieces, and toss with the scallions, red onion, and sliced mushrooms. Pour the dressing over top, and toss well. Scatter with the bacon and croutons, and serve at once.

Scarpazzone (Spinach Pie)

SERVES 6

For the pastry:

2 cups	all-purpose flour	500 ml
1/4 cup	white sugar	50 ml
1/2 tsp	baking powder	2 ml
1/4 tsp	salt	1 ml
1/2 cup	cold unsalted butter, cubed	125 ml
2	large eggs, beaten	2

For the filling:

2 lb	fresh spinach, rinsed and trimmed	1 kg
4 Tbsp	butter	60 ml
1 Tbsp	olive oil	15 ml
4 oz	pancetta, cubed	125 g
1	large sweet onion, chopped finely	1
1	large garlic clove, chopped very finely	1
2 oz	mortadella sausage, diced	50 g

This recipe takes some time, but it is worth the effort. Use baby leaf spinach rather than the spinach packaged in cellophane if you can, as it will have more flavour. The foolproof pastry, made in a food processor, can stand the abuse of even a first-time pastry maker.

1/3 cup	grated fresh parmesan	80 ml
1/2 tsp	freshly grated nutmeg	2 ml
	salt and freshly ground black pepper	
2	large eggs, beaten	2
2 Tbsp	fine dry bread crumbs	25 ml

For the glaze:

1	egg, beaten with a pinch of salt	1

To make the pastry: Combine the dry ingredients in the bowl of a food processor, and pulse 2 or 3 times to blend. Add the cubes of butter, and pulse until the mixture resembles fine bread crumbs. Then switch to an automatic pulse, and add the eggs, until a ball of dough forms. Remove the dough, and knead it on a lightly floured surface for 1 minute, until smooth. Wrap tightly in plastic, and refrigerate for up to half an hour. (If you make the dough ahead of time, refrigerate until an hour or so before you need it, and allow it to come back almost to room temperature before using.)

To make the filling: Blanch the spinach in batches for 1 minute in a large pot of lightly salted boiling water. Refresh under cold running water, and drain thoroughly, using your hands to squeeze out any excess water. Chop coarsely.

Heat the butter and olive oil in a large frying-pan, and add the pancetta. Cook for 1 minute, stirring constantly, and then add the chopped onion and a pinch of salt. Sauté over a low heat for 10 minutes, until the onion has softened but not browned. Add the garlic, and cook for another minute. Stir in the mortadella, and cook for 5 minutes more, stirring frequently.

Add the drained, chopped spinach, and sauté for at least 5 minutes, stirring frequently. Transfer the mixture to a bowl, and add all but 1 tablespoon of the parmesan, the nutmeg, and salt and pepper to taste. Set aside until almost cool, and then fold in the beaten eggs.

Preheat the oven to 400°F (200°C), and grease an 8-inch (20-cm) springform pan. Remove the pastry from the refrigerator, and divide it into 2 parts, one approximately a third larger than the other. Roll out the larger piece into a 12-inch (30-cm) circle, and transfer into the pan, pressing it into the corners without stretching it (it will come only about halfway up the sides). If it tears, simply patch it. Mix together the bread crumbs with the remaining tablespoon of parmesan cheese, and sprinkle over the pastry bottom. Spoon in the spinach mixture.

Roll out the remaining pastry into an 8-inch (20-cm) circle, and lay it over the pie. (Or, for a really spectacular creation, make a lattice crust.) Pinch together the edges to seal, turning them in towards the middle as you crimp. Brush with the egg glaze, and prick the surface all over with a fork. Bake in the centre of the oven for 45-50 minutes, until golden brown. Allow to cool for about 10 minutes before removing the sides of the pan and transferring the beautiful pie to a serving plate. Serve warm.

SPINACH IN THE MICROWAVE
Microwaving greens keeps them bright, lively, and full of nutrients. Wash 1 pound (500 g) spinach and lightly shake off excess water. Place in a microwave-safe casserole, cover, and cook on high for 4 minutes, stir, and cook for a further 1-2 minutes, until nearly tender. Let stand, covered, for 5 minutes.

Baked Eggs Florentine

In my book, the perfect baked egg is one with the white just set and a yolk that runs like crazy when broken with a fork. You'll need 6 ramekins to make individual starters, or you can use one large ovenproof dish and serve two eggs per person for a main course. Make sure you have lots of toast or warm crusty bread on the side.

1 1/2 lb	fresh spinach, rinsed and trimmed	750 g
1/3 cup	heavy cream	80 ml
	freshly ground nutmeg	
6 tsp	butter	30 ml
6	small slices cooked ham	6
6	large eggs	6
	salt and freshly ground black pepper	

Preheat the oven to 350°F (180°C). Pour about 1/2 inch (1 cm) of water into a large roasting pan, and set it on the centre rack of the oven. Grease 6 ramekins or 1 large ovenproof dish.

Pack the rinsed spinach into a large, heavy-based saucepan, cover, and cook over a low heat for 3-5 minutes, until wilted. Drain well, squeezing out excess liquid. Chop finely, and mix with the cream, nutmeg, and salt and pepper.

Line the greased ramekins or single dish with the slices of ham, then spread the cooked spinach thickly over top. Using the back of a spoon, make a hollow in the centre of each ramekin, or make 6 good-sized hollows in the single dish. Carefully crack the eggs into the hollows, dot each with a teaspoon of butter, and set the ramekins or dish in the water in the roasting pan. Bake for 10-12 minutes, until the whites have just set. Serve at once.

RAMEKINS IN THE MICROWAVE
Cook the spinach in a covered casserole on high for 5 minutes. Stir and let stand, covered, while you grease the ramekins and line them with ham.

Drain the spinach, squeezing out excess liquid, chop it finely, and mix in a bowl with the nutmeg, cream, salt, and pepper. Divide among the ramekins, make a well in each, and carefully crack an egg into each well. Pierce the egg yolks with a wooden toothpick to prevent bursting. Dot with butter, cover with vented plastic, and place, evenly spaced, in the microwave. Cook at medium (50%) for 5 minutes, turning each ramekin and moving those in the centre to the edge and vice versa once.

Let stand for 1-2 minutes, until the yolks have the desired consistency. If they still seem too runny, cook for a few seconds more. The whites will be less well-done than the yolks, but they'll firm up during the standing time.

Stir-Fried Spinach with Garlic, Figs, and Pine Nuts

Spinach takes only a few minutes to stir-fry, so have your table set and your guests ready. You can substitute plump raisins for the figs.

1 Tbsp	virgin olive oil	15 ml
2	shallots, sliced thinly	2
1	large garlic clove, chopped finely	1

2 lb	fresh spinach, rinsed, dried, and chopped or torn coarsely	1 kg
3 Tbsp	toasted pine nuts	40 ml
3 Tbsp	chopped fresh figs	40 ml
1 Tbsp	balsamic vinegar	15 ml

TOASTED PINE NUTS
There are two ways to toast pine nuts. You can roast them on an ungreased baking sheet in a 350°F (180°C) oven for 3-4 minutes, or you can sauté them for a few minutes in a dry frying pan. Don't overdo it, as they'll brown up a little more after you remove them from the heat.

Heat the oil in a wok or large frying pan, and sauté the shallots and garlic for 2-3 minutes. Add the spinach, stirring briskly for 1-2 minutes, until just wilted. Remove from the heat, toss in the toasted pine nuts and figs, then drizzle the balsamic vinegar over top. Serve at once.

Sprouts

Sprouts are one of nature's finest snack foods. Crunchy, nutritious and tasty, you can't go wrong sneaking a bag of fresh sprouts into the movie theatre. And make sure they are fresh, because that really is the key to their goodness. Whether you're throwing a handful of alfalfa sprouts into a sandwich or salad, or stir-frying hardier mung bean sprouts, you want them to be crisp and sweet-smelling.

SMALL SPROUTS, BIG FLAVOUR
Alfalfa and clover sprouts are wonderful in savoury sandwiches, particularly roast beef or pork. I also like them with egg salad.

An increasing number of sprout varieties have become available as growers experiment with sprouting various types of seeds. The most common of the small varieties are alfalfa, clover, and radish sprouts, all of which should be eaten raw. Alfalfa sprouts are the tiniest, with 2-3 inch (5-7 cm) tails, tender, moist, and delicately crisp. Clover sprouts are a little longer, 3-5 inches (7-13 cm), with tiny, bright green leaves that taste bittersweet and a bit grassy. Radish sprouts, extremely hot and peppery, are sold in combination with alfalfa sprouts, usually under the label of "spicy" sprouts. Since these pale green sprouts are more robust than their more delicate cousins, you can toss them into salads without fear of crushing them, or combine them with shredded cheese and serve them in an omelette.

The larger sprout varieties are suitable for steaming, stir-frying, or tossing into a soup or casserole. The most familiar is the mild, fresh-tasting mung bean sprout, which is commonly used in Asian cooking — in stir-fries, noodle dishes, and spring rolls. Others legumes, such as aduki, lentils, garbanzos (chickpeas), yellow beans, and soy beans, can also be sprouted successfully. Often these are combined to make a variety called "crispy" sprouts, because the seeds only partially sprout, and so one gets to enjoy the crunchy seeds themselves.

Whatever variety of sprouts you buy, make sure they are crisp and fresh-looking. Refrigerate delicate sprouts in their plastic containers, and use as needed. They will keep for up to 5 days. Crispy sprouts and mung bean sprouts should be used within a day or two of purchase, as they will rapidly grow slippery and sour-smelling. If you've left them a bit too long, pick through them and refresh the freshest sprouts in a sink full of cold water. Drain well and use them in a cooked dish.

Stir-Fried Mung Sprouts, Red Pepper, and Tofu with Black Bean Sauce

SERVES 4

1 Tbsp	vegetable or peanut oil	15 ml
1 tsp	sesame oil	5 ml
2	shallots, sliced very thinly	2
1	garlic clove, chopped finely	1
1 Tbsp	finely chopped fresh ginger	15 ml
1-2	finger hot peppers, seeded and chopped finely	1-2
8 ounces	firm tofu, drained and cut in 1/2-inch (1-cm) cubes	250 g
2	large sweet red peppers, seeded and cut in 1/2-inch (1-cm) squares	2
3 cups	fresh mung bean sprouts	750 ml

For the sauce:

3 Tbsp	rice wine or dry sherry	40 ml
1 Tbsp	red wine vinegar	15 ml
1 Tbsp	soy sauce	15 ml
1 Tbsp	black bean sauce	15 ml
2 tsp	sugar	10 ml
2 tsp	cornstarch	10 ml

To retain their crunch, bean sprouts should be stir-fried just long enough to heat them through. You can substitute a pound (500 g) of raw, peeled shrimp for the tofu if you prefer.

Mix the sauce ingredients in small bowl, and set aside.

Heat the oils in a wok or large skillet, and stir-fry the shallots for 3 minutes. Add the garlic, ginger, and hot peppers, and cook over a high heat for 1 minute. Add the tofu, and stir-fry until golden brown. Stir in the sweet pepper, and cook for 2 minutes more. Now add the sauce, stirring well to coat the tofu and peppers. Stir in the bean sprouts, and cook for 1 minute more. Serve at once.

Garden Wraps

SERVES 4

2 cups	fresh mixed small sprouts (alfalfa, clover, and spicy)	500 ml
4	tomatoes, chopped	4

1/2	English cucumber, chopped	1/2
4	scallions, chopped finely	4
3	carrots, peeled and grated	
1 cup	grated cheddar cheese	250 ml
4 large or 8 small	California wraps	4 large or 8 small

For the dressing:

1	garlic clove, chopped finely	1
1	shallot, chopped finely	1
	zest and juice of 1 lemon	
1/2 cup	sour cream	125 ml
1/2 cup	mayonnaise	50 ml
2 Tbsp	chopped fresh mint	25 ml
1 Tbsp	chopped fresh dill	15 ml
	salt and pepper	

Combine the dressing ingredients in a large bowl, and whisk to blend well. Fold in the vegetables and grated cheese. Divide the salad mixture among the wraps, and roll them up. Serve at once.

Winter Squash

Winter squash is an excellent source of vitamin A and folate and a fair source of vitamin C. The darker the flesh, the more nutrients it contains.

Despite the fact that most squash varieties are available year-round, we still tend to think of them in two categories — winter and summer. It is more accurate, perhaps, to distinguish them as hard-shell and soft-shell. Winter squash are harvested in the fall, when their rinds have hardened, and they keep well under the bed all winter, or so says the Yankee lore of New England and the Maritimes. Summer squash are cultivated for their soft, immature fruit, and are frequently eaten with their skins left on. If you're not clear about the difference, sit on one. Only summer squash will, well, squash. You can read more about them on pages 155-157.

The many different types of winter squash vary wildly in appearance but somewhat less so in use and flavour. Among the most popular squash are the acorn, sweet dumpling, buttercup, butternut, Hubbard, and spaghetti squash. (Pumpkins are also squash, but they have a chapter of their own, pages 114-116.) When buying winter squash, choose one that is hard and feels heavy for its size. Don't worry if you see dry, scabby patches, but make sure there are no soft spots, mould, or cracks. Whole squash will keep for up to a month in a cool, dark, dry place. Cut squash can be kept in the refrigerator, wrapped tightly, for a week.

Acorn squash are small and heart-shaped, the perfect size for a romantic dinner for two. Also known as pepper squash, their smooth thin skin varies in colour from deep green to white to orange, and sometimes a combination of all three. They have pale orange flesh — tender, moist, and fibrous — with a relatively large seed cavity. The orange or golden acorn is sweeter and more flavourful and can be substituted for pumpkin in most recipes. Cut acorn squash in half lengthways, and, using a spoon, scrape out the seeds and fibres. Place them, cut sides down, on a greased baking sheet, and bake at 375°F (180°C) for 30-45 minutes, or until soft. You can eat them right out of the shells, with butter and seasoning, or scoop the flesh out and use it in a recipe. Two other varieties of single-serving squash are the sweet potato squash, a fat sausage with green and white stripes, and the sweet dumpling, which looks like a small drum and is also striped with green and white. Both of these squash have orange flesh with a rich, nutty flavour.

Buttercup squash are identified by the small, pale cap they wear on their blossom end. They're shaped like small pumpkins, and the skin is usually a deep, ivy green, with faint stripes in the same colour as the cap. If you find one with a mottled, grey-blue skin, chances are it is a Kabocha, a Japanese strain of buttercup squash, or a Queensland blue squash, or a New Zealand grey pumpkin. All have pale orange flesh, dry and fine in texture, and are all good to steam, as their flesh turns tender and more creamy than when baked or roasted. The blue varieties have very thin skin; they can be sliced in thin wedges and sautéed in their skin, which deepens in colour when cooked. Halve buttercup squash carefully, remove the seeds and fibres, and steam the halves, placed cut sides down on a steamer rack in a large pot, for 15-20 minutes. You can also steam a whole squash, which will take about twice the time. If you prefer a drier texture, place the squash, cut sides up, in a roasting pan with about an inch of water. Brush the flesh with a little olive oil, season with salt and pepper, and cover tightly with foil. Bake at 350°F (170°C) for 40-60 minutes.

Butternut squash look a little like a water balloon, with a cylindrical neck and bulbous bottom. Their pale beige to deep yellow skins are fairly thin, and as only the bulb end contains seeds, you can be sure of getting your pound (actually 4-6 pounds) of flesh. And the flesh is superb — rich, sweet, and dry, perfect for baking or using in soups and stews. They should be split lengthways if you want perfect halves, or you can chop the neck off and then split the bulb end to remove the seeds.

The old-fashioned Hubbard squash range in size from the traditional 8-20 pounders (3-8 kg) to the new, fashionably small ones, weighing in at only 2-4 pounds (1-2 kg). They have hard, warty skin that can be anything from deep green to blue-grey to golden orange in colour. With a deep orange flesh that is sweet, fine-grained, and dry, Hubbards are excellent when mashed with butter, salt, pepper, and a little nutmeg. Or to spice things up a bit more, try adding garlic and cayenne pepper.

Cook a yellow, watermelon-shaped spaghetti squash, crack it open, and you can pull out seemingly miles of tender, golden strands. Like pasta, it is mild in flavour, making a great canvas for many different sauces. Look for very hard squash with smooth yellow skin. Avoid any with lumps and bumps, and those with a greenish hue may be immature. The larger the squash, the denser the pasta-like strands, which can range in texture from angel-hair to thick spaghetti. Use a fork to comb and pull the stands away from the skin, and serve hot. The strands can also be cooled and sautéed in butter to reheat.

HOW TO BUTCHER A SQUASH
Buttercup and Hubbard squash have very thick, hard rind, so be careful when cutting one open. Place it on a damp cloth to prevent it from sliding around, and use a long, sturdy, sharp knife and a mallet to split the squash vertically, to one side of the stalk.

HOW TO COOK
SPAGHETTI SQUASH
To steam, halve lengthways and scoop out the seeds. Halve again lengthways, and place the pieces, cut sides down, on the steamer rack. Cover and cook for 20-30 minutes, until your finger makes a dent in the skin. To bake these squash whole, simply pierce several times with a sharp knife to allow the steam to escape, and cook for 45-60 minutes at 350°F (170°C). Remove from the oven and cut in half to prevent further cooking.

Baked Baby Acorn Squash
with Walnut Vinaigrette

SERVES 2

Walnut vinaigrette brings out the nutty flavour of roasted squash. You can substitute other small, thin-skinned winter squash, and the vinaigrette tastes equally delicious tossed with cooked strands of spaghetti squash.

1	acorn squash	1
1 Tbsp	butter	15 ml
	salt and freshly ground black pepper	

For the vinaigrette:

1	small garlic clove, chopped	1
1/2 tsp	salt	2 ml
1 Tbsp	balsamic vinegar	15 ml
4 Tbsp	walnut oil	60 ml
4 Tbsp	vegetable oil	60 ml
2 Tbsp	toasted walnuts, crushed	25 ml
1 Tbsp	chopped fresh cilantro	15 ml

Preheat the oven to 375°F (190°C). Halve the squash across its middle, and scoop out the seeds and pith. Line a baking pan with foil, and butter it generously. Place the squash halves, cut sides down, on the pan. Add a few tablespoons of water to the pan, and bake for about 20 minutes. Turn the squash over, baste with the pan juices and bake for 10-15 minutes longer, until the flesh is tender.

To make the vinaigrette: Crush the garlic and salt to a paste. Combine it with the remaining vinaigrette ingredients in small jar with a tightly fitting lid, and shake thoroughly. Drizzle over the roasted squash, and serve at once.

Curried Squash and Sweet Potatoes
with Cashews

SERVES 6

Serve this heart-warming dish over freshly cooked basmati rice.

2 Tbsp	butter	25 ml
2 Tbsp	vegetable oil	25 ml
2	red onions, chopped finely	2
5	garlic cloves, chopped finely	5
2 Tbsp	grated fresh ginger	25 ml
1 tsp	ground cumin	5 ml
2 tsp	toasted coriander seeds, crushed	10 ml

1 tsp	ground cardamom	5 ml
2-3 tsp	chili powder	10-15 ml
1 cup	toasted cashews	250 ml
1 lb	squash, peeled, seeded, and cut in 1-inch (2.5-cm) cubes	500 g
1 lb	sweet potatoes, peeled and cut in 1-inch (2.5-cm) cubes	500 g
1	medium-sized turnip, peeled and cut in 1-inch (2.5-cm) cubes	1
3/4 cup	hot chicken or vegetable stock	175 ml
	salt and pepper	
1 1/4 cups	plain yogurt	300 ml
2 Tbsp	chopped fresh cilantro	25 ml

Heat the butter and oil in a large skillet, and sauté the onions for 5 minutes. Stir in the garlic, ginger, spices, and cashews, and cook for 2 minutes more. Add the squash, sweet potatoes, and turnip, and stir well to coat. Cover, reduce the heat, and cook for 10 minutes. Pour in the stock, bring to a simmer, and cook for 10 minutes, until all the vegetables are tender and the liquid has reduced. Season to taste with salt and pepper, stir in the yogurt and cilantro, and serve at once.

Squash, Corn, and Black Bean Soup

SERVES 6

3 Tbsp	olive oil	40 ml
2	onions, chopped finely	2
2	garlic cloves, chopped finely	2
1 Tbsp	paprika	15 ml
1 1/2 lb	winter squash, peeled, seeded, and cut in 1-inch (2.5-cm) cubes	750 g
12 oz	plum tomatoes, chopped coarsely	375 g
3 cups	chicken or vegetable stock	750 ml
1 cup	fresh or frozen corn	250 ml
1 cup	cooked or canned black beans	250 ml
1/4 cup	chopped fresh cilantro	50 ml
	salt and freshly ground black pepper	

This hearty, "down-home" soup makes a terrific winter supper.

Heat the olive oil in a large saucepan, and sauté the onions and garlic for 5 minutes, until softened. Stir in the paprika, and cook over a high heat for 1 minute. Stir in the chopped squash, cover, reduce the heat and cook for 10 minutes. Add the tomatoes and stock, bring to a boil, reduce the heat, and simmer for 10-15 minutes, until the squash is tender. Transfer half the soup to a food processor or blender, and purée. Return it to the pan, stir in the corn and black beans, season to taste with salt and pepper, and cook for 5 minutes longer. Stir in the cilantro, and serve.

Sweet Potato

Sweet potatoes are rich in vitamin A and contain good amounts of vitamin C.

In case you're confused about when a sweet potato is a sweet potato and when it is a yam, turn to page 153. Yams have their own chapter, a pretty big hint that these tubers are two distinct creatures. This popular confusion is relieved neither by the existence of a sweet potato variety called the Louisiana yam, nor by the knowledge that the sweet potato isn't a potato at all. To make matters even more complicated, you may also find sweet potatoes sold by their Spanish name, boniato, which often designates an irregularly shaped, white-fleshed variety.

The sweet potato is a New World vegetable, native to South America and commonly associated with southern cooking and "soul food." It comes in a variety of shapes — round and fat, long and skinny, knobbly or smooth. The skin can range in colour from golden brown to copper or pale pink to deep purple, while the flesh may be white, yellow, orange, red, pink, or even purple. The most common variety is copper-skinned with bright orange flesh. The flavour will vary depending on the variety; as a general rule, lighter-fleshed sweet potatoes are more delicate, nutty rather than sweet, while darker ones have the distinctly spicy-sweet taste most of us expect.

Available year-round, sweet potatoes are grown all over the world. Mexico, Florida, and Central and South America produce most of the sweet potatoes sold in North America, but Asia is by far the largest producer, growing 90% of the world's crop. Look for clean, well-shaped tubers with an even colour, and avoid soft or bruised ones, which are already spoiling. They will keep best in a cool, dark place, but not in the refrigerator, for up to 2 weeks.

Sweet potatoes should not be peeled: simply give them a scrub and then cook as you would white potatoes, slipping off their skins afterwards if desired. (If you prefer to peel them first, submerge them in acidulated water, as their flesh will begin to discolour as soon as it is exposed to air.) They boil, bake, roast, and fry beautifully, cooking a little faster than white potatoes. Bake unpeeled sweet potatoes in the microwave on high for about 5 minutes each (depending on size), halve them lengthways, and scrape out the flesh and mash it, perhaps with boiled white potatoes, olive oil, and basil pesto, or with butter, cream, and a generous grating of fresh nutmeg. If you like the skin crusty, bake them in the regular oven, then split them open and pack in the butter and sour cream or yogurt. They can be quartered lengthways, brushed with olive oil, and roasted, on their own or mixed with other roots.

Braised Sweet Potatoes and Apples with Crunchy Pancetta Topping

SERVES 4

1 Tbsp	butter	15 ml
1 Tbsp	olive oil	15 ml
1 lb	sweet potatoes, peeled and cut in 1/4-inch (5-mm) slices	500 g
2	large apples, cored and cut in 1/2-inch (1-cm) slices	2
1/4 cup	brown sugar	50 ml
1/4 tsp	salt	1 ml
3 Tbsp	apple juice or cider	40 ml
1/4 tsp	paprika	1 ml
6-8	strips of pancetta or bacon, chopped and fried until crisp	6-8

Heat the butter and olive oil in a large skillet or frying pan, and toss in the sweet potatoes and apples. Stir in the brown sugar and salt, and cook for 5 minutes. Add the apple juice or cider, cover, and reduce the heat. Cook for 20-25 minutes, stirring occasionally, until the potatoes are softened and the liquid is absorbed. Season with paprika, and serve with the crisp pancetta or bacon bits scattered over top.

IN THE MICROWAVE
In a microwave-safe casserole, combine the butter, oil, sweet potatoes, and apple slices, tossing to coat well. Cover and cook on high for 2 minutes. Stir in the sugar and salt, cover, and cook another 1-2 minutes. Add the cider, cover, and continue to cook, stirring occasionally, until the sweet potatoes are softened, 4-6 minutes. Season with paprika, sprinkle with bacon or pancetta bits, and serve.

Spicy Sweet Potato Chips

SERVES 2

These chips are wonderful served with a creamy garlic dip.

1 lb	sweet potatoes	500 g
1 Tbsp	freshly squeezed lemon juice	15 ml
1/4 cup	flour	50 ml
1/4 tsp	each cayenne pepper, ground cumin, ground coriander, and salt	1 ml
	vegetable oil, for deep-frying	

Peel and slice the sweet potatoes thinly, dropping them in a bowl of water acidulated with the lemon juice as you go along. Combine the flour and seasonings on a plate. Preheat the oil in a deep-fryer or wok. Drain the sweet potato slices, and dip them in the seasoned flour. Fry in batches for 3-4 minutes, until golden and crisp. Drain on paper towel, and serve warm.

Sweet Potato Curry

SERVES 4

FRIED SWEET POTATOES
I like to cut sweet potatoes into matchsticks or small cubes and fry them in butter and oil until golden and crunchy. Served with a squeeze of lime juice and lots of salt and pepper, these are heavenly.

2 lb	sweet potatoes	1 kg
2 Tbsp	peanut oil	25 ml
1	onion, chopped	1
1	garlic clove, chopped finely	1
1	finger hot pepper, seeded and chopped finely	1
1/2 tsp	fresh grated ginger	2 ml
1 Tbsp	curry powder	15 ml
1/2 cup	unsweetened coconut milk	125 ml
1/4 cup	fresh lime juice	50 ml
1/2 cup	chicken stock	125 ml
	salt and freshly ground black pepper	
2 Tbsp	chopped fresh cilantro, to garnish	25 ml

Peel the sweet potatoes, cut them into 1-inch (2.5-cm) cubes, parboil them in lightly salted water until slightly softened, and drain.

Meanwhile, heat the peanut oil in a wok or large skillet, and sauté the onion for 5 minutes, until softened. Stir in the garlic, pepper, ginger, and curry powder, and cook for 2 minutes more. Add the coconut milk, lime juice, and chicken stock, and bring to a boil. Reduce the heat, and simmer for 15 minutes, stirring occasionally. Adjust the seasoning to taste, and stir in the cubed sweet potatoes. Cover and cook for 10-15 minutes, until the potatoes are tender. Serve hot, garnished with cilantro.

Swiss Chard

One cup of cooked Swiss chard has only 35 calories. An excellent source of vitamin A, potassium and fibre, it also contains good amounts of vitamin C and calcium. It is naturally high in sodium, so it should be eaten in moderation if this is a dietary concern.

Although the word chard comes from the Latin for thistle, this vegetable is in fact a kind of beet cultivated for its greens rather than for its roots. To confuse things even more, Swiss chard doesn't appear to have originated in Switzerland. Anyway, the name distinguishes it from another variety, ruby or rhubarb chard, which has vivid red rather than pale green or white ribs. And you're actually getting two vegetables for the price of one, as Swiss chard's thick, pale ribs are generally cooked separately from the ruffled greens, which are akin to spinach leaves in both taste and appearance. So if you like spinach, beets, or both, you'll love Swiss chard.

Available off and on throughout the year, Swiss chard peaks from early summer through October. As with all greens, the leaves are extremely perishable and should be fresh and crisp when brought home. Use them as soon as possible, and certainly within 2 days. If you separate the leaves from the ribs, you can keep the ribs for a few days longer, wrapped well and stored in the vegetable crisper.

Rinse Swiss chard thoroughly in a sink full of tepid water, swishing the leaves around and allowing any grit or sand to sink to the bottom. Lift out, spin or pat dry, and use a sharp knife or scissors to trim the leaves from the ribs, pulling off any fibrous strings. Tear the leaves into pieces of uniform size, and slice the stems on the diagonal. Swiss chard is very delicate and should always be steamed, never boiled. Cook it like spinach, with just the water clinging to its leaves after washing.

With its distinctive, beet-like taste, Swiss chard can be used in a mixed green salad. Like bok choy, Swiss chard adds flavour and colour to soups and stews (add it just a few minutes before serving to retain its texture), as well as making a great stir-fry ingredient. This green also holds its own in creamy dishes, as the fat counterbalances its slightly acid taste.

MICROWAVED SWISS CHARD Cooking Swiss chard in the microwave preserves its texture and colour as well as its nutrients. Wash 1 pound (500 g) leaves, stem them, cut them into 1-inch (2.5-cm) strips, and chop the stems. Place in a 2-quart (2-L) microwave-safe casserole with 1/4 cup (50 ml) water, cover, and cook on high for 5-7 minutes, stirring occasionally, until the chard is almost tender enough. Let stand, covered, for 3 minutes to finish cooking.

Chard and Sausage Pie with Rosti Topping

SERVES 6

Use stored potatoes rather than new ones to make the rosti topping, as their starchiness helps to hold the rosti together.

1 Tbsp	olive oil	15 ml
1	onion, chopped finely	1
2	garlic cloves, chopped finely	2
1/2 lb	fresh lean sausages, chopped finely	250 g
2 lb	Swiss chard	1 kg
1/2 cup	chopped fresh parsley	125 ml
	salt and freshly ground black pepper	

For the rosti topping:

1 1/2 lb	medium-sized potatoes, scrubbed	750 g
3 Tbsp	melted butter	40 ml
1/4 cup	grated parmesan cheese	50 ml
	salt and freshly ground black pepper	

Boil the potatoes, whole and unpeeled, in lightly salted water for 12 minutes. Drain and set aside. Remove the stems from the chard, and shred the leaves.

Heat the olive oil in a large skillet, and sauté the onion and garlic for about 5 minutes, until softened but not browned. Add the chopped sausage, and cook for 10 minutes, stirring frequently until browned. Stir in the chard, season with salt and pepper, and cook for 5 minutes more. Stir in the parsley, and remove from the heat.

Preheat the oven to 400°F (200°C). Peel the potatoes, and grate them coarsely into a bowl. Pour in the butter, and toss well to coat, seasoning with salt and pepper.

Transfer the sausage and chard mixture to a deep pie pan or shallow baking dish, and spoon the potato mixture over top, spreading it evenly and pressing lightly to seal the edges. Sprinkle the grated parmesan over top, and bake for 45-50 minutes on a high oven shelf, until the rosti topping is golden brown. Serve hot.

Swiss Chard with Lemon Butter and Pistachios

SERVES 4

2 lb	Swiss chard, rinsed and trimmed	1 kg
3 Tbsp	butter	40 ml
1	garlic clove, chopped finely	1
	zest and juice of 1 lemon	
3 Tbsp	finely chopped pistachios	40 ml
	salt and freshly ground black pepper	

IN THE MICROWAVE
Cook the Swiss chard in the microwave (see page 142), drain, squeeze out excess liquid, and chop coarsely. In the casserole used for cooking the chard, mix the butter, garlic, and lemon zest. Cook on high for 1 minute, stirring once. Add the chard, and toss to coat. Sprinkle with the lemon juice, and reheat for 1 minute. Scatter the pistachios over all, season with salt and pepper, and serve.

Bring a large pot of lightly salted water to a boil and blanch the chard for 1 minute. Drain well, squeezing out any excess water from the leaves, and then chop coarsely. Melt the butter in a skillet over a medium heat, and stir in the garlic and lemon zest. Add the chard and sauté for about 5 minutes, until tender. Sprinkle the lemon juice over top, and increase the heat. Cook for a few minutes longer, until the liquid reduces. Stir in the pistachios, and serve at once.

Tomatillos

Tomatillos contain a lot of vitamin A, some vitamin C, and niacin.

The tomatillo is yet another vegetable (that is to say fruit, or actually berry) which both is and isn't what it seems. In appearance it resembles an unripe cherry tomato, and it is, in fact, sometimes called a Mexican green tomato. Like the tomato, eggplant, and sweet pepper, the tomatillo is a member of the nightshade family, but just as a tomato isn't an eggplant or a pepper, the tomatillo isn't a tomato. It is a physalis, and these are all easily identified by the papery husks that encase them like miniature Chinese lanterns. (The Cape gooseberry is a more commonly known physalis, so if you've seen these you know what I'm talking about.)

Fans of Mexican food will know about tomatillos, a fundamental ingredient in green salsa. However, it is only in recent years that fresh tomatillos have become available. If you can't find them in your regular supermarket, ask the produce manager to get some in, or try a Latino specialty shop. They should be unripe, and if they are purple or yellow it means they are starting to ripen and won't have the distinctive sour taste that adds zest to the fiery sauces and stews in which they are used. Their husks should be fresh and not fully open, and when you pull them back, the tomatillo should be hard and slightly sticky.

Store tomatillos in their husks. In a paper bag in the refrigerator, they will last for up to two weeks. To prepare, simply pull back and discard the husks, remove the stems, and rinse. Very tart when raw, tomatillos are usually used in this state only in stews and cooked sauces, where they cook along with everything else. Otherwise, cook them before adding them to a recipe; this softens them and allows their citrusy flavour to develop. You can simmer them gently (don't boil) until just tender, which will take 5-15 minutes, or roast them in their husks in a very hot oven for 10-15 minutes. A good addition to gazpacho and guacamole, they can also be used in place of lemon or lime juice to give extra zing to a dish.

Tomatillo Salsa

MAKES 4 CUPS (1 L)

1 lb	tomatillos, with husks	500 g
3	tomatoes	3
1	garlic clove, peeled	1
2-3	chipotles, seeded	2-3
1	onion, peeled and quartered	1
1 cup	fresh cilantro leaves	250 ml
2 Tbsp	freshly squeezed lime juice	25 ml
	salt	

This salsa is great with barbecued meat, fish, and vegetables. Chipotles add a lovely smoky hot flavour to the citrusy taste of the tomatillos.

Preheat the broiler. Place the tomatillos and tomatoes on a baking pan, and slide them under the broiler for a few minutes, until they begin to char. Remove from the oven, and cool. Remove the husks from the tomatillos, and skin the tomatoes. Combine the tomatoes and tomatillos in a food processor with the garlic, chipotles, onion, and cilantro. Pulse until chopped finely. Stir in the lemon juice, season to taste with salt, and refrigerate until using.

Tomatillo and Avocado Salad

SERVES 4

2	avocados	2
1 1/2 tsp	freshly squeezed lemon juice	7 ml
1/2 lb	tomatillos, husked, rinsed, and diced finely	250 g
1	sweet onion, chopped coarsely	1

The raw tomatillos retain their acidic quality, which contrasts nicely with the creaminess of avocado.

1/4 cup	fresh cilantro	50 ml
1	garlic clove, peeled and chopped	1
1/3 cup	olive oil	80 ml
	salt and freshly ground black pepper	

Peel and stone the avocados, and cut in 1-inch (2.5-cm) cubes. Place in a serving bowl, and sprinkle with lemon juice. Add all but 2 tablespoons of the tomatillos, along with the onion. Combine the reserved tomatillos with half of the cilantro, the garlic, and a pinch each of salt and pepper in a food processor or blender. Pulse to form a paste. Gradually add the olive oil, and pulse to blend. Pour over the salad, and toss gently to blend. Refrigerate until chilled before serving.

Tomatoes

Round, ripe, and red, the tomato is a sexy little number. The "love apple," as it was long called in England, was viewed with suspicion until early in the 20th century and grown largely as an ornamental fruit (which it is). A member of the deadly nightshade family, the tomato was suspected at worst of being poisonous and at best (which, for the English, was not much better) as encouraging an excessive sexual appetite. The Italians, not surprisingly, embraced the tomato much earlier, and it's hard to imagine Mediterranean cooking without this passionate ingredient.

Although I'm an Englishman, born and bred, a good tomato — juicy, succulent, flavourful — makes me weak at the knees. I can't walk past a display of cherry toms without filching one and popping it right into my mouth. Although nothing beats a tomato eaten straight from the vine, we're lucky these days to have vine-ripened tomatoes available year-round, albeit at a price. Ripe tomatoes do not transport easily, so most of the tomatoes that you get during winter are either picked green and ripened with gas instead of sunlight, or else grown in greenhouses. Neither of these methods produces the earthy flavour of the vine-ripened tomato, so you'll have to decide between your money and your mouth.

There are dozens of tomato varieties, and each has its own best way of being used. The large beefsteak tomatoes are rich and juicy — great for slicing thickly and stuffing in sandwiches or hamburgers, grilled, or stuffed and baked. Plum tomatoes are the oblong, sometimes misshapen fruit so popular in Italy. They are great in sauces but also a flavourful choice for salads. My favourite, the cherry tom, is ideal for a snack, a salad, or to toss in a stir-fry at the last minute. You can leave them whole or slice larger ones in half. You can sometimes get yellow, gold, and orange tomatoes, which are sweet and flavourful. There has been a recent surge in the popularity of green tomatoes, which, like green peppers, are simply unripe. Green tomatoes are tart, even sour, and will make your mouth pucker if you eat them raw. However, they are used for preserves and cooking, as anyone who has seen the movie *Fried Green Tomatoes* will know.

Tomatoes are an excellent source of vitamin C, and one medium-sized fruit makes a nutritious snack at only 25 calories.

When buying tomatoes, choose ones that are heavy for their size and firm but not hard. Use your nose. A tomato should smell like a tomato — fruity and earthy. Tomatoes with their stems still attached (sometimes clustered on a vine) will keep fresh longest. In summer, you have more choice over whether to buy tomatoes prime for eating or a little less ripe for use another day. During the winter, you'll probably have to let them ripen at home. Place them stem-end down in a paper bag, leave it in a sunny place for a few days, and they'll continue to ripen. A ripe tomato will keep for several days in a cool place, but please don't condemn them to the refrigerator, as the cold will blanch their flavour.

Some recipes call for peeled tomatoes, and although I more often than not ignore that instruction, it is easily obeyed. Put them in a bowl and cover with boiling water. Leave them for less than half a minute, drain them, and plunge them into very cold water until they're cool enough to handle. The skins will slip right off once you make a slit with a sharp knife. As for seeding tomatoes, slide your finger down either side of cut wedges, or else cut ripe tomatoes horizontally and squeeze the halves in your fist. Do it into a strainer set over a bowl to catch the juices — otherwise you're likely to throw out the flavour along with the seeds.

SUN-DRIED TOMATOES
Sun-dried tomatoes are a tasty and versatile ingredient to have on hand. Buy a bottle of them preserved in oil, and replenish them with the less expensive dried variety as you use them up.

Tomato, Olive, and Bocconcini Tart

SERVES 6

The shell of this tart is lined with bocconcini, or "baby" mozzarella, which forms a creamy contrast to the sweet tang of fresh tomatoes. If you use regular mozzarella, you'll end up with something distinctly chewy, so if you have to substitute, you're better off with goat's cheese or some other soft cheese.

4 oz	bocconcini, sliced	125 g
4-5	tomatoes, sliced thickly	4-5
8	black olives, halved	8
8-10	basil leaves	8-10
1	large garlic clove, chopped finely	1
2 Tbsp	olive oil	25 ml
2 tsp	balsamic vinegar	10 ml
1/2 tsp	each salt and freshly ground black pepper	2 ml

For the crust:

1/2 cup	all-purpose flour	125 ml
1/2 tsp	salt	2 ml
1/2 cup	cold butter, cubed	125 ml
1	egg, beaten	1
2-3 Tbsp	cold water	25-40 ml

To make the pastry: Combine the flour and salt in a mixing bowl, and cut or rub in the butter until the mixture resembles coarse bread crumbs. Stir in the egg yolk, and sprinkle in enough water to form a dough. Gently form the dough into a ball, cover with plastic wrap, and refrigerate for 1 hour.

Preheat the oven to 375°F (190°C). Roll out the pastry on a lightly floured surface, and ease it into an 8-inch (20-cm) flan pan. Prick with a fork, and line with a sheet of parchment weighed down with dried beans. Bake for 10-12 minutes, until barely golden. Remove from the oven, and set aside to cool.

Distribute the cheese over the bottom of the baked tart shell, and then arrange the tomatoes in concentric circles over top. Tuck the olives, basil leaves, and garlic in around the tomatoes, and drizzle with the olive oil and vinegar. Season with the salt and pepper. Bake for 40-45 minutes. Remove from the oven, and allow to cool for 10 minutes before serving.

Oven-Roasted Ratatouille

SERVES 6-8

Tomatoes are the foundation of this classic French stew. Instead of cooking it on the stovetop, I like to roast the vegetables in the oven, which helps them to retain their shape as well as giving them a superb flavour and texture. You can serve this hot or at room temperature, and you'll want lots of good bread to sop up the juices.

2 lb	cherry tomatoes	1 kg
1	large red onion, sliced thickly	1
2	zucchini, cut in 1-inch (2.5-cm) cubes	2
1	large eggplant, cut in 1-inch (2.5-cm) cubes	1
3	sweet peppers, seeded and cut in 1-inch (2.5-cm) pieces	3
4-6	garlic cloves, peeled	4-6
1/2 cup	chopped fresh basil	125 ml
3	sprigs fresh thyme, cut in half	3
2 Tbsp	chopped fresh oregano	25 ml
6 Tbsp	olive oil	90 ml
2 Tbsp	balsamic vinegar	25 ml
	salt and freshly ground black pepper	

Preheat the oven to 475°F (240°C), and set the oven rack to the highest position.

Arrange the vegetables in a very large, shallow roasting pan, tucking the garlic cloves and fresh herbs in and around them. Combine the olive oil and vinegar, and drizzle over the vegetables. Season liberally with salt and black pepper, and bake for 30-40 minutes, turning the vegetables occasionally. They should be slightly browned and very soft. Transfer to a serving platter, and allow to cool slightly before serving.

Tomatoes Stuffed with Spicy Rice and Pine Nuts

SERVES 4-8

This recipe will stuff 8 large tomatoes. Serve 1 or 2 per person, depending on whether it's a main course or a starter.

3 Tbsp	olive oil	40 ml
1	large sweet onion, chopped finely	1
2	garlic cloves, chopped finely	2
1 tsp	toasted coriander seeds, crushed	5 ml
1/2 tsp	ground cumin	2 ml
1/2 tsp	ground turmeric	2 ml
1/2 tsp	paprika	2 ml
1/2 tsp	salt	2 ml
1/2 tsp	freshly ground black pepper	2 ml
1 cup	white rice	250 ml
1 1/2 cups	hot vegetable stock	375 ml
1/2 cup	feta cheese, crumbled	125 ml
1/4 cup	raisins	50 ml
1/2 cup	toasted pine nuts	125 ml
	zest and juice of 1 lemon	
8	large beefsteak tomatoes	8
2 tsp	sugar	5 ml

Heat 2 tablespoons of oil in a large skillet, and sauté the onion and garlic for 5 minutes, until softened but not browned. Stir in the spices, salt, and pepper, and cook for 1 minute. Add the rice, and stir well to coat with oil. Pour in the hot stock, bring to a simmer, cover, and cook for 20 minutes, until the rice is tender and the liquid is absorbed. Remove from the heat, and stir in the feta, raisins, pine nuts, and lemon zest and juice.

Preheat the oven to 350°F (180°C). Slice the tops off the tomatoes, reserving the "lids," and scoop out the seeds and core. Place the tomatoes in a large roasting pan, and sprinkle a pinch of sugar inside each one. Divide the rice stuffing among the tomatoes, and top with the reserved lids. Drizzle with the olive oil, and bake for 25-30 minutes. Serve hot or cold.

Fresh and Sun-Dried Tomato Sauce

SERVES 4

3 Tbsp	olive oil	40 ml
1	onion, chopped finely	1
1	garlic clove, chopped finely	1
2	celery ribs, trimmed and chopped finely	2
1 lb	fresh tomatoes, skinned, seeded, and chopped coarsely	500 g
4 oz	sun-dried tomatoes in oil, drained and chopped finely	125 g
1/2 cup	dry white wine	125 ml
4 oz	goat's cheese, cubed	125 g
8	large black olives, halved	8
1/4 cup	chopped fresh flat-leafed parsley	50 ml
	salt and freshly ground black pepper	

IN THE MICROWAVE
In a microwave-safe casserole, mix the oil, onion, garlic, and celery, and cook on high for 2-4 minutes, stirring once. Add the fresh and sun-dried tomatoes and the wine, and cook 3-5 minutes, stirring once. Then cover and cook on medium (50%) for 8-10 minutes. Stir in goat's cheese and olives, and season to taste with salt and pepper. Allow to stand until the cheese is melted. Garnish with parsley, and serve.

Heat the oil in a large saucepan or skillet and sauté the onion, garlic, and celery for about 8 minutes, until softened but not browned. Add the fresh and dried tomatoes and white wine. Simmer for 30 minutes, stirring occasionally. Stir in the goat's cheese and olives, until the cheese melts. Season to taste with salt and pepper, and add the parsley just before serving with fresh cooked pasta.

Turnips

Turnips are packed full of vitamin C.

A sweet young turnip is a welcome guest at my dinner table any time. However, turnips have a rather rustic reputation. Some people still associate them with cattle fodder (which they are), forgetting or never knowing just how delicious they can be. North Americans also tend to get them mixed up with rutabagas, which are also tasty but not the same vegetable. Turnips are generally smaller and creamier in texture and have smooth, white skin tinged with green. Very young turnips and French turnips, or navets, can be eaten raw.

Turnips are available year-round, but unlike rutabagas, which benefit from the cold growing season, the best ones are found in spring and fall, perhaps with their leafy green tops still attached; these can be braised or boiled and served with a bit of butter. Choose smaller turnips, heavy for their size, with smooth, unblemished skins. If the turnip has its greens, or if you're buying turnips for their greens, make sure they are fresh and brightly coloured.

Turnips don't have the extended shelf-life that rutabagas enjoy, but they will keep well for 2-3 weeks when wrapped in plastic and refrigerated. Remove any greens before storing, and use these within a day or two. Very young turnips shouldn't need peeling, as the skin is thin and tender. Simply scrub them before using. I like to braise small whole turnips in chicken stock, with a little butter and port for good measure. Larger turnips can be treated the same way, once they are peeled and sliced. Sauté sliced turnips in butter and sugar to caramelize them, and serve with bacon and eggs. Or roast them with other root vegetables, on their own or around a roast of meat.

Don't shy away from this wonderful root. Invite a few turnips for dinner, and while you're at it, ask a rutabaga along for the ride.

TURNIP SALAD? YOU BET! *Turnips can be chopped or grated and added raw to a salad — try them in place of shredded cabbage in a slaw.*

Steam or boil whole turnips until just tender, and blanch in cold water. Grate, dress with a creamy vinaigrette, and let the salad rest for a while to allow the flavours to blend.

Turnips Braised in Cider and Honey

SERVES 4

2 lb	turnips	1 kg
1 Tbsp	butter	15 ml
1 cup	apple cider	250 ml
1 Tbsp	honey	15 ml
	salt and freshly ground black pepper	

If you're using baby turnips, leave a short stem on each, and don't bother peeling them. Large turnips should be peeled and chopped in 1/2-inch (1-cm) cubes or wedges.

Melt the butter in a skillet or large frying pan, and stir in the turnips to coat them all over. Pour in the cider, and stir in the honey and a sprinkling of salt. Bring to a simmer, cover, reduce the heat, and cook for 15 minutes, until just tender. Remove the lid, and increase the heat. Toss or stir the turnips, until the liquid has reduced to a syrupy glaze. Season with pepper, and serve at once.

Turnip and Cranberry Salad

SERVES 4

This salad makes a flavourful accompaniment to baked ham, or you could garnish it with crisply fried pancetta.

1 lb	small turnips, scrubbed and grated coarsely	1 kg
2	carrots, peeled and grated	2
3	ribs celery, chopped finely	3
2	scallions, chopped finely	2
1/4 cup	dried cranberries	50 ml
	fresh mint sprigs, to garnish	

For the dressing:

2 Tbsp	sherry vinegar	25 ml
1 Tbsp	coarse-grained prepared mustard	15 ml
1 tsp	sugar	5 ml
1/2 cup	vegetable oil	125 ml
3 Tbsp	sour cream	40 ml
3 Tbsp	heavy cream	40 ml
	salt and freshly ground black pepper, to taste	

To make the dressing: Whisk together the vinegar, mustard, sugar, and vegetable oil in a large bowl. When well blended, beat in the sour cream and heavy cream. Season to taste with salt and pepper.

Toss the salad ingredients with the dressing until mixed and coated. Garnish with sprigs of fresh mint, and chill until ready to serve.

MICROWAVED TURNIPS
Peel and cube 1 pound (500 g) turnips. Place in a 1 1/2-quart (1.5-L) microwave-safe casserole with 3 Tbsp (40 ml) water and 1/4 tsp (1 ml) salt. Cover and cook on high for 7-9 minutes, and let stand, covered, for 3 minutes.

Watercress

As its name suggests, watercress is a cress that grows in water. Cresses belong to the mustard family, and their name comes from the Greek word *grastis*, meaning "green fodder." Other cresses include winter cress, curly cress, and garden cress, but only watercress is commonly available. It grows wild along the banks of fast-flowing rivers, and it is now cultivated worldwide. It has a clean, peppery flavour that can perk up a green salad; it makes a gorgeous soup; and in a classic Béarnaise sauce it goes beautifully with red meat, fish, and eggs.

You'll usually find watercress in amongst the herbs, although now that supermarkets are carrying wider varieties of salad greens it may be tucked in with the lettuces. Look for compact bunches of shiny, deep green leaves, with few thick stems. You can store watercress in water like cut flowers, or trim the thick stems and refrigerate the leaves, wrapped in plastic. As with other delicate salad leaves, watercress is perishable and should be used within a day or two of purchase. It should be very clean already, but you can rinse the leaves in cool water and pat dry.

Because they have such a pungent flavour, cresses are usually classified as herbs, since we tend to use them sparingly. However, watercress is the mildest of the cresses and can be treated as you would other robust greens such as arugula, bearing in mind that when cooked it loses some of its bite. I tend to add it to sauces and soups just before serving, so as not to sacrifice that characteristic sharpness.

MACHO WATERCRESS
I'm a fan of watercress sandwiches, not the dainty, crustless variety served to very thin ladies at garden parties, but lots of green leaves stuffed between thick slabs of buttered crusty bread.

Watercress Sauce

MAKES 1 1/2 CUPS (375 ML)

1	small garlic clove, peeled	1
2	egg yolks	2
1 tsp	dry mustard	5 ml
1 tsp	salt	5 ml
1/4 tsp	freshly ground black pepper	1 ml
1 cup	vegetable oil	250 ml
2 tsp	freshly squeezed lemon juice	10 ml
1 tsp	white wine vinegar	5 ml
1 cup	watercress leaves, rinsed and dried	250 ml

This delicately flavoured sauce is excellent with salmon, poached eggs, angel hair pasta, new potatoes, or any lightly steamed green vegetable.

Combine the garlic clove, egg yolks, mustard, salt, and pepper in a blender or food processor, and pulse to form a paste. Gradually add the vegetable oil while continuing to pulse, and then add the lemon juice, wine vinegar, and watercress leaves. Pulse until the leaves are chopped finely. Serve at once, or refrigerate and whisk well with a tablespoon of water before using.

Not-So-Dainty Egg and Watercress Sandwiches

SERVES 2

4	hard-boiled eggs, peeled and chopped finely	4
1/4 cup	mayonnaise	50 ml
1/2 cup	watercress leaves, chopped coarsely	125 ml
1 Tbsp	finely chopped celery	15 ml
	a generous squeeze of lemon juice	
	salt and paprika	

These are not the barely-there dainties served at tea with the duchess. Egg salad spiked with peppery watercress is spooned onto toasted Italian bread seasoned with garlic and olive oil.

For the toast:

4	thick slices Italian bread	4
1	garlic clove, peeled and halved	1
1 Tbsp	olive oil	15 ml

Combine the salad ingredients in a bowl, and mix well. Refrigerate if not using immediately.

Toast the bread, and rub with the cut sides of the garlic clove. Drizzle with the olive oil. Divide the egg and watercress salad among all four slices, serving the sandwiches open-faced.

Yams (Ñame)

More than a few Frootique customers asking for yams are treated to a lesson on the difference between a yam and a sweet potato, which is often what they actually want. In fact some people have been confusing the two for such a long time that they won't believe me until I show them the tubers side by side. There's no mistaking the shaggy, dark, bark-covered yam for its smooth-skinned namesake. And truth be told, the two aren't even related botanically — the yam came from Africa, while the sweet potato originated in South America. The confusion started 300 years ago when transported slaves from West Africa used the word *nama*, or *nyama*, to describe the American sweet potato, the vegetable most similar to their indigenous tuber. And before you leap to the wrong conclusion, the yam's other common moniker, *ñame*, comes from the Spanish, who translated the West African name as *igname*.

Few people outside of North America would make the yam/sweet potato mistake, because from Africa to Latin America, India to the Caribbean, and Asia to the South Pacific, yams have long been a staple. And although cookbooks frequently suggest using the yam and the sweet potato interchangeably, the yam has a white or yellow flesh, crisp rather than mealy, and its flavour is not sweet so much as mildly nutty. The aggressive spices and seasonings of ethnic cuisines are well-suited to the relatively bland taste of the yam.

Yams are available year-round and can vary wildly in shape — looking like anything from a slightly deviant potato to an extraterrestrial creature — as well as size. You're unlikely to find really huge ones in your super-market, since the six-man variety is not easily transported, six men being needed to carry it. Generally speaking, choose a firm yam that weighs in under a pound (500 g) and has an unwrinkled skin. The skin will be rough, sometimes with small, whisker-like roots. If you're not quite sure of your choice, ask the grocer to cut one open, or split the skin with your fingernail. The flesh should be smooth and juicy.

Yams will keep for at least a week when stored in a cool, dry place. A cut yam will seal itself, forming a scar over the exposed skin which can be removed when you use the rest of the tuber. To prepare for cooking, chop yams in large pieces and peel them thickly. Submerge peeled pieces in a bowl of cold water acidulated with a tablespoon of lemon juice to prevent discoloration. You can boil, bake, or fry yams, although, unlike sweet potatoes, plain yams need something more than butter and salt to liven them up. Serve them with salsa or a garlicky dressing.

FRIED YAMS

Before frying yams, parboil them until barely tender, and chop them in finger-sized pieces. Fry them in plenty of olive oil, to which you can add chopped garlic and a few drops of chili oil. Season generously with chopped fresh cilantro, salt, and pepper. Serve with a spicy sauce or a bowl of aïoli for a real feast.

Yams Baked with Citrus Butter

SERVES 4

2 lb	yams, peeled and cut in 1-inch (2.5-cm) cubes	1 kg
2 Tbsp	olive oil	25 ml
1/4 tsp	chili powder	1 ml

1/3 cup	butter	80 ml
	zest and juice of 1/2 lime	
2 Tbsp	water	25 ml
1 Tbsp	finely chopped fresh cilantro	15 ml
	salt and freshly ground black pepper	

Preheat the oven to 375°F (190°C).

Toss the yams with the olive oil in a shallow roasting pan. Season with chili powder, salt, and pepper. Bake for 45 minutes, giving the pan an occasional shake to cook the yams evenly. Meanwhile, melt the butter, and stir in the lemon juice, water, and cilantro. Pour the mixture into the pan with the yams, shake the pan, and bake for 15 minutes more, until the liquid has evaporated and the yams are tender. Serve hot.

Hearty Yam Soup

SERVES 6

This is a thick soup, flavoured with bacon and allspice. You can add other vegetables you have on hand, such as potatoes, turnips, or squash.

1 Tbsp	olive oil	15 ml
8	strips bacon, chopped coarsely	8
1	onion, chopped coarsely	1
2	celery ribs, chopped coarsely	2
2 lb	yam, peeled and chopped in 1/2-inch (1-cm) cubes	1 kg
1 tsp	fennel seed, crushed	5 ml
4 cups	ham or chicken stock	1 L
	salt and freshly ground black pepper	
	chopped celery leaves, to garnish	

Heat the olive oil in a large saucepan, and sauté the bacon and onion for 5 minutes. Add the chopped celery, yam, and fennel seeds, and stir to coat. Reduce the heat to minimum, cover, and leave for 15 minutes to allow the vegetables to "sweat" and release their flavour. Add the stock, season with salt and pepper, and bring to a boil. Reduce the heat, and simmer for about 20 minutes, until the yam is tender. Serve hot, garnished with a few chopped celery leaves.

IN THE MICROWAVE
Toss the yams and the olive oil together in a 2-quart (2-L) microwave-safe casserole. Cover and cook on high for 6-8 minutes, stirring once. Sprinkle with chili powder, dot with butter, and add the lime juice, cilantro, and salt and pepper. Cover and cook for 4-6 minutes more, or until tender, stirring once. Let stand, covered, for 3 minutes before serving.

IN THE MICROWAVE
In a 2-quart (2-L) casserole, cook the bacon on high for 6-8 minutes, until lightly browned. Drain, add the onion, cover, and cook for 2 minutes, stirring once. Add the celery, yams, fennel seed, and 1/4 cup (50 ml) of the stock. Cover and cook on high for 10-12 minutes, or until the vegetables are tender, stirring once. Stir in the remaining stock, season to taste with salt and pepper, and cook, uncovered, on high for 10-12 minutes, stirring twice, until hot. Garnish with chopped celery leaves, and serve.

Zucchini and Other Summer Squash

Zucchini is the most familiar summer squash. People with vegetable gardens are well-acquainted with zucchini — as are their families, friends, and neighbours, who are on the receiving end of the plant's overwhelming bounty. Most of us groan at the sight of zucchini by early September, although a month later we're happy enough to see them in the supermarket and glad that they're available all winter long. Other summer squash, which are distinguished from their winter elders (see pages 135-139) by their tender, digestible skins and succulent flesh, include the crookneck and the pattypan squash.

Because we've grown so used to them, it is odd to realize that zucchini have been a familiar sight to most North Americans for only about 30 years. Before that, you might have seen them at Italian specialty markets, or on a holiday in the Mediterranean, where they have long been prized for their versatility and delicate flavour. In North America we call them zucchini — meaning small gourds — because they arrived with Italian immigrants, while the Brits still know them by their French name, *courgette* — "small marrow" — which is basically what they are.

There are numerous varieties of zucchini, but the two most commonly available are the Italian-style zucchini — slender, sometimes ridged, and either straight or slightly curved, with glossy, mottled green skin — and the Middle Eastern variety, which is paler in colour and more blocky in shape. The Italian ones have a faintly nutty flavour, and the Middle Eastern are sweeter. The bright yellow zucchini has slightly firmer flesh than the green variety but is otherwise similar.

The crookneck squash looks like a goose, with a fat bottom and a long neck, bent just before the stem; it is bright yellow with bumpy skin. Pattypan squash are round and flat with a scalloped edge. Both are seasonal, available from June through August, and both have a much sweeter flavour than zucchini.

Like all summer squash, zucchini should feel firm, with smooth skin and no blemishes or soft spots; the smaller the squash, the more tender its flesh. Zucchini will keep for at least a week on a refrigerator shelf. It's easy to prepare — simply rinse well, trim away the stem, if necessary, and slice it or cut it in fingers to use in salad or eat with a dip. Cooked zucchini makes a wonderful side dish. Once you've had your fill of it by itself, try adding it to casseroles, gratins, and soups, or scrape out the seeds and stuff and bake the big ones. All summer squash go particularly well with other summer vegetables such as tomatoes, sweet peppers, eggplants, garlic, and fresh herbs, which is why they turn up in ratatouilles. Zucchini also can be grated and used in cakes and breads, adding moisture and usually reducing the fat.

Don't lock your door and close the curtains the next time you see your neighbours coming with baskets of zucchini. Accept the gift with glee, and invite them in for dinner.

HOW TO COOK ZUCCHINI
The best way to cook zucchini is quickly, and with as little liquid as possible.

Slice zucchini in rounds or strips, or leave very small ones whole. Steamed lightly or sautéed in butter, zucchini makes a delicious side dish, needing nothing more than a squeeze of lemon juice and some salt and pepper.

Larger zucchini can be sliced thickly, brushed with olive oil, seasoned, and thrown on the grill.

Zucchini Fritters with Tzatziki

SERVES 4

4	medium-sized zucchini	4
1	small onion	1
2	large eggs, beaten	2
3 Tbsp	all-purpose flour	40 ml
1/4 tsp	salt	1 ml
1/4 tsp	freshly ground black pepper	1 ml
2 Tbsp	finely chopped fresh mint	45 ml
	olive oil, for shallow-frying	

For the tzatziki:

1 cup	plain yogurt	250 ml
1/2	English cucumber, peeled and chopped finely	1/2
1	garlic clove, chopped finely	1
2 Tbsp	chopped fresh mint	25 ml
	salt, to taste	

Grate the zucchini and onion into a colander, allowing the liquid to drain away. Combine the eggs, flour, salt, pepper, and mint in a mixing bowl to form a smooth batter. Stir in the grated zucchini and onion.

Heat 2-3 tablespoons of oil in a large skillet over a medium heat, and drop the batter in by spoonfuls (you'll need to cook the fritters in batches). Fry for 1-2 minutes, and then turn and cook the other sides, until golden brown. Drain on paper towel, transfer to a serving platter, and keep warm while you cook the remaining batter.

To make the tzatziki: Combine the ingredients in a small bowl, and stir well.

Zucchini and Watercress Soup

SERVES 4-6

1 Tbsp	butter	15 ml
2	shallots, chopped finely	2
1	large potato, peeled and chopped finely	1
4	medium-sized zucchini, chopped coarsely	4
3 cups	hot chicken stock	375 ml

ZUCCHINI BLOSSOM TREATS
In produce markets, you can sometimes find very young zucchini with their blossoms still attached, or maybe you know a gardener trying to hold back the zucchini tide. Gently stuff blossoms with a mixture of soft or grated cheese, garlic, and herbs, twist the petals together at the top, and then bake them or dip them in batter and fry them to make delectable fritters.

Blossoms won't last for more than a day in the refrigerator, so use them immediately.

The mild favour of zucchini is spiked with peppery watercress, creating a delicious soup that can be enjoyed hot or cold. If you wish, you can substitute milk for the cream or increase the amount of stock and halve the cream.

In a covered 2-quart (2-L) casserole, cook the butter and shallots for 1 minute. Stir in the potato and zucchini and 1 cup (250 ml) of the stock. Cover and cook on high for 6-8 minutes, until the vegetables are tender, stirring once. Add the remaining stock and lemon juice, and cook on high for about 2 minutes, until hot.

Add the watercress, and purée in batches until smooth. Return to the casserole, add the cream, and heat on high for 2-3 minutes, until the soup is hot but not boiling. Season with salt and pepper, and serve hot or cold, garnished with watercress.

1 Tbsp	lemon juice	15 ml
1/2 cup	watercress, chopped coarsely	125 ml
1 cup	cream	250 ml
	salt and freshly ground black pepper	
	a few watercress leaves, for garnish	

Melt the butter in a large saucepan, and sauté the shallots for 3-4 minutes, until softened. Stir in the potato and zucchini, and cook for 5 minutes longer. Pour in the stock and lemon juice, and simmer for 15-20 minutes. Add the chopped watercress, and transfer the soup to a food processor or blender. Purée in batches until smooth. Return the soup to the saucepan, and stir in the cream. Heat through gently, and season with salt and pepper. Serve hot, or refrigerate and serve chilled, garnished with watercress leaves.

Baked Zucchini Stuffed with Feta and Mint

SERVES 4

This makes a super accompaniment to roast lamb.

4	medium-sized zucchini	4
3 Tbsp	olive oil	40 ml
2	shallots, chopped finely	2
1	garlic clove, chopped finely	1
1/2 cup	fresh bread crumbs	125 ml
1 cup	feta cheese, crumbled	250 ml
3 Tbsp	chopped fresh mint	40 ml
	freshly ground black pepper	

Preheat the oven to 400°F (200°C).

Halve the zucchinis lengthways, and scrape out the flesh, leaving a 1/4-inch (5-mm) shell. Chop the flesh, and squeeze or drain most of the liquid from it. Heat 2 tablespoons of olive oil in a skillet, and sauté the shallot and garlic for 3 minutes, until softened. Add the drained zucchini, and cook for 3 minutes more. Remove from the heat, and stir in the bread crumbs, feta, and mint. Season to taste with pepper; the feta is probably salty enough to make additional salt unnecessary.

Place the zucchini shells in a shallow baking dish, and divide the filling among them, packing it in fairly firmly. Add a few tablespoons of water to the dish, and drizzle the remaining tablespoon of olive oil over the zucchini. Bake for 30 minutes, and let stand for 5 minutes before serving.

Herbs

Not that long ago, when a recipe called for almost anything other than parsley we would automatically reach into the cupboard for a small jar of dried leaves. These days, many recipes call for fresh herbs, and we tend to use them much more liberally than in the past. I'm a huge fan of cooking with fresh herbs, which can literally transform a ho-hum dish into something lively and memorable. While gardeners and rural dwellers may enjoy a vast variety of cultivated and wild herbs, I've included only those that are commonly available in supermarkets.

It is not always easy to know when a herb is a herb and when it is a vegetable. For culinary purposes, usually we think of herbs as flavouring or seasoning ingredients. They are often too pungent or strong-tasting to eat on their own, and because they generally are used in small quantities, they impart little if any nutritional value. As always, there are many exceptions to the rules, and one can argue that both tabbouleh and pesto use herbs as primary rather than secondary ingredients. On the other hand, salad greens such as arugula and watercress are used sparingly to accent or flavour other ingredients, but we consider them to be vegetables. What makes a herb a herb and not a spice is more easily defined: herbs, whether fresh or dried, are the leaves and stems of a plant, while spices are a plant's roots, seeds, or nuts. Thus, dill weed is a herb, and dill seed is a spice.

Fresh culinary herbs can be bought cut or sometimes potted in soil. The latter will obviously last longer, although even these are not intended to grow indefinitely. Simply snip or tear off the leaves as you need them, and keep the soil damp. Cut herbs with stems can be treated as fresh cut flowers, and placed in a vase of water for several days (after removing any elastic bands or twist-ties). Leaves also can be wrapped loosely in paper towel and stored in a perforated plastic bag in the refrigerator. These bags are available at most supermarkets; the perforations allow air to circulate, which helps to delay decomposition. You can just as easily snip a few holes in a plastic freezer bag.

The key to cooking with fresh herbs is to add them at the last minute, especially delicate leafy herbs, which will quickly lose their flavour and colour when cooked. On the other hand, herbs can also be used to infuse a stock, soup, or sauce with flavour. I like to add a sprig of mint to the cooking water when I boil potatoes and will toss in some dill when I'm poaching fish. Whenever I use herbs in a cooked dish, I save a few sprigs for garnish, which also adds a bit of last-minute zest.

While I encourage you to use fresh herbs wherever possible, as a general rule of thumb, you can replace any measure of finely chopped fresh herbs with a third the amount of dried herbs. Woody or more hardy herbs such as rosemary, bay, and oregano hold more flavour when dried than do delicate, leafy herbs like basil, cilantro, and dill. And don't expect dried herbs to last forever; if you can't remember the last time you bought dill flakes, chances are they're not doing much to flavour your beet salad!

Basil

I can still remember a time when more than half my friends thought of *Fawlty Towers* rather than pesto when they heard me talking about basil. Times have changed. Basil is one of the most popular herbs, with a growing number of varieties available. Sweet basil is used extensively in Italian cooking, while spicy basil is a fundamental herb in Thai cuisine. Basil's spicy-sweet aroma is very alluring, and it is not surprising that it's a common base note in perfumes.

Basil can be found in almost any supermarket; if it's not where you expect to find it, ask for it. If you're lucky you'll have more than one variety to choose from. Rub a leaf between your fingers to release the oils, and sniff to find out whether it has a sweet and citrusy or a spicy fragrance. Small-leaf basil, or bush basil, has an intense, clean aroma and sweet, lemon-like flavour. I like to throw a handful into a bowl of strawberries or fruit salad. Larger leaves will have less flavour, but they make a beautiful addition to leafy salads. Purple-leaf basil is pungent and spicy, a terrific last-second addition to Asian-style soups and stir-fries.

In any case, choose bright, fresh-looking leaves, and buy just as much as you need, as this delicate herb will not last long. Wrap basil loosely in paper towel before storing in a plastic bag in the refrigerator, where it should keep fresh for two or three days. Alternatively, consider buying a basil plant for your kitchen. Although they usually don't grow well indoors, the plant will survive longer than cut leaves, and you can pick fresh leaves as you need them.

Nowadays, a call for "Basil!" makes everyone think of pesto. Although I like to experiment with various combinations of herbs, true pesto is made with basil. Try stirring pesto into almost any soup or stew for a last-minute burst of flavour. Mash it with potatoes, or thin it with a little olive oil and drizzle over any steamed vegetables. You'll find you can hardly remember life before basil.

Basil is the most delicate of herbs and will soften and turn black if it is kept too cold, so try to find the least-cold place in your refrigerator for it.

Basic Pesto

MAKES 2 CUPS (500 ML)

You can substitute various combinations of herbs for the basil, but this recipe is for a true pesto.

3	garlic cloves, peeled	3
1/4 cup	toasted pine nuts	50 ml
2 cups	packed fresh basil leaves	500 ml
1/2 cup	virgin olive oil	125 ml
1/2 cup	grated parmesan cheese	125 ml
	salt and freshly ground black pepper	

INSTANT PESTO
Take advantage of summer's bumper basil crops to whip up a few batches of pesto. Drop it by spoonfuls into ice-cube trays and freeze. Transfer the cubes to a freezer bag or container, and use as needed.

SWEET POTATO CURRY
page141

**ZUCCHINI AND
WATERCRESS SOUP**
page156

SCALL
BASIL
page16

Combine the garlic and pine nuts in a food processor or blender. Pulse to form a coarse paste. Add the basil leaves with a little of the oil, and pulse until as smooth or coarse as you like. Add the remaining oil and the parmesan, and pulse to combine. Season to taste with salt and pepper. Refrigerate until using; it will keep for a week.

Scallops Wrapped in Basil and Prosciutto

SERVES 2

This makes a very quick, easy, and deliciously extravagant dinner for two. Serve these kebabs with Pesto Mashed Potatoes (see page 112) and a crisp green salad. You can easily increase the recipe to serve more people; you'll need 2 skewers per person. Soak bamboo skewers in water for 30 minutes before cooking, or use thin lengths of lemon grass to add extra flavour.

12	large fresh basil leaves	12
12	large scallops	12
12	slices prosciutto	12
12	cherry tomatoes	12
1 tsp	olive oil	5 ml
1 tsp	melted butter	5 ml

Roll a scallop in a basil leaf and then in a slice of prosciutto, securing the package with a skewer. Then slide a cherry tomato onto the skewer, follow with another wrapped scallop, and so on, ending up with 3 wrapped scallops and 3 tomatoes on each skewer.

Heat a griddle or large frying pan over a high heat, and brush lightly with the oil and melted butter. Cook the kebabs on each side for 2-3 minutes, until the prosciutto is browned and the scallops are cooked through. Serve at once.

Bay

Bay leaves have a distinguished history, culinary and otherwise. Ceremonial wreaths of these fragrant leaves were bestowed upon the heads of ancient Greek and Roman athletes, warriors, and poets. And bay leaves have long been one of the three herbs in a classic *bouquet garni*, used to flavour stocks and casseroles. More frequently available and used in their dried state, bay leaves have an intense woodsy aroma and spicy flavour when they're fresh. Unlike many other herbs, bay leaves are always cooked, and they're usually removed before serving.

If you happen upon fresh bay leaves, buy some. Although you're unlikely to use them all when still fresh, they will probably remain more aromatic over a longer period of time than any dried ones you have in your cupboard. A bay tree makes an amazing house plant and supplies your kitchen at the same time.

Aside from using bay in marinades, soups, or stews, try adding a leaf to the water when cooking potatoes, rice, or pasta. Use fresh leaves sparingly, as the aroma may infuse itself more stridently than you expect.

Winter Vegetable Stew

3 Tbsps	olive oil	40 ml
8	pearl onions or small shallots, peeled	8
2	garlic cloves, chopped finely	2
2-3	bay leaves, chopped very finely	2-3
1	red finger hot pepper, seeded and chopped finely	1
1/2 Tbsp	paprika	7 ml
1 lb	potatoes, cut in 1-inch (2.5-cm) cubes	500 g
3	carrots, peeled and sliced in 1/2-inch (1-cm) rounds	3
3	turnips, peeled and chopped in 1/2-inch (1-cm) cubes	3
1	rutabaga, peeled and chopped in 1-inch (2.5-cm) cubes	1
1	tart apple, peeled, cored, and chopped in 1-inch (2.5-cm) cubes	1
3	tomatoes, chopped coarsely	3
2 tsp	sugar	10 ml
2 cups	dry red wine	500 ml
1 cup	water	250 ml
	salt and freshly ground black pepper	
	sour cream or plain yogurt, to garnish	

Finely chopped bay leaves softened with garlic and onions lend a warm spiciness to winter roots.

BOUQUET GARNI
The classic herbs for a *bouquet garni* are bay, thyme, and parsley. Tie the stems of fresh herbs together, and drop them in your stew, soup, stock, fish poaching water, or casserole. Remove the bouquet after the herbs have imparted their wonderful flavour and aroma and before serving.

To make a *bouquet garni* from dried herbs, heap the ingredients on a square of cheesecloth, and tie the corners diagonally to make a neat bundle.

Preheat the oven to 350°F (180°C).

Heat the oil in an oven- and flameproof casserole dish or dutch oven. (Or you can use separate dishes for stovetop and oven.) Sauté the onions or shallots for 5 minutes. Add the garlic, bay leaves, hot pepper, and paprika, and cook for 3 minutes more. Add the vegetables and apple, stir to coat them with the oil and spices, and cook for a few minutes. Add the sugar, wine, water, and salt and pepper to taste

Cover and transfer to the oven. Bake for 1 hour, reduce the heat to 275°F (160°C), and bake for 1 hour longer. Remove from the oven, and allow to rest for 10 minutes before serving with a dollop of sour cream or plain yogurt.

Chives

Chives look like miniature scallions and in fact are a member of the *allium*, or onion, family. Their subtle sweet-onion flavour makes them a pleasant addition to scrambled eggs and omelettes as well as salads and soups. They can also be snipped with scissors and blended with soft butter as a mild alternative to garlic spread. Garlic chives, sometimes called Chinese chives, have flat, broad stems and a distinct garlic flavour. More robust than common chives, these are good in stir-fries and other spicy dishes, and they can be braised in a little butter and white wine and served as a side dish.

Chives are a favourite with gardeners as well as cooks, as the hardy perennial grows in grassy clumps with pretty mauve flower heads. If you're growing chives for the kitchen, you'll have to cut stems that aren't in bloom, since the flowering stems are much less flavourful and tender. On the other hand, chive blossoms are edible and make a colourful salad garnish, and fancy restaurants sometimes serve the flowers lightly battered and deep-fried.

There's no comparison between the flavour of fresh chives and that of the dried herb, and fresh chives are available year-round. Look for plump, sprightly bunches with no blemishes or wilted stems. You can sometimes find them with tiny, tightly closed flower buds, which indicate that the chives are young and sweet, though the stems of mature flower heads (whether in full bloom or not) will be tough. Store chives in a perforated plastic bag in the refrigerator for up to a week, snipping them from their root ends as needed.

Chive and Potato Filo Parcels

MAKES 16

Make these cork-shaped parcels small enough to enjoy as finger food, or make larger ones to serve alongside soup. Use whatever combination of herbs you like; here I've added basil to soften the sharper flavour of the chives.

4	sheets filo pastry	4
2-3 Tbsp	melted butter	25-40 ml

For the filling:

2 Tbsp	butter	25 ml
1/3-1/2 cup	milk	80-125 ml
2 cups	mashed potatoes	500 ml
1/2 cup	snipped fresh chives	125 ml
2 Tbsp	chopped fresh basil	25 ml
	salt and freshly ground black pepper	

Preheat the oven to 350°F (180°C), and lightly grease a baking sheet.

Heat the milk and butter until the butter melts, and then beat with the mashed potatoes. Stir in the herbs, and season with salt and pepper to taste.

Lay out a single sheet of filo pastry, covering the rest with a damp tea towel to keep them from drying out. Brush the sheet with melted butter, and use scissors or a sharp knife to cut it horizontally and then vertically to create 4 rectangles. Place a spoonful of the potato mixture near one end of each rectangle, and roll it up like a cigar, tucking the ends in and sealing the side edge with a little melted butter. Transfer to the baking pan, and brush with butter. Repeat with the remaining pastry and filling. Bake for 20 minutes, until golden and crisp. Cool for a few minutes, and serve warm or cold.

Thai Noodles with Bean Sprouts and Garlic Chives

SERVES 4

10 oz	dried rice noodles	300 g
1 Tbsp	freshly grated ginger	15 ml
2 Tbsp	soy sauce	25 ml
2 tsp	sesame oil	25 ml
2-3 tsp	Thai peanut sauce	10-15 ml
2 Tbsp	peanut or vegetable oil	25 ml
1	large garlic clove, crushed lightly	1
1	sweet onion, cut in wedges	1
4 oz	tofu, sliced thinly	125 g
1 cup	bean sprouts	250 ml
1	bunch garlic chives, snipped in 2-inch lengths	1
2 Tbsp	chopped fresh cilantro	25 ml
1 Tbsp	crushed peanuts, to garnish	15 ml

Stir-fries are all about preparation. Take the time to have the ingredients ready, and then shout, "Dinner's on!" just before you throw everything in the wok. In my house, this gives me about 5-10 minutes to actually cook the food and get it to the table.

Pre-soak the noodles according to package directions, rinse in cold water, and drain. Combine the ginger, soy sauce, sesame oil, and peanut sauce in a bowl, and toss the noodles in the mixture. Leave for 5 minutes, and then drain, reserving the liquid.

Heat the peanut or vegetable oil in a wok or stir-fry pan, and fry the garlic until golden. Remove and discard, and then stir-fry the onion wedges for 4-5 minutes, until softened and brown. Add the tofu, and stir-fry for 2-3 minutes, to brown. Stir in the drained noodles, and cook for 5 minutes more. Add the sprouts, chives, and cilantro, and drizzle with the reserved marinade. Toss to heat through, garnish with the crushed peanuts, and serve at once.

Cilantro

I love it, I love it, I love it! If I had to choose *the* herb of the 1990s, it would have to be cilantro. Ten years ago this zesty green beauty was still unknown to many people, and you'd have been hard-pressed to find it in your local supermarket. However, the increasing influence of both Asian and Latin American cooking has driven cilantro to stellar heights of popularity.

Cilantro is also known as coriander, although in North America this term usually refers to the dried seeds, which are used mainly as a curry and pickling spice. The plant's lacy green leaves somewhat resemble flat-leafed or Italian parsley, and cilantro is variously called Mexican or Chinese parsley. Whatever you call it, you can't mistake its pungent fragrance and grassy, citrus-like flavour. It is a primary ingredient in Mexican salsas and Indian chutneys, and it is featured in most Asian recipes, especially soups and stews.

Available year-round, cilantro should be bought and used as fresh as possible. Unlike parsley, which can keep well for some time, cilantro is extremely perishable. Choose bright green, leafy bunches with thin stems. Wrap the stems in moist paper towel, and place the whole bunch in a plastic bag in the refrigerator, where it should stay fresh for a few days. Don't rinse the leaves until just before using, and then spin or pat them dry.

Cilantro makes a super garnish for grilled fish or chicken, and a handful of leaves added to a broth or stew just before serving will add a delicious fragrance and flavour. You can't really make a salsa without cilantro, and there are few hot or spicy dishes that don't benefit from its tangy freshness. Cilantro leaves are generally used raw or added to cooked dishes at the last minute to release their flavour and aroma.

If you find cilantro with its roots attached, don't throw them out. Chop them finely, and sauté them alongside onions, garlic, and hot peppers when cooking spicy dishes.

HOW TO KEEP
CILANTRO FRESH
Buy cilantro with its roots still attached if you can, and treat it the way florists treat cut flowers. Store it upright in a vase of water in the refrigerator. Put a plastic bag over the leaves so they won't dry out, and rinse them and pat them dry just before using.

Citrus Salad with Cilantro and Coconut Dressing

SERVES 6

This fruit salad has an unusual spicy-sweet dressing. You can use regular or low-fat coconut milk, but make sure it is unsweetened.

4	oranges, tangerines, and/or satsumas, peeled	4
1	sweet grapefruit, peeled	1
1 cup	chopped fresh pineapple	250 ml
2	firm bananas, peeled and sliced	2
1/2 cup	chopped fresh cilantro	125 ml

For the dressing:

1 cup	unsweetened coconut milk	250 ml
2 Tbsp	honey	25 ml
1 tsp	toasted coriander seeds, crushed	5 ml
	zest and juice of 1/2 lemon	

Divide the oranges and grapefruit into segments. Separate the flesh from the membranes using a sharp knife, and catch any juices over a large bowl. Cut the segments into bite-sized pieces, and set aside. In the bowl with the citrus juices, whisk the dressing ingredients together, and then fold in the fruit and cilantro. Refrigerate until serving.

Grilled Salmon with Hot Pepper and Cilantro Yogurt Sauce

SERVES 4

You can substitute any other fish fillets for the salmon in this quick and easy dish. Save a few cilantro sprigs for garnish.

4	salmon fillets	4
2	shallots, chopped finely	2
1-2	green or red finger hot peppers, seeded and chopped finely	1-2
3 Tbsp	chopped fresh cilantro	40 ml
1 Tbsp	freshly squeezed lime juice	15 ml
1/2 cup	plain yogurt	125 ml
	salt and freshly ground black pepper	

Preheat the broiler.

Rinse the salmon fillets, pat them dry, and arrange them in an ovenproof dish. Beat together the remaining ingredients, and spread the mixture over the fish. Place the dish on the second-highest oven rack, and cook for 8-10 minutes, until the fish flakes when prodded with a fork and the yogurt sauce is beginning to brown.

IN THE MICROWAVE
The microwave will cook this dish to perfection, though it doesn't give a grilled effect. Arrange the salmon fillets in a shallow microwave-safe dish, cover with vented plastic wrap, and cook on high for 2 minutes. Peel back the plastic, and spread the mixture of remaining ingredients over the salmon. Replace the plastic wrap, and cook for 5-6 minutes more, until the fish flakes. Let stand, covered, for 2-3 minutes before serving.

Dill

Even the most inexperienced cook can identify the fragrance of the herb that flavours the ubiquitous pickle. Dill is one of the prettiest herbs around — with its slender stems and lacy green fronds — and one of the most common, used by "plain" cooks all over the world. Scandinavians are particularly fond of dill, perhaps because it grows well even in harsh climates, and its seeds are as useful as its leaves for flavouring everything from fish, poultry, and vegetables to baked goods.

Fresh dill is vastly more flavourful than the dried herb and has a distinctive licorice-like flavour, with a hint of celery and parsley. Because it is so easily available, I would never buy dried dill, and I'd rather substitute dill seed and fresh parsley or even celery leaves if I had no fresh dill on hand.

When buying dill, choose sprightly green stems and leaves, avoiding any that are pale or limp. Wrap them loosely in paper towel, store in a plastic bag in the refrigerator, and use within four or five days. Snip the leaves and tiny stems from the larger stems with scissors. The stems can be chopped finely and added to soups and stocks. I like to throw a sprig or two of dill in the water when cooking potatoes or carrots, and then toss the cooked vegetables with fresh snipped leaves. The same thing can be done when poaching fish. And don't forget dill when it comes to salads. Toss the feathery sprigs in with green salads, sliced tomatoes, beets — almost any salad vegetable you can think of.

Beet Salad with Dill

SERVES 4

Scandinavians combine beets and dill in almost every dish imaginable. This simple salad demonstrates why this marriage is made in heaven.

2 lb	very small beets, trimmed and scrubbed	1 kg
1/2 cup	sour cream	125 ml
1/2 cup	plain yogurt	125 ml
2 Tbsp	freshly squeezed lemon juice	25 ml
1/4 cup	snipped fresh dill	50 ml
1 tsp	prepared horseradish	5 ml
	salt and freshly ground black pepper	

Cover the beets with cold water, and bring to the boil. Cook for 10-12 minutes, until just tender. Drain, blanch in cold water, and slice thinly.

Combine the sour cream, yogurt, lemon juice, dill, and horseradish in a large bowl. Season to taste with salt and pepper. Fold the sliced beets into the dressing, and refrigerate for at least 2 hours, until chilled.

Potato and Dill Casserole

SERVES 6-8

3 lb	potatoes, peeled and quartered	1.5 kg
3	shallots, peeled and halved	3
1/4 cup	butter	50 ml
1 cup	grated white cheddar cheese	250 ml
2	eggs, beaten	2
1/4 cup	chopped fresh dill	50 ml
1 tsp	caraway seeds	5 ml
	salt and freshly ground black pepper	

Dill adds great flavour to any potato dish. Make this one ahead and refrigerate until you want to bake it.

Bring a large pot of lightly salted water to the boil, and cook the potatoes and shallots for 20-30 minutes, until tender. Drain well, and mash with the butter and three-quarters of the cheese. Beat in the eggs and dill, and season to taste with salt and pepper.

Meanwhile, preheat the oven to 350°F (180°C), and lightly butter a casserole dish. Transfer the mashed potato mixture into the dish, and use a fork to rough up the surface. Sprinkle with the remaining cheese and caraway seeds, cover, and bake for 30 minutes. Remove the lid, and bake for 10-15 minutes longer, until golden brown. Serve hot.

Lemon Grass

Lemon grass is relatively new to the North American scene. We can find it in our supermarkets thanks to the rise in popularity of Southeast Asian foods, especially Thai, Malaysian, and Indonesian. As its name suggests, lemon grass resembles coarse, heavy grass, and it has a subtle sweet-and-sour citrus flavour which provides balance to hot curry spices.

Fresh lemon grass is sold in single stems, anywhere from six inches to two feet (15-60 cm) long. The outer leaves, coarse and dry but very aromatic, can be used to flavour soups and stocks. They should be removed, like bay leaves, before serving. Only the innermost tender heart of the lemon grass is chopped finely and used like a spring onion, adding flavour to everything from curries to stir-fries, sauces, marinades, and salad dressings. Choose short, fresh-looking green stems with a pungent lemon-lime aroma. Wrap them in foil or plastic and refrigerate for up to two weeks.

Stalks of lemon grass make excellent skewers that impart a delicious flavour to kebabs.

A trick for getting the most aroma and taste from lemon grass is to bruise the leaves by crushing them with the flat blade of a knife before chopping them.

Don't reserve lemon grass for cooking. Steep it in boiling water, add honey to sweeten, and you have a delicious hot drink. Malaysian women bathe in lemon grass water after childbirth, a pleasure I can't recommend on the basis of experience!

Lemon Grass Vinaigrette

MAKES ABOUT 1 CUP (250 ML)

This vinaigrette is quick to make, although it must be steeped overnight to let the flavours develop. Serve it over a salad of grilled chicken, mango slices, and tender greens. Remember to remove the tough outer leaves of the lemon grass.

1/3 cup	coarsely chopped lemon grass	80 ml
1	red finger hot pepper, chopped	1
3/4 cup	vegetable oil	125 ml
3 Tbsp	freshly squeezed lime juice	40 ml
3 tsp	soy sauce	15 ml
2 tsp	honey	10 ml

Combine the lemon grass and hot pepper in a food processor or blender, and pulse to chop them very finely. Add the oil, and pulse to combine. Transfer to a small bowl, cover, and leave to marinate overnight. The next day, strain the oil through a fine sieve, and discard the pulp. Mix the flavoured oil with the remaining ingredients, and whisk until blended.

Lemon Grass, Rice, and Chicken Coconut Soup

SERVES 4-6

6 cups	chicken stock	1.5 L
1/2 cup	Thai fragrant or jasmine rice	125 ml
2	boneless, skinless chicken thighs	2
2	6-inch (15-cm) stalks lemon grass, peeled and bruised	2
1 inch	fresh ginger, peeled and sliced very thinly	2.5 cm
3	shallots, peeled and sliced thinly	3
1	fresh green finger hot pepper, chopped finely	1
1/2 cup	unsweetened coconut milk	125 ml
2 Tbsp	freshly squeezed lemon juice	25 ml
2 Tbsp	chopped fresh cilantro	25 ml

Combine the stock, rice, chicken thighs, lemon grass, sliced ginger, shallots, and hot pepper in a saucepan, and bring to a boil. Reduce the heat, and simmer for 15 minutes. Remove the chicken thighs, and slice them thinly. Bring the soup back to a simmer, cover, and cook for 5 minutes more, until the rice is tender. Remove and discard the lemon grass. Stir in the sliced chicken, lemon juice, and coconut milk, and heat gently. Garnish with the cilantro, and serve hot.

Mint

Everyone who brushes their teeth will be familiar with the taste of mint, which is by far the most popular flavouring ingredient in toothpaste. The Elizabethans also valued mint for its teeth-whitening and breath-freshening properties. Long before them, the Romans believed in the stimulating qualities of the fresh herb and showered their dinner guests with mint leaves to encourage hearty appetites. We still use mint in a bewildering array of cosmetic and medicinal products, as well as in the kitchen. Mint is used to flavour tea, candy, liqueurs, and cough medicines, and its fragrance graces everything from shampoo to air fresheners.

There are any number of mint varieties, including spearmint, peppermint, and orange mint. This is definitely a herb that you want to get between your teeth as well as under your nose to see if it appeals before buying. Spearmint is the most commonly used variety in cooking, and it is also used to make mint juleps, teas, sauces, and jellies. Any cuisine that features lamb makes use of mint in cooking, but it is also good with fish and poultry, as well as with vegetables. Peas, potatoes, carrots, cucumbers, and tomatoes all have an affinity with mint. Add a few leaves to the cooking water, and then chop some more into melted butter to season simply prepared vegetables. Combine chopped mint with plain yogurt to serve as a cooling sauce with spicy dishes, or add whole leaves to balance a salad of bitter or tangy greens. And if you forget your toothbrush, chew on a mint leaf before you greet your loved one with a kiss.

Minted Lemon Curd

MAKES 1 CUP (250 ML)

If you've never had fresh lemon curd, you're in for a treat. You can spread it on toast or between cake layers, or use it instead of jam to make tartlets.

	zest and juice of 2 large lemons	
2/3 cup	sugar	150 ml
3	large eggs, beaten	3
1/2 cup	unsalted butter, cubed	125 ml
1/4 cup	lightly packed fresh mint leaves, chopped finely	50 ml

Combine the lemon juice and zest, sugar, and eggs in the top of a double boiler or in a heatproof bowl set over a pan of barely simmering water. Whisk well to combine, and then add the butter. Cook slowly, stirring frequently, for 20 minutes or until thickened. Stir in the mint, remove from the heat, and cool. Pour into a jar, and use within a week.

IN THE MICROWAVE
Mix the lemon juice and zest, sugar, and butter in a 4-cup (1-L) bowl. Cover and cook on high for 3-4 minutes. Stir well. If the sugar isn't dissolved, cook for 1 minute longer.

In a separate bowl, beat the eggs, and whisk in 1/4 cup (50 ml) of the hot lemon mixture. Pour the egg mixture back into the lemon mixture, and beat well. Cook on high, uncovered, for 30 seconds at a time, stirring after each cooking period, for about 2 minutes, until the lemon curd is thick and creamy. Stir in the mint, cool, and enjoy.

Strawberry and Mint Granita

SERVES 6

This is a fresh-tasting version of the snow cones you can buy at carnivals; serve it in ice cream soda glasses or clear glass bowls. Mint and strawberries are a great combination, but you can substitute fresh sweet basil for a different flavour.

1 lb	ripe fresh strawberries, cleaned and hulled	500 g
3/4 cup	super-fine granulated sugar	175 ml
2 cups	water	500 ml
3 Tbsp	freshly squeezed lemon juice	40 ml
1/2 cup	lightly packed fresh mint leaves, chopped finely	125 ml
6	whole mint leaves, to garnish	6

Combine the strawberries and sugar in a food processor or blender, and purée until smooth. Add water and lemon juice, and pulse until combined. Strain the mixture through a sieve into a shallow plastic container, and discard the seeds. Stir in the chopped mint, cover, and freeze for 2 hours. Give the mixture a good stir, and return it to the freezer for at least 1 hour and up to 3 hours. Spoon into glasses or bowls, and garnish each with a mint leaf. If you want to freeze the granita for longer than 3 hours, you'll need to thaw it for 30 minutes in the refrigerator before serving.

MICROWAVE-DRIED HERBS
The microwave oven makes drying summer's bountiful crop of fresh herbs as easy as picking them, and herbs preserved this way taste much more like fresh herbs than the commercially dried variety.

Use the freshest herbs available. Rinse thoroughly, and dry in a salad spinner. Scatter 2 cups (500 ml) of leaves or sprigs in an even layer on a double thickness of paper towel on the floor or turntable of your microwave. Do not cover.

Cook on high for about 4 minutes. (The time will vary from herb to herb, so you'll need to practice a little.) When the herbs are dried to the right degree, they'll lose their bright colour and crumble easily.

Store in tightly covered glass jars in a cool, dark place.

Marjoram and Oregano

Marjoram and oregano are so closely related that it only makes sense to discuss them together. Oregano, in fact, is simply the Italian name for wild or hardy marjoram, and this is the stuff that is used so commonly in Italian and other Mediterranean cooking. It has a spicy fragrance, with a hint of cloves and pine. Its leaves are green (sometimes striped with yellow) and narrow, growing in clumps on tender stems. Sweet marjoram, in contrast, has a sweet, almost peppermint smell and a tart, resinous flavour. Its leaves are similar to oregano leaves, but they're smaller and a paler shade of green. Unless you purchase your herbs from a nursery or specialist market (or grow your own), you'll probably be buying a hybrid of sweet marjoram and wild marjoram, which will be called oregano. This is true of both dried and fresh herbs, and oregano is one of the few dried herbs that I tend to have on hand.

Oregano is a must in many Italian dishes, including ratatouilles and tomato-based sauces. It also complements mushrooms, eggplants, and other earthy-flavoured vegetables, as well as meat and poultry.

Simple Slow-Cooked Tomato Sauce with Oregano

MAKES 2 CUPS (500 ML)

This simple tomato sauce is very pure. Serve it with fresh hot pasta and a sprinkling of parmesan for a truly beautiful and basic dish.

2 lb	ripe plum tomatoes, sliced	1 kg
2 Tbsp	butter	25 ml
2 Tbsp	olive oil	25 ml
1	small onion, peeled and halved	1
1/4 tsp	sugar	1 ml
2 Tbsp	finely chopped fresh oregano	25 ml
	salt and freshly ground black pepper	

Place the tomatoes in a saucepan, cover tightly, and cook over a very low heat for 40 minutes. Push through a fine sieve, and discard the seeds and skin. Return the tomatoes to the pan and stir in the butter, olive oil, onion, sugar, and oregano. Bring to a simmer, and cook for 30 minutes, stirring occasionally. Remove and discard the onion, and season the sauce to taste with salt and pepper.

IN THE MICROWAVE
Cut the tomatoes in half and place them in a 2-quart (2-L) casserole with 1 Tbsp (15 ml) of water. Cover, cook on high for 8-10 minutes, and let stand, covered, for 5 minutes. Push through a fine sieve, and discard the seeds and skin. Return the tomatoes to the casserole, and stir in the butter, olive oil, onion, sugar, and oregano. Cover and cook on high for 5 minutes, until the onion is soft and the sauce is thoroughly heated. Discard the onion, and season to taste.

Warm Mushroom and Gnocchi Salad

SERVES 2

8 oz	fresh gnocchi	250 g
1 Tbsp	olive oil	15 ml
1 Tbsp	butter	15 ml
1	shallot, chopped finely	1
1	garlic clove, chopped finely	1
1/2 lb	oyster or chanterelle mushrooms, cleaned and halved	250 g
2	plum tomatoes, chopped coarsely	2
1 Tbsp	chopped fresh oregano	15 ml
	salt and freshly ground black pepper	
2 Tbsp	grated fresh parmesan cheese	25 ml
	oregano leaves, to garnish	

Cook the gnocchi in a pan of salted boiling water according to package directions, drain, and set aside.

Heat the olive oil and butter in a skillet, and sauté the shallot and garlic for 3 minutes, until softened. Raise the heat, and stir in the mushrooms. Cook for 3 minutes, until golden brown, and then add the tomatoes and oregano. Cook, stirring frequently, for 5 minutes more. Remove from the heat, and stir in the gnocchi. Season to taste with salt and pepper, and serve scattered with the parmesan cheese and a few oregano leaves.

Parsley

Even those who shy away from buying fresh herbs often chuck a bunch of parsley into their shopping baskets. This is the most familiar of the herbs, one that we all feel comfortable using to garnish and flavour anything from salads to soups, sandwiches to grills and casseroles. Parsley might even seem a bit boring compared to more exotic sprigs like cilantro. However, its fresh but mild flavour and colourful appearance make this herb a must-have in the kitchen for both beginning and more sophisticated cooks.

There are two main varieties of parsley. Curly-leafed parsley is the most recognizable, with its decorative, tightly furled leaves that are most commonly used as a raw garnish. Flat-leafed, or Italian, parsley looks like a cross between cilantro and celery leaves. It has a more intense flavour and is often preferred over its curly cousin for use in cooking. Both are available year-round.

Parsley keeps best when it is placed in a jar of water, much like cut flowers. Rinse the leaves just before using, and spin or pat them dry. The stems can be chopped and added to soups and stocks. One way to chop the leaves is to stuff them in a measuring cup and use scissors to snip them down to size. When chopping large quantities, I like to use a *mezzaluna*, which is a curved, double-handled blade. It allows you to chop quickly and efficiently without reducing the herbs to a pulp. Don't reserve the leaves just for garnish; parsley has a clean, slightly peppery flavour that makes a wonderful base for soups and sauces. Because parsley is inexpensive, it makes an economical addition to pestos and herb breads, as well as balancing stronger-tasting herbs and spices. Curly parsley can be deep-fried and served as a crisp garnish on grilled fish.

Parsley is rich in vitamin C and A and iron. Chock-full of chlorophyll, parsley leaves are a great breath freshener — save your garnish to munch on after a garlicky meal. Rumour has it that parsley stems are an aphrodisiac.

Parsley Pesto

MAKES ABOUT 2 CUPS (500 ML)

1 cup	packed parsley leaves, heavy stems removed	375 ml
1	large garlic clove, peeled	1
1/4 cup	walnut pieces	50 ml
2 tsp	freshly squeezed lemon juice	10 ml

Parsley pesto has a fresh taste all its own. In this recipe, walnuts are used instead of the usual pine nuts, but you can use either. Toss this with hot pasta, or use it as a condiment for grilled shrimp, fish, or chicken.

1 cup	olive oil	250 ml
	salt	

Combine the parsley, garlic, and walnuts in a blender, and pulse until chopped finely. Add the lemon juice, and gradually add the olive oil, pulsing until the mixture emulsifies. If the pesto is too thick, blend in a tablespoon of cold water. Season to taste with salt.

Tabbouleh

SERVES 4-6

1 cup	bulgur wheat	250 ml
2 cups	boiling water	500 ml
3	large ripe tomatoes, chopped finely	3
1/2	cucumber, peeled and chopped finely	1/2
2 cups	packed fresh parsley, chopped finely	500 ml
1 cup	lightly packed fresh mint, chopped finely	250 ml
1	bunch scallions, chopped finely	1
1	onion, chopped finely	1

For the dressing:

1/2 cup	freshly squeezed lemon juice	125 ml
1/2 cup	olive oil	125 ml
1	large garlic clove, crushed	1
1/2 tsp	ground allspice	2 ml
1/2 tsp	salt	2 ml
	freshly ground black pepper	

Parsley stars in this zesty Middle Eastern salad, its fresh, slightly peppery flavour balancing the sweetness of the mint and the sharpness of the garlic.

Tabbouleh makes a great accompaniment to grilled chicken or fish. Or, for a light meal, serve it in lettuce- or radicchio-leaf bowls, accompanied by warm pita and hummus.

Place the bulgur in a large bowl, and cover with the boiling water. Stir well, and leave for 30 minutes to soak. Drain well. Stir in the chopped tomatoes, cucumber, parsley, mint, green onions, and onion.

To make the dressing: Combine the ingredients in a jar with a tightly fitting lid, and shake thoroughly. Pour over the salad, and toss to coat. Allow to stand at room temperature for at least 1 hour before serving. Alternatively, refrigerate overnight, and bring to room temperature before serving.

Cream of Parsley Soup

The fresh taste of parsley holds its own in this cream soup, which is particularly good with toasted parmesan crostini.

3 cups	packed fresh parsley	750 ml
2 Tbsp	butter	25 ml
2	shallots or 1 small onion, chopped very finely	2
2 Tbsp	flour	25 ml
4 cups	chicken stock	1 L
1 Tbsp	chopped fresh mint	15 ml
2 cups	cream	500 ml
	a pinch of freshly grated nutmeg	
	salt and freshly grated black pepper	

IN THE MICROWAVE
Melt the butter in a 2-quart (2-L) microwave-safe casserole. Add the parsley stems and shallot, stir to coat, and cook, covered, on high for 2-3 minutes. Stir in the flour, cover, and cook for 1 minute. Add the stock, mixing well, and cook on high for 3 minutes, stirring once or twice. Add the mint and the parsley leaves, and cook for 2 minutes more. Stir in the cream, season with nutmeg, salt, and pepper, and bring back to serving temperature.

Trim the stems from the parsley, and chop them very finely. Chop the leaves, and set aside. Heat the butter in a large saucepan, and sauté the stems and chopped shallot or onion for about 5 minutes, until softened but not brown. Stir in the flour, and cook for 3 minutes longer. Pour in the stock, and bring it to a simmer, stirring frequently.

Add the chopped mint and parsley, and simmer gently for 5 minutes. Stir in the cream, and season with nutmeg, salt, and pepper. Heat through gently, and serve at once.

Rosemary

Rosemary for remembrance, so the old saying begins. Trouble is, I never can remember the rest of it. What I *do* remember is a mouth-watering shish kebab I once had — tender bits of lamb skewered on rosemary twigs, pervaded with their woodsy aroma. It was served with crunchy potatoes, roasted in olive oil and seasoned liberally with black pepper, rosemary and garlic. Makes my knees weak just to think of it.

Rosemary is essentially a Mediterranean herb, popular in Greek and Italian cooking. The Romans introduced the plant to the rest of Europe during the Middle Ages, where it was cultivated mainly as an ornamental shrub, and rosemary is still a favourite with gardeners, with its dense, aromatic pine-like needles and pale blue flower clusters.

This is one of the few herbs that retains a lot of its character when dried, but you'll still find a big difference between fresh rosemary and the stuff you buy in bottles, especially in terms of its aroma. Fresh rosemary smells of both the woods and the ocean, and no wonder: its Latin name, *ros marinus*, means "dew of the sea." It's available year-round, so look for fresh, sprightly twigs with greyish-blue to bright green leaves. This fairly hardy herb will last for at least one week if popped into a plastic bag and stored in the refrigerator.

You can add a couple of whole rosemary twigs to a marinade or stew to infuse the dish with a warm, peppery flavour and heavenly scent. Or chop it finely with sea salt, garlic, and olive oil to make a paste for smearing on meat or fish before cooking. For those of you who like to jam it up in the kitchen, try adding rosemary to crab-apple jelly; it's great on toast, served with cheese, or as a condiment with grilled or roasted meats.

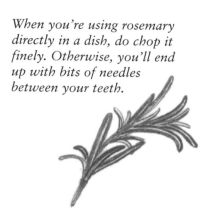

When you're using rosemary directly in a dish, do chop it finely. Otherwise, you'll end up with bits of needles between your teeth.

Rosemary and Black Olive Focaccia

SERVES 4-6

1 cup	warm water	250 ml
1 Tbsp	sugar	15 ml
1 Tbsp	dry yeast	15 ml
1 tsp	salt	5 ml
1/4 cup	whole wheat flour	50 ml
2 - 2 1/2 cups	all-purpose flour	500 - 625 ml
4	sprigs rosemary	4
4 Tbsp	olive oil	60 ml
2 Tbsp	balsamic vinegar	25 ml
2 Tbsp	coarsely chopped black olives	25 ml
1 tsp	coarse sea salt	5 ml
	sliced tomatoes for garnish (optional)	

Home-made focaccia bread is one of my all-time favourites. Add a bowl of olives, a bottle of red wine, and you've got a snack that will keep your friends loyal for life. This recipe combines the woodsy aroma of rosemary with the sea-salty flavour of black olives, but you can pretty much toss whatever you like on top. Pine nuts, feta cheese, and basil is another great combination.

Combine the water and sugar in a small bowl. Sprinkle the yeast over top, give it a quick stir, and leave to proof for 5 minutes, until frothy.

Meanwhile, in a large bowl, mix the teaspoon of salt with the whole wheat flour and 1 cup of the all-purpose flour. Strip the rosemary needles from their twigs, and chop half of them very finely. Stir the chopped rosemary into the salt and flour. Make a well in the centre of the dry ingredients, and pour in the proofed yeast and 2 tablespoons of olive oil. Stir well to combine, and then gradually stir in enough of the remaining flour to make the dough come away from the sides of the bowl. Turn out onto a floured surface, and knead for 10 minutes, adding flour as necessary, until smooth and elastic.

Wipe out the mixing bowl and grease it with oil. Place the dough in the bowl, turning it once to coat with oil. Cover with a tea towel, and set aside in a warm place to rise until doubled in size, about 1 1/2 hours.

Punch down the risen dough, and stretch it out to fit in a greased baking sheet. Cover again and leave for another 45 minutes.

Preheat the oven to 375°F (180°C). Use your thumb to make random indentations in the dough, and then drizzle with the remaining olive oil and the balsamic vinegar. Scatter the chopped olives, sea salt, and rosemary needles over top. Leave for 5 minutes, and then bake for 20-25 minutes, until puffy and golden brown. Garnish with sliced tomatoes, if you like, and serve warm, sliced or torn in pieces.

Grilled Lamb Chops with Rosemary and Parmesan Crust

SERVES 4

1/2 cup	fresh rosemary	125 ml
1/2 cup	fresh parsley	125 ml
2-4	garlic cloves	2-4
1/4 cup	freshly grated parmesan cheese	50 ml
1/4 cup	olive oil	50 ml
1 Tbsp	salt	15 ml
1 Tbsp	cracked black peppercorns	15 ml
8	lamb chops	8

Lamb and rosemary are wonderful partners. Prepare and marinate the chops the night before you cook them, and you've got dinner ready in a flash. You can also use the herb and cheese paste to coat a loin roast.

Combine the herbs, garlic, parmesan, olive oil, salt, and peppercorns in a food processor, and pulse until the mixture forms a coarse paste. Rub the paste generously on both sides of the chops, cover, and refrigerate for several hours or preferably overnight.

Preheat the broiler, and set the rack about 3-4 inches (7-10 cm) from the heat. Grill the chops for 4-6 minutes on each side, and serve at once.

Sage

Known as the healing herb, sage's name comes from the Latin word *salvere*, "to save." Sage also means wise, and any truly sage cook will want to have this fresh herb on hand. While we often turn to sage when making stuffing for a Sunday bird, this aromatic herb can be added to many other recipes. With its strong flavour — a bit musky, like resin and lemon peel — sage should be used sparingly, whether you chop a few leaves into a tomato salad, blend finely chopped leaves with soft cheese, or use sage to flavour focaccia bread. I like to place whole sage leaves on chicken breasts or pork chops and pan-fry them in butter.

Fresh sage is available year-round and can be grown successfully indoors throughout the winter months. It is a bushy plant, with leaves that are narrow, slightly fuzzy, and a pale greenish-grey in colour (sage green, in fact). I much prefer fresh sage to dried, as drying almost eliminates its lemony scent, leaving a strong, camphor-like aroma. You can infuse fresh sage leaves in hot water to make a refreshing tea, good for an upset tummy as well as for freshening your breath. Get wise, and experiment with sage. It's not just for the birds.

Pork Chops with Sage and Pepper Crust

SERVES 4

3 Tbsp	finely chopped fresh sage	40 ml
1 Tbsp	peppercorns, crushed	15 ml
3 Tbsp	dry bread crumbs	40 ml
1 tsp	fine lemon zest	5 ml
1	egg, beaten	1
4	pork chops	4
2 Tbsp	olive oil	25 ml
2 Tbsp	butter	25 ml
	salt	
2	tart apples, cored and sliced in thin rings	2
1	onion, sliced thinly	1

Pork, sage, and apples is a traditional combination. Here sage combined with cracked pepper forms a savoury crust for lean pork chops. Apples fried with onions make a delicious topping.

On a plate, combine the sage, peppercorns, bread crumbs, lemon zest, and a pinch of salt. Dip the chops in the beaten egg, and then press them into the crumb mixture to coat both sides. Heat half the oil and butter in a skillet or frying pan over a high heat, and brown the chops on both sides. Reduce the heat, and cook for about 8-12 minutes more per side, depending on their thickness.

Meanwhile, heat the remaining oil and butter in another pan, and sauté the apples and onion until soft and golden. Serve on top of the cooked chops.

Cannellini and Tomato Stew with Sage

SERVES 6

2 Tbsp	olive oil	25 ml
1	sweet onion, chopped	1
3	garlic cloves, chopped finely	3
2 Tbsp	chopped fresh sage	25 ml
1	tart apple, peeled, cored, and chopped	1
2 cups	chopped fresh or canned tomatoes	500 ml
3 cups	cooked or canned cannellini beans	750 ml

Sautéing the sage in olive oil with the onion and garlic brings out its flavour. Serve this hearty stew over thick slices of garlic-seasoned toast.

1 Tbsp	freshly squeezed lemon juice	15 ml
	salt and freshly ground black pepper	
6	thick slices ciabatta or other Italian-style white bread	6
1	garlic clove, peeled and halved	1

IN THE MICROWAVE
In a 2-quart (2-L) microwave-safe casserole, combine the olive oil, onion, and garlic, and cook on high, uncovered, for 4 minutes, stirring once. Add the chopped apple, and cook for 1 minute more. Stir in the sage and tomatoes, and cook for 4 minutes, stirring once. Add the beans, and heat through; this will take 4-6 minutes.

Heat half of the oil in a large saucepan, and sauté the onion, chopped garlic, and sage for 3 minutes. Stir in the chopped apple, and cook for 2 minutes more. Add the tomatoes and beans, and bring to a simmer. Cook for 10-15 minutes, stirring occasionally.

Meanwhile, toast the bread, and rub both sides with the cut garlic clove. Drizzle with olive oil, season with salt and pepper, and set each piece of toast in the bottom of a wide soup plate. Stir the lemon juice into the stew, season to taste, and ladle generously over the toast. Serve at once.

Tarragon

Tarragon is a herb that we associate most closely with classic French cooking, and the best tarragon come from the French plant. Russian and Mexican varieties are also called "false" tarragon, as their flavour can't hold a candle to the real thing.

Fresh tarragon is sold in sprigs of soft, narrow leaves, which have a peppery, licorice flavour and fragrance. It is used to flavour classic French sauces such as Béarnaise and tartar, as well as poultry and fish dishes. I like to add a sprinkling of tarragon to simply prepared vegetables, especially carrots, potatoes, peas, or cauliflower. Like the other classic aromatic herbs — rosemary, sage, and thyme — tarragon is best used on its own or in combination with lighter herbs such as parsley and chives.

Unlike more delicate herbs such as basil, fresh tarragon is more subtle than the dried herb. When added to cooked dishes, its flavour intensifies. One of the most popular ways to preserve the flavour of fresh tarragon is to infuse it in vinegar. You can simply add a few sprigs to a bottle of white wine vinegar and note how the flavour grows stronger with age. Tarragon vinegar makes a beautiful vinaigrette, and you can add a splash to the water when poaching fish or chicken.

Carrot Soup with Tarragon and Ginger
SERVES 4-6

3 Tbsp	butter	40 ml
3	shallots, chopped finely	3
1/2 Tbsp	grated fresh ginger	7 ml
1 lb	carrots, peeled and shredded	500 g

3	sprigs fresh tarragon, leaves stripped and stalks reserved	3
4 cups	boiling water	1 L
1 tsp	sugar	5 ml
	salt and freshly ground black pepper	
1/4 cup	cream	50 ml

Melt the butter in a large saucepan over a medium heat, and sauté the shallots for 3 minutes. Stir in the ginger, shredded carrots, half the tarragon leaves, and the stalks. Cover, reduce the heat to low, and cook for 10 minutes. Pour in the boiling water, and add the sugar and a pinch of salt and pepper. Bring to a boil, and then reduce the heat and simmer for 30 minutes. Remove and discard the tarragon stalks, transfer the soup to a food processor or blender, and purée until smooth. Return to the saucepan, and stir in the cream and the remaining tarragon leaves. Adjust the seasoning to taste, and reheat gently before serving.

Pickled Cauliflower and Onions with Tarragon

MAKES 1 QUART (1 L)

Tarragon goes particularly well with cauliflower, and these pickles are a treat. They need to marinate for at least three weeks to develop their flavour, and they will keep well for up to three months. If you use 2 small jars rather than 1 large one, divide the ingredients between the jars, and use 2 small garlic cloves and 2 small hot peppers.

1	garlic clove, peeled	1
12-15	pearl onions, peeled	12-15
1 lb	cauliflower florets	500 g
3	springs fresh tarragon	3
1	bay leaf	1
1	red finger hot pepper	1
2 cups	white vinegar	500 ml
1 Tbsp	pickling salt	15 ml

Sterilize a 1-quart (1-litre) canning jar and its 2-piece lid.

Place the garlic, onions, cauliflower florets, tarragon, bay leaf, and hot pepper in the sterilized jar. Combine the vinegar and salt in a saucepan, and bring to a full boil. Pour into the jar to cover the ingredients.

Wipe the jar rim perfectly clean, carefully set the lid in position, and screw the ring down tightly. Cool for several hours or overnight. If the lid has sealed

IN THE MICROWAVE

In a 2-quart (2-L) microwave-safe casserole, combine the shallots and ginger, and cook on high, uncovered, for 2 minutes, stirring once. Stir in the shredded carrots, half the tarragon leaves, and the tarragon stalks. Cover and cook on high for 6-8 minutes. Pour in the boiling water, add the sugar, salt, and pepper, and cook for 5 minutes. Remove and discard the tarragon stalks, and purée the soup until smooth. Return it to the casserole, and stir in the cream and the remaining tarragon leaves. Adjust the seasoning, reheat (but do not (that is, if the dome is concave), move the jar to a cool, dark place; if it's still convex, move the jar to the refrigerator. Store for at least three weeks before using.

Thyme

Thyme, parsley, and bay are the three herbs that make up a *bouquet garni*, the classic herbal posy used to flavour stocks and soups. There are literally hundreds of varieties of thyme, but the four most commonly cultivated for culinary use are common thyme, lemon thyme, silver thyme, and caraway thyme. Common or garden thyme has a strong, resinous flavour and adds warmth to many meat and fish dishes. It is also used to flavour vegetables, particularly full-bodied roots such as potatoes and carrots. Silver thyme, more mild in flavour and aroma, perhaps tastes better with lighter fare such as eggs, rice, and grains. Lemon thyme is also popular with cooks, with its mild flavour and sweet, citrusy fragrance. I like to add lemon thyme to vinaigrettes and sprinkle the fresh leaves on tomato salads. Caraway thyme, as its name suggests, has a warm, nutty flavour, with a touch of aniseed and lemon. This is a particularly nice herb to blend with soft cheese or to use in flavouring baked goods such as focaccia bread or herb muffins.

Use your nose when choosing thyme, and pick one with a scent that appeals. Usually thyme leaves are stripped from their stems and used raw or added towards the end of cooking. However, you can use whole sprigs to infuse a stock or sauce and remove them before serving. Heavy stems make good kebab skewers for barbecuing or grilling fish and vegetables.

Roasted New Potatoes with Thyme

SERVES 6-8

4-5	sprigs fresh thyme	4-5
3 lb	small new potatoes, scrubbed	1.5 kg
1/4 cup	olive oil	50 ml
	salt and freshly ground black pepper	

Preheat the oven to 400°F (200°C).

Strip the leaves from the sprigs of thyme, and place the stems in a large pot of salted water. Bring to a boil, and add the potatoes. Cook for 10 minutes, and then drain well, discarding the thyme stems.

Place the potatoes in a large, shallow roasting pan, and drizzle with the olive oil. Season generously with salt and pepper, and scatter half the thyme leaves over top. Toss well to coat, and roast near the top of the oven for 30-35 minutes, until golden brown and crisp. Toss with the remaining thyme leaves, and serve at once.

Marinated Olives

A ho-hum olive will improve dramatically when left to marinate for at least 48 hours. This marinade is flavoured with thyme sprigs, coriander seeds, and orange peel.

1 1/4 cups	olive oil	300 ml
2	shallots, chopped finely	2
2	garlic cloves, chopped finely	2
3	sprigs fresh thyme, leaves stripped and stems reserved	3
1	basil leaf	1
2-inch	strip orange peel	5-cm
1/2 tsp	toasted coriander seeds	2 ml
1 lb	black, green, or mixed olives	500 g

Combine all the ingredients in a large jar or bowl, and mix well. Leave (in the fridge or out, it doesn't matter) for at least 48 hours to marinate. To serve, strain the olives, and remove the thyme stems, bay leaf, and orange peel.

THYME MANAGEMENT
Thyme sprigs will keep well for up to two weeks when stored in the refrigerator. Wrap the sprigs in a paper towel, and then pop them in a plastic bag. To refresh tired-looking thyme, spray it with a mist of water, but never store waterlogged sprigs, as they will begin to decompose.

Index